CW01648993

RKETING

Q&A

Questions & Answers

International Aspects of Marketing

MARKETING

Q&A

Questions & Answers

International Aspects of Marketing

Peter Doust

Financial Training

First published in Great Britain 1986 by Financial Training Publications Limited, Avenue House, 131 Holland Park Avenue, London W11 4UT

© Peter Doust, 1986

ISBN: 1 85185 004 X

Typeset and produced by Graham Burn, Leighton Buzzard, Beds.
Printed by Pendragon Press, Cambridge

All rights reserved. No part of this book may be reproduced or transmitted in any form or by any means, electronic or mechanical, including photocopying, recording, or any information storage or retrieval system without prior permission from the publisher.

Contents

Introduction

This introduction primarily refers to Part I of this book, which consists of questions and answers relevant to Part II of the examination for the Institute of Marketing. All these questions and answers have been specifically written for students who are taking the International Aspects of Marketing examination paper for the Diploma Stage of the Institute of Marketing examinations.

There are 85 questions and answers in Part I, and five case studies with suggested solutions in Part II. The first part is arranged in nine chapters which cover all aspects of the Institute of Marketing syllabus, broken down as follows:

— the global approach;
— comparative analysis of world markets;
— world marketing infrastructures, and international and multi-national organisations;
— marketing planning and control;
— information collection, analysis and interpretation;
— international selling and distribution;
— exporting and importing;
— multi-national marketing strategy;
— international trade regulations.

At the beginning of each chapter students will find an expanded breakdown of each chapter showing the exact syllabus requirements of the Institute of Marketing.

Although the questions follow the Institute of Marketing syllabus, they will also be of use to those studying marketing on courses such as: HND Business Studies; BA in International Marketing; and any course covering the international aspects of marketing.

Students will find these questions and answers particularly useful if used in conjunction with the textbooks recommended by the Institute of Marketing.

Students are reminded that the aim of the International Aspects of Marketing examination paper is to enable them to acquire expertise in applying marketing techniques in countries other than their own, and thereby to acquire practice in dealing with international marketing situations.

Regardless of what method of study a student has followed, these questions and answers will provide him with an essential tool that, if properly used, will assist in a greater understanding of the course, with an improved chance of success in the examination.

The greatest benefit will be shown if students:

(a) Thoroughly read each question, breaking it down into its component parts.

(b) Establish a list of the theory or theories required in fully covering all aspects of the question.

(c) Establish a skeleton answer, giving just headings and subheadings.

(d) Finally, write your full answer, giving real life examples wherever possible.

The Institute of Marketing assumes that students of international marketing are already familiar with the principles of marketing, and the Institute of Marketing states the following objectives for this course of study.

Candidates should be able to:

(a) Compare and contrast export, international and multi-national marketing.

(b) Differentiate between the marketing policies appropriate to industrialised, developing and underdeveloped economies.

(c) Demonstrate the major differences between national and multi-national marketing planning.

(d) Identify sources of information, methods of information collection and methods of information analysis suitable for international marketing operations.

(e) Identify the factors which distinguish product, price and promotional policy formulation for overseas markets as opposed to the domestic market.

(f) Formulate methods of monitoring and controlling overseas selling and distribution.

(g) Identify the major organisational changes to be made when a company moves from international to multi-national selling.

(h) List the main methods, procedures and documentation requirements for exporting from the United Kingdom.

(i) Identify and discuss the impact of cooperative and restrictive measures to regulate international trade.

The Institute suggests that one way of approaching this examination paper could be to consider it as an advance marketing practice paper, specifically in the international dimension. By this, they imply that the student is conversant with subject areas included in the certificate stage and is able, for example, to formulate marketing plans and research procedures, as well as consider behavioural and financial aspects. In this examination paper, this expertise will be overlaid and added to with the particular circumstances of international operations; but the basic expertise is very relevant to Section 1, the mini-case, where a frequent cause of failure by students has been their inability to use previously acquired knowledge within the context of the case material.

The Institute says that one of the most important considerations is that the examiners expect candidates, when confronted with any international marketing situation, to have a clear idea where to start and how to tackle the problem. They realise that, in practice, detailed information will be obtained, but they expect candidates to know what information they will need and how they will get it, even if not necessarily carrying it in their heads.

They make a further point: that they expect candidates to be aware of the marketing implications of world affairs, social trends, etc. Therefore, students must read and view intelligently and in a questioning way, with this in mind.

Finally, the examiners also apply the judgement: 'If this were submitted to me as, say, a marketing director by a member of my staff, would it be acceptable?' In other words, credit will be given for answers which are well presented and are pragmatic, not merely academic.

International marketing refers to a wide range of activities involved in conducting business transactions across national boundaries. International, as opposed to multi-national, suggests a comprehensive approach to the operations of both large and small companies engaged in business overseas. It is from this perspective that you need to commence your consideration of international marketing as it has developed, and as it must change and grow in the future.

Good luck in your examination.

1 The global approach

INTRODUCTION

This chapter covers that part of the syllabus concerned with a global approach to markets: national, export, international and multi-national markets compared; the origins of world trade, the development of world markets, and the forces underlying the development of international business. It also looks at and compares world markets by showing the methods available to analyse markets: the economic dimensions; income, wages, GNP trade and competitive patterns. Social-cultural patterns are considered: population, education, literacy; ethnic, occupational, consumption patterns, etc. Finally, political, legal, geographical and natural resources dimensions, together with the stages of market development, are examined.

QUESTIONS

1 Explain the theory of 'comparative advantage'.

2 Why is international marketing of growing importance?

3 A significant method of business offering an entry into a foreign market in the 1980s is a contractural agreement. A popular method in this category is 'licensing'. Discuss the advantages and disadvantages of 'licensing'.

4 The dominant considerations of 'host' countries vary from region to region, and from industry to industry. What factors do you consider are the most dominant?

5 What is 'the World Bank?'

6 In international business, there are numerous forms of market agreement amongst different countries. The most common forms are: free trade areas; customs union; common market; economic union; and political union. Write notes on each of these forms.

7 Given the present volatile atmosphere in which multi-national corporations operate, what are the strategic implications for multi-national operators in the future?

8 Most companies commence their international business activities by exporting. Why?

9 Describe the importance of the economic environment for international marketing.

10 Are 'international managers' different from 'domestic managers'?

ANSWERS

1 Economists such as Adam Smith, Ricardo, and Stuart Mill, are all credited with offering economic justification for international trade.

In its most simple form, modern trade takes place because a foreign country is able to provide a material, a product or a service more cheaply than the domestic industry can supply it. For example, if the delivered price of a Japanese television set is less than the cost of a United Kingdom television set, it makes economic sense to import television sets from Japan.

Ricardo advanced the concept of relative or comparative costs as the basis of international trade. He emphasised that labour costs more than any other aspect of production. In summation, the theory of competitive advantage states that even if a country is able to produce all of its goods at lower cost than another country can, trade still benefits most countries, based on comparative, not absolute, costs. In other words, countries should concentrate efforts on producing goods that have a comparative advantage compared to other countries, and then export those goods in exchange for goods that command advantage in their own countries.

One country may be absolutely more efficient in the production of every good than is the other country; and this means the other country has an absolute disadvantage in the production of every good. But so long as there are differences in the relative efficiencies of producing the different goods in the two countries, we can always be sure that even the poor country has a comparative advantage in the production of those commodities in which it is relatively most efficient; this same poor country will have a comparative disadvantage in those other commodities in which its inefficiency is more than average. Similarly, the rich, efficient country will find that it should specialise in those fields of production where it has a comparative advantage, planning to import those commodities in which it has a comparative disadvantage.

A well-known example used to illustrate comparative advantage is the case of the best solicitor in a town, who also happens to be the best typist in that same town. Will he or she not specialise in law and leave the typing to a secretary? How can he or she afford to give up precious time from the legal field where his or her comparative advantage is very great, to perform typing activities at which he or she is efficient, but in which he or she lacks comparative advantage? To look at it from the secretary's point of view, he or she is less efficient than the solicitor in both activities but his or her relative advantage compared with the solicitor's is least in typing. Relatively speaking, the secretary has a comparative advantage in typing.

So it is with countries. Suppose the United Kingdom produces food with one-third the labour that other members of Europe do, and clothing with one-half the labour. Then it is clear that the United Kingdom has comparative advantage in food and comparative disadvantage in clothing — this, despite the fact that the United Kingdom is absolutely most efficient in everything. By the same token, Europe has comparative advantage in clothing.

The key to this concept is the word 'comparative', which implies that each and every country has both definite 'advantage' in some goods, and definite 'disadvantage' in other goods.

2 In the 1980s we are seeing that international business is increasingly treated not simply as an additional route to growth, but rather is considered as shaping business strategy for all businesses, even those with strictly domestic markets.

Whereas the reasons for the international globalisation of markets have been different in many industries, its implications have been the same for every industry. Most important, companies in global industries have had to reshape their strategies in very basic, fundamental ways. In order to compete profitably, they have often been obliged to redesign their whole system of doing business to take advantage of the fact of the international and global aspects of their markets. In choosing technological processes, they follow the example of the Japanese with plain-paper copiers, for example, and search the world for the technology offering the greatest promise for most markets.

In planning a new product, these companies tend to design a product or service to be marketable in the maximum of countries, to serve an identifiable world market segment — the best example of this is the Toyota Car Company in Japan — or to be easily adaptable to slightly different markets.

In working out a manufacturing or production strategy, they pick the lowest cost source. Examples of this could well be Malaysia for very simple electronics; Sri Lanka for textiles; Japan for advanced electronics; the United Kingdom for personal computers; mainland Europe for precision machinery. They then design a manufacturing system geared to the scale requirement of the world market.

If scale is important to product economies, companies in global industries design a marketing system that gives them the broadest coverage and quickest penetration of world markets, even if it means signing cross-marketing agreements with their competitors, selling under manufactures' names, or marketing through distributors and retailers they cannot really control.

In short, they have thought hard about what global operations mean to the economics of their businesses, about where the economic leverage points in the business will be, and about how they must shape their own business systems to take advantage of these points. The successful ones have acted accordingly.

Initially, the USA played a dominant role in shaping world economic events; but this is no longer the case. In the future, businesses will confront changes quite different from the kind of changes that they are most familiar with. These new kinds of changes in the world environment are taking place at an increasingly fast pace. No business can now hope to survive simply by examining changes as unusual occurrences — rather, a well-organised system is needed to deal with world events.

3 Some of the advantages of licensing can clearly be established as:

(a) Licensing requires very small capital and serves as a very quick and easy entry into foreign markets.

(b) In many countries, particularly the developed communist countries, licensing is the only way to get entry into that market.

(c) Licensing provides an extension of the product lifecycle for products in the maturity stage of their lifecycle in the home economy.

(d) Licensing is an extremely good alternative to foreign production marketing in an environment where there is world-wide inflation, a shortage of skilled labour, increasing foreign and domestic regulation, and increasingly difficult international competition.

(e) Licensing royalties are guaranteed and periodic, whereas shared income from investment fluctuates and is risky.

(f) Domestically based companies can benefit from product development abroad without the expense of research through technical feedback arrangements.

(g) When exports are no longer profitable because of intense competition, licensing provides an alternative.

(h) It can also overcome high transportation costs, which makes some exports non-competitive in overseas target markets.

(i) Licensing cannot be expropriated.

(j) In many countries manufactuers of security and military equipment, or any product critical to the national interest, may be compelled to enter into licensing agreements.

There are, however, a number of disadvantages; the main ones are as follows:

(a) To attract licensees, a company must possess a distinctiveness either in technology, trade-mark, company or brand name that is of particular attractiveness to potential foreign users.

(b) The licensor has no control over production and marketing by the licensee.

(c) Royalties are negligible compared to equity investment potential. Royalty rates very seldom exceed 5% of gross sales, mainly because of the host country's government restrictions.

(d) The licensee may lose interest in renewing the contract unless the licensor holds interest through innovation and technology.

(e) There is a danger of creating competition in third, or even home markets if the licensee violates territorial agreements. Taking legal action in these situations is very time-consuming and expensive, and there is no international body that can adjudicate.

4 There are many forces that will be strong in most host countries over the next decade. It is suggested that they are:

(a) Increasing government involvement in both economic planning and management — to an increasing extent, the governments of lesser developed countries will manage their economic growth process through the use of plans designed by well-trained technocrats and based on economic development concepts with which the world has been experimenting over the last three or four decades.

(b) Closer government/private sector cooperation — as governments play an increasing role in the economic planning and implementation process, there will be a tendency to move towards the highly successful model of government/private sector cooperation, rather than emulating the American/European model.

(c) A greater articulation of national interest — many years of debate at both national and international meetings are resulting in each country being able to articulate its own set of national interest much more clearly than in the past.

(d) The perception that technology is the key to success in the development process — the lesser developed countries will increasingly perceive technology to be the critical element in the development process (one of the best examples of today is Saudi Arabia). As a result, they will become more aggressive in their efforts to obtain technological know-how from multinational organisations.

(e) The heightened selectivity and sophistication of the lesser developed countries — previous trial and error in the development process, and experiences with foreign investors, will increase the ability of the lesser developed countries to determine what kind of foreign investement they want for what reasons, and under what conditions.

(f) Multi-national corporations will be tolerated to the extent that they can demonstrate good economic value. With the possible exception of countries such as Korea and Taiwan, which at the moment view foreign investment as important, countries will view foreign investors as political liabilities to be tolerated only in relation to their demonstrable economic value.

(g) The increased use of social benefit/cost analysis. To a greater extent than in other parts of the world, South America has utilised social benefit/cost analysis to screen potential foreign investors. As nations in the rest of the world become more selective in the type of foreign investment they accept, as well as more sensitive to the non-economic cost benefits associated with any new project, these techniques will be utilised not only to screen future investments, but also to monitor existing investments.

(h) The closure of an increasing number of sectors — as the ability of the lesser developed countries' enterprises grows, the trend will be to close more economic sectors to foreign companies.

(i) The pressure to employ more nationals — even in those countries where the local population is extremely small in relation to business activities (e.g. Saudi Arabia), foreign investors will be increasingly required to utilise nationals in senior positions.

(j) The pressure for greater local ownership and participation — although methods may vary, most countries will continue to push for larger local ownership, and often for controlling ownership. One of the best examples here is the indigenisation programme of the Federal Government of Nigeria.

(k) Increasing competition from foreign firms — in many industries the forces already stated will create increasing competition abroad from local companies in their own domestic markets. In some industries it may also cause international competition. Furthermore, many highly sophisticated European and Japanese multi-national companies will be competing in the United States for a larger share of the US market.

(e) The legitimisation of authoritarian rule — most African, Latin American, Middle Eastern and Asian governments did not gain power through democratic means, and many of those that have experimented with democracy have reverted to more authoritarian structures. It is unlikely that this trend will be reversed. Many authoritarian regimes are likely to try to broaden their base and avoid contact that will prove embarrassing internationally.

(m) Unstable transition periods — the tide of authoritarian control will create unstable transition periods in not only their own domestic economies, but also in many other countries.

5 (This is a very straightforward question requiring a factual and straightforward answer.)

The World Bank, officially called the International Bank for Reconstruction and Development, was founded along with the International Monetary Fund in 1944, at a United Nations Monetary and Financial Conference of 55 governments. The World Bank began operating in June 1946 and membership in the Bank is open to all members of the IMF (International Monetary Fund). Currently there are 129 member countries. The Bank is owned and controlled by its member governments. Each member country subscribes to shares for an amount relative to its economic strength. The largest shareholder in the World Bank is, at the moment, the United States.

The primary purpose of the Bank is to provide financial and technical help for the development of poorer countries. Currently it lends about £6 billion a year to help raise the standard of living in poorer countries. The scope of the Bank's operations has increased phenomenally during the past two decades. For example, in the late 1970s it provided more than five times as much financial help to developing countries than in any year of the 1960s. The Bank provides support for a wide variety of projects related to agriculture, education, industry, electricity, rural development, tourism, transportation, population planning, urban development, water supply, and telecommunications. The Bank lends money only for productive purposes, and seriously considers prospects of repayment before granting the loan.

While the countries who are members subscribe to the share capital of the World Bank, the Bank relies mainly on private investors for its financial resources through borrowing in various capital markets. In this way, private investors become involved in the development efforts of developing countries. Since the Bank obtains most of its funds on commercial terms, it charges its borrower a commercial rate of interest. Loans are usually repayable over a 20-year trading period.

In discussing the World Bank, mention must be made of the International Development Association. The reason for this is that in the 1950s it became obvious that many of the poorer countries needed loans on much easier terms than the World Bank could provide. The International Development Association was established in 1960 to help meet this need. It was made an affiliate of the World Bank, and was to be administered in accordance with the Bank's established methods.

Almost all of the International Development Association's loans are granted for a period of 15 years without interest except a small charge to cover administrative overheads. Repayment of loans does not start until after a 10-year period of grace. The major portion of the Internationl Development Association's resources emerges from three sources: transfers from the World Bank's net earnings; capital subscribed in convertible currencies by independent Development Association members; and finally, contributions from the Association's richer member countries.

6

Free trade area

The free trade area type of agreement requires different countries to remove all tariffs among its members. Let us assume that there are three nations A, B and C, that agree to a free trade area agreement and abolish all tariffs amongst themselves to permit free trade. Beyond the free trade area, A, B and C, may impose tariffs as they choose. For example, if nation X trades extensively with B, B may have very low tariffs for goods imported from X, while A and C impose high tariffs on goods from X. Under a free trade area agreement, B is free to continue its preferred relationship with X, while A and C are at liberty to decide their own external tariff policies. EFTA (European Free Trade Area) and LAFTA (Latin American Free Trade Area) illustrate the free trade area type of agreement.

Customs union

In addition to requiring abolition of internal tariffs among members, customs union further obligates the members to establish common external tariffs. To continue with the example (countries A, B and C), under a customs union agreement, B would not be permitted to have a special relationship with country X. A, B and C would have to have a common tariff policy towards X. A customs union agreement exists among Caribbean countries. Their cooperative effort started as a free trade area, and later developed into a customs union.

Common market

In a common market type of agreement, not only do members abolish internal tariffs amongst themselves and levy common external tariffs, but also they permit free flow of all factors of production among themselves. Countries A, B and C, under a common market agreement, would not only remove all tariffs and quotas among themselves, and impose common tariffs against other countries such as country X, but would also allow capital and labour to move freely within their boundaries as if they were one country. This means, for example, a resident of country A is free to accept a position in country C without a work permit.

Likewise, an investor in country B, is at liberty to invest money in country A, country B, or country C without restriction from either home or host government when transferring funds for investments.

Economic union

Under an economic union agreement, common market characteristics are combined with the harmonisation of economic policy. Member countries are expected to pursue common fiscal and monetary policies. Ordinarily this means a synchronisation of money supply, interest rates, regulation of capital market, and taxes. In effect, an economic union calls for a supernational authority to design an economic policy for an entire group of nations. Thus the European Economic Community, to a great extent, can be called an economic union. This terminology can be justified by the fact that the EEC has a common agricultural policy.

Political union

This is the ultimate market agreement among nations. It includes the characteristics of economic union and requires, additionally, political harmony among the members. Essentially, it means nations merging with each other to form a new nation.

In its purest form, an example of political union does not exist. However, in the 1950s Egypt, Yemen and Syria formed a political union, but it did not last for very long. To a degree, the Commonwealth of Nations and the Council for Mutual Economic Assistance (COMECON) can be characterised as politically based agreements. In the future, in a very limited sense, the European Economic Community with a European Parliament could be considered a political union.

7 If we understand the historical, present and future changes in the international environment of multi-national corporations, we can then discuss what strategies should be adopted to plan the course in what can only be considered as a very uncertain environment.

The most important strategy is to formulate programmes with greater flexibility. The days when the multi-nationals dictated terms, ran the operation, and took out exorbitant returns on their investments with little concern for the impact on the host nation, are gone forever. All countries, regardless of their economic state of development, have become keenly aware of the economic world around them, and are not likely to accept the arrangements characteristic of what has gone on in the past. Multi-national corporations must be prepared for long, hard negotiation, often under very disadvantageous conditions, and must also be ready to make numerous concessions if they expect to gain access to foreign markets.

Beyond gaining access, they must be prepared to contribute actively, in ways never before imagined, to the growth and prosperity of the people of the host nations. If the multi-nationals attempt to do less than is expected of them, the results will most likely be expulsion of the company and nationalisation by the host country of the multi-national corporation's assets. Additionally, the multi-national should be tolerant of, as well as being sensitive to, the policies and desires of its own country. It is increasingly evident that the home govenment can offer a great deal of aid to the multi-nationals in the form of both technical and research activity, as well as protection against the dangers of expropriation. The knowledge that a home government is supportive and protective of its multi-national corporations will only further enhance their position in dealing with foreign governments. To attain this end, the multi-national corporation should also attempt to enhance its image both at home and abroad by educating the public on the positive aspects of its activities.

Finally, multi-national corporations must continue to grow and expand in the world to keep themselves competitive with the multi-nationals of other nations. One must remember that developing countries may have very large, often state-owned, multi-national corporations of their own. It is obvious that resource scarcities are here to stay, so it will be the responsibility of the multi-nationals to use their financial strength and technical ability to undertake the search for new ways to meet the basic needs of the world. At the same time, it is vital they follow a growth and development strategy which includes locating and extracting resources in the cheapest possible manner in order to meet world-wide consumer and industrial demands.

In conclusion, the multi-nationals must develop strategies that stimulate their growth and competitiveness, while at the same time stemming public apprehension about the misuse of their power. This is not an easy task, but it is a task that must be done. World-wide, governments will force multi-national corporations to temper their strategies in the interests of their publics. Obviously, multi-national corporations and public objectives will often be in conflict, but the ultimate search should be for the optimal strategic blend. Flexibility and constant change of individual strategies will achieve more than unwavering commitment to any one long-term strategy.

8 Most companies begin their international activities by exporting, often in the following manner. Initially requests are received from overseas markets in what is often a very disorganised way. A more systematic attempt to sell off excess production in times of over-supply may lead that company to contact an agent or importer in a foreign country. Such an approach is usually opportunistic and not designed to provide any longer-term basis for sales. Investment is low, risks are low, and profits highly unpredictable.

The recognition that profits are available in foreign markets, plus growing experience with handling such orders, may lead to the exporters deciding to go after markets on a slightly longer-term basis. This is where the first significant investments are made. Several trips abroad are made and an agent is taken on. Orders begin to trickle in. All goes well until the firm encounters a period of short supply in its own domestic market, and faces the question whether or not to allocate output to overseas agents. It is quite common at this stage for the overseas agent to be abandoned; unfortunately this can result in a costly process of reimbursing that agent later on. There comes a point at which export must be considered as a long-term investment into entering foreign markets. Exporting is often carried on until a sufficiently large market is built up in the foreign country to justify investment in production facilities in that country. Exporting is also often seen as a useful way of learning how to operate in international markets. Unfortunately, the key management skills involved are essentially those of marketing, and as the export operation is almost entirely a marketing one, often a domestic company entering into the early stages does not have these areas of expertise.

One of the main factors influencing the decision to export is, of course, the tariffs on the goods concerned. High import tariffs tend to encourage domestic companies to go the manufacturing route, as do other trade barriers. Many markets are closed to exporters for balance of payment reasons in the foreign country concerned.

The choice between agents or direct sales facilities frequently has to be made at this stage. Agents usually offer a quick entry with little investment or risk and have the advantage of knowing the country and the customers. On the other hand, they are usually limited in the attention that they can give to the product, are less subject to controls, and are sometimes very ill-equipped to handle technical problems. Many countries, indeed, impose stringent penalties for terminating agency contracts, so it is worth while looking at this aspect very carefully before becoming tied to a particular agent. Generally speaking, the agent appears to be declining in relative importance, particularly in goods requiring any knowledge or understanding of technical aspects.

9 If international marketing executives are considering entry into foreign markets, they must be aware of the economic environment that exists in those foreign markets. There are several economic considerations that might govern the decision either to enter or not to enter a particular country. These include the country's economic development, and the purchasing power of the various segments within the market.

The stage of economic development is very significant — it will determine the potential for a wide variety of goods. Two very well-known examples are Pepsi-Cola and Singer sewing machines. The potential of these two products does not seem to be affected by the level of economic development — they are purchased in the least developed countries and the most advanced countries. But most other companies are affected by economic potential. It might be asked whether marketing is relevant in less-developed countries because of their lack of purchasing power, but the conclusion would be that international marketing is relevant regardless of economic development as long as it is geared to customer needs. The less developed countries would not be good markets for motor cars, but they might be excellent markets for motor bikes.

Countries can be categorised as:

(a) less developed;
(b) developing;
(c) industrialised;
(d) post-industrialised economies.

These classifications vary according to the gross national product, the rate of literacy, the evolution from an agricultural to an industrial economy (as applies in most developing countries), the evolution from industrial to service economies (as in post-industrial economies), and the range and quality of products that are demanded by the markets within those countries.

Yet another consideration in economic development is whether the economy is based upon free market exchanges, or a centrally-planned economy. Most countries have elements of both. The United Kingdom and the European Economic Community are regarded as free market economies, but exert significant control over utilities, telecommunications and transportation. Russia and most of the COMECON countries are based on a central planning authority, but private enterprise exists in the exchange of certain items and in selling 'black market' goods. An international marketer must recognise the latitude that exists in setting prices, distributing and promoting products. The large American oil company, Amoco, recognised the degree of centralised planning in mainland China and directed its advertising not to final consumers, but to the decision-makers in the various government ministries that oversee the exploration of petroleum products.

Finally, the purchasing power of the target segments must be considered. The level of economic development indicates the general purchasing power of a country. Marketing managers must evaluate the purchasing power of the target segments abroad. These are likely to vary among countries. In the post-industrial countries, purchasing power is more homogeneous than in other economies because of a higher standard of living. In the less developed countries, extreme variations in purchasing power are very common. It would not be surprising to see a Rolls-Royce or a Mercedes in Ghana or Peru, because of the existence of a very powerful, but small, elite. The largest market for Lamborghini is Portugal, one of the poorest European countries, because of the existence of a wealthy status-conscious elite.

10 The basic nature of marketing does not change from domestic to international marketing, but marketing outside of national boundaries poses special problems. Unlike domestic marketing, international marketing requires operating simultaneously in more than one kind of environment, coordinating the operations, and using the experience gained in one country for making decisions in another. The demands are, therefore, tough and the stakes are high. International marketing managers must not only be sensitive to different marketing environments internationally, but also be able to balance marketing moves world-wide in order to seek optimum results for the company.

New technology, disappearing trade barriers, and changing cost relationships, have affected the competitive patterns of industry world-wide. Therefore, only companies with global perspectives are operating successfully. A very few world companies sell world products to increasingly brand-conscious consumers. One of the best examples to use in illustrating the impact of the environment upon international business is the wrist-watch industry. The globalisation of the watch industry has made five countries — Switzerland, Japan, Hong Kong, the United States and the Soviet Union — dominate the scene by emphasising brand names. Manufacturing operations are specialised by country according to costs of specific processes, sub-assemblies, and component parts.

It has been suggested that the number of American managers stationed abroad will most likely not diminish within the next decade. Concurrently, it has been found that a very high percentage of individuals who become chief executives of multi-national organisations do so without ever having had international experience. It has also been shown that many managers with international responsibilities have had no training in international studies prior to their employment, and have not participated in management development programmes with international content. In other words, they lack preparation for their international responsibilities. These sorts of findings emphasise the importance of formal training in international business, with particular emphasis on training and marketing, because marketing problems in overseas business surpass in complexity those in any other areas. Recent research has shown that marketing errors in international business outweighed those in other areas by a very wide margin.

One aspect of the complexity of UK, US and European marketing centres around the strategic shortage of materials. These shortages occur either because of depletion by use or because they were limited in the first place. Therefore, they have to depend on other nations for many minerals; some are not available from land sources in Europe of the United States, for example, platinum, titanium manganese, cobalt. As the Middle East oil embargo proved, dependence upon outside sources for strategic materials involves high risks.

Traditionally, marketing managers have been accustomed to gearing production and distribution strategies to never-ending natural resources. But increasingly in the future, a new marketing perpective is essential. Shortages of materials will affect marketing in many different ways, including the following:

(a) Scarcities are likely to alter the speed, direction and motivation behind economic growth, which is the company's reason for operation.

(b) Scarcities are likely to affect taste and lifestyle, for example, moving demand away from those products and services that are wasteful materials, too energy-intensive or pollute the environment.

(c) Scarcities are apt to make inflation endemic, and as a result, distort demand patterns.

(d) Scarcities require recuperation and the recycling of wastes.

(e) Scarcities influence advertising tremendously, and to a lesser extent, distribution.

2 Comparative analysis of world markets

INTRODUCTION

This chapter covers that part of the syllabus relating to a comparative analysis of world markets: methods of comparative analysis and economic dimensions — income, wages, gross national product, trade and competitive patterns, etc.; socio-cultural patterns — population, education, literacy, ethnic, occupational, consumption patterns, etc.; political, legal, geographical and natural resource dimensions; stages of market development.

QUESTIONS

1 While international marketing personnel must be aware that culture influences all aspects of an environment, they must also know that cultures change over time. Describe the basis of cultural change.

2 Expropriation is the harshest of all forms of political intervention. When is this most likely to occur and how can organisations best avoid it?

3 Both the stability of a government and its ability to govern its own economy are significant factors to consider in international business. What criteria would you establish to analyse a country's situation in these areas?

4 The conceptual analysis of marketing opportunity centres around two sets of criteria: cost/benefit and risk/reward. Explain.

5 Describe how you would set about selecting a new international market.

6 How would tax controls, exchange controls, and import restrictions be used as a form of political intervention?

7 What is the Eurodollar?

8 How do market agreements between countries affect international marketing?

9 What factors would you consider in attempting to determine your possible competitive advantage over other companies?

10 'One of the most common errors made by the international executive in evaluating a foreign country is in ignoring the cultural and social factors of that country.' Discuss.

ANSWERS

1 The matter of cultural change is a controversial one and different anthropologists would specify different reasons for it. While it may be disputed, one way of looking at cultural change is through economic development and Maslow's 'hierarchy of needs' theory. Maslow ranked five human needs, from low to high, in the following order: physiological needs of food, water, shelter, and sex; safety needs, protection, security, stability; social needs, affection, friendship, acceptance; ego needs, prestige, success, self-esteem; and the need for self-actualisation. As a country begins to move from a subsistence economy, where fulfilment of physiological needs has been the major goal, to a situation where basic needs are easily achievable, new needs take precedence. This change forces cultural adjustment. In other words, as the economic well-being of society satisfies one level of needs, it gives rise to new needs whose satisfaction requires cultural change.

Consider the role of a South-East Asian homemaker. In a village economy, she would be fully confined to the home; but a job for her husband in a factory in a nearby city enables the family to move into that city. This move assures the family of basic needs fulfilment. There would be no more dependence on the farm for survival, but instead, a weekly wage-packet. At this time safety needs become important. Safety requires buying groceries at the works' shop as soon as they are available. In many developing countries, items such as cooking oil, sugar and soap are often in short supply. Thus, while the husband is at work, the wife must shop. This imposes a new role on the wife, a cultural change that results from economic prosperity. No longer are activities confined within the home; now she can go out alone to shop; something that back in the village would have been culturally totally prohibited.

Whether all aspects of a culture change when a single aspect changes is a question that may be answered by referring to Hall's classification of culture aspects into formal, informal and technical. Formal aspects constitutes the core of a culture. They are most deeply rooted and are extremely difficult to change. Formal aspects are taught as absolute rights or wrongs. Non-observance of formal aspects cannot be forgiven. Informal aspects are traits that one learns by being a member of the society. Everyone is supposed to be aware of these aspects. If an informal aspect is not adhered to, an expression of disapproval or concern would be shown. In other words, accommodation is feasible in relation to informal aspects. Technical aspects are transmitted in the form of instruction and have reasons behind them. Change can be most easily accomplished in technical cultural aspects. So long as change can be reasoned in a logical fashion, no emotions stand in the way.

The definition of a formal, informal or technical cultural aspect will vary from country to country. For example, take the case of cigarette smoking among middle class, teenage girls. In India, this matter would be concerned with a formal aspect of the culture and completely rejected. In Latin America, it would be in conflict with an informal aspect of the culture. While parents might not like their daughters smoking, they might accept it after registering their disapproval. In West Germany and Sweden, a young girl smoking could be categorised as a technical aspect. Parents might not mind if the cigarettes are low tar and, therefore, on technical grounds, they will have resisted smoking for health reasons. Once it is agreed that the cigarettes will be low tar, there would be no objection to the girls smoking.

2 Let us first establish what is meant by expropriation. It is the official seizure of foreign property by a host country whose intention is to use the seized property in the public interest. Expropriation is recognised by international law as the right of sovereign states, provided the expropriated companies are given prompt compensation, at fair value, in convertible currencies.

The second part of this definition points out the source of much of the controversy associated with expropriation. Other terms used interchangeably with expropriation are nationalisation, indigenisation, and socialisation. Nationalisation refers to a transfer of the entire industry within that country from private to public ownership, with no discrimination as to foreign ownership or local ownership. Socialisation, also referred to as communisation, differs from nationalism in that it is a transfer of all the industries within the country. Indigenisation refers to the transfer and ownership from foreign to local control. Confiscation means expropriation without compensation.

Patterns of expropriation have been differentiated according to industry, geographic region, type of ownership, technology, degree of vertical integration, assets size and politico-economic situation. Based on geographic region, Latin America has accounted for 49% of all expropriations between 1960 and 1980, followed by the Arab countries, with just under 30%, Black African with 13%, and South-East Asian nations with 11%. A study by the United Nations of foreign firm take-overs in the 1960s and 1970s shows that two-thirds of all take-overs were accounted for by just 10 countries, including Argentina, Chile, Peru, Iraq, Libya, Algeria, and Cuba.

For a long time it was believed that ownership shared with host nations through joint ventures was advantageous. This has been proved false. Although on an admittedly small data base from which strict conclusions would not be permitted, it has been found that joint ventures with host country governments, as opposed to wholly owned foreign subsidiaries, have a greater rate of expropriation. Furthermore, joint ventures with foreign multi-nationals are eight times worse, although they have a better chance of obtaining compensation for the expropriated properties.

Technology can serve as a defence against expropriation if the technology of the enterprise cannot be duplicated by the host country or cannot be made operable by the expropriators. However, former employees are sometimes induced to work for these expropriated businesses through salary incentives. Low technology industries, on the other hand, are easily taken over, even though this seldom happens because such enterprises are unattractive, lacking the glamour of technological advancement sought by the developing countries.

If a company is vertically integrated with the parent company so that the parent company controls either the supplies for production or the market for the product, the company is then an unlikely target for expropriation. This relative safety comes from the obvious fact that the enterprise would be unoperable or its output unmarketable without the parent company and thus no longer of economic value to the host country. Brand names and trade marks are also important; without a brand identification, it would be difficult to market products successfully.

Another area to be analysed and compared is that of asset size. According to some researchers, a firm with very large total assets has a much better chance of being expropriated than a firm with small assets, the reason being that the political and economic gains from expropriation of a small company would not justify the cost to the host country with regard to reactions of the business community, world lending institutions, and foreign governments.

The politico-economic backdrops against which expropriations have taken place, have been associated with sweeping and violent upheavals, which transform the basic governmental structure and politico-economic ideologies of the nation involved. Recent trends have shifted from those of ideologies and politics, to the more functional need for economic development desired by the less developed countries. In the light of this trend, expropriations have become more selective, directed toward those foreign-owned enterprises whose policies or aspirations have conflicted with the economic plans and priorities of the developing nation. To lessen vulnerability in this area, a company should assess the proper behaviour necessary to fit in with the economic interests and objectives of the host nation.

3 In many countries there are frequent changes of government. In such a climate, a foreign business finds that the government has changed by the time it is ready to implement an agreement. In other words, the government with whom the intitial agreement was arranged was different from the one currently in office. Such changes may create difficulties in implementing the agreement because the new government may not subscribe to the commitments made by its predecessor.

Thus, it is important for international marketers to try to determine, in advance of making agreements, whether the current government will continue to be in office to implement agreements made with it. In a democratic situation, the encumbent party strengths and/or the alternative outcomes for the next election can be weighted to assess the likelihood of a change in government. In other situations a variety of symptoms could point towards the instability of a government:

(a) public unrest, demonstrations, riots, or other demonstrations of social tension;
(b) government crises, opposition forces tring to topple the government;
(c) armed attacks by one group of people on another, or from a neighbouring country;
(d) guerrilla warfare;
(e) politically motivated assassinations;
(f) coup d'état;
(g) irregular change in top government leaders.

A report covering these factors would provide good evidence of a government's stability or instability.

Another factor to be examined is the quality of the host government's economic management. A country that manages its economic affairs according to sound economic principles, whether through free economies or socialist policies, other things being equal, will provide a more favourable environment than a country governed by political emotions and corrupt practices. The economic environment of a country should be studied in the political context with particular reference to:

(a) the ability of the government to sustain its internal and external debt;
(b) the country's pursuit of stable and diversified growth;
(c) the country's ability to generate an adequate amount of foreign exchange;
(d) the nature of the various fiscal and monetary means used to steer the economy;
(e) the quality of the long-term planning of economic policy and its implementation.

Take as an example, a country that continues to live on borrowed funds, either from private sources or from international agencies like the IMF, and frequently defaults on payments or demonstrates poor economic management.

4

Cost benefit analysis

Cost benefit criteria answer a series of questions that stress markets, competition, and the financial implications of doing business in a foreign country.

Markets Will people want our products? More importantly, will they want them enough to pay a price that will yield us a profit? Is the market large enough for the company to venture in?

Competition What kind of competition will we have to face, and will the rules apply equally to all? Concern about equal treatment within a market comes from situations of altered market-place. In many countries, altered market-place competition comes from host governments, through direct ownership of competitors, subsidisation, or participation. In such cases, the foreign business is usually at a disadvantage since it is pitted against inefficient local business but cannot compete on an equal footing.

Financial examination How many resources, and how much of each, must be committed and what will be their cost? What return may be expected, and how long might it take to recover the investment?

Of course, there are other cost/benefit criteria. The level of training and skills of a national workforce is an important consideration, as well as the availablility of educated, experienced local managers. Most multi-national corporations have learned the value of having local or regional executives in host countries. For example, the Rander Organisation in Japan shares a joint venture that is manned entirely by Japanese workers and executives. In addition, transportation, communications systems, and the availability of local resources, especially energy, must be considered. This list could go on, but the above illustrate some of the assessable conceptual factors influencing market entry decisions.

Risk/reward criteria

The risk/reward criteria emphasise the overall, constantly changing mix of situations in the social, political and economic climates of a host country. In terms of economics, the macroeconomic characteristics of a country will almost always affect the specific economics of business. The national economic objectives of a country, therefore, also figure in a company's decision to explore entry there. For example, the company needs to know how fiscal policy — the control of the nation's economy through taxes — translates into business taxation, or how incomes policy, wage/price guidelines, may affect future wage and price controls. The company also needs to know about a country's monetary policy — the control of the nation's economy through increasing or decreasing interest rates by the central bank. Does the country's policy place restrictions on international cash transactions, such as the repatriation of profits? What is the outlook, for example, for the cost and availablility of credits? Is the currency strong, and more important, what is the inflation situation?

5 There are over 150 countries in the world; of these the majority may appear to offer entry markets. Many countries go out of their way to attract foreign investment by offering lures ranging from tax exemptions to low-waged, ample, skilled labour. These inducements, valid as they may be in certain individual cases, have repeatedly led to hasty foreign market entry.

A good basis for decision is arrived at through a comparative analysis of different countries, with long-term economic environment having the greatest weight. In the first place certain countries, on account of their political situations (for example, Iran), would be considered unsuitable for market entry. It might help to consult one of the various indices that rate different countries for business attractiveness. Many banks and commercial institutions produce such lists. The final choice should be based on the company's own assessment and risk preference. Further, markets which are either too small in terms of population and per capita income, or economically too weak, should be eliminated. For example, a number of countries with populations less than 20 million and annual per capita incomes below £2,000 are of little interest to many companies because of the limited demand potential.

The markets surviving this screening are then assessed for strategic attractiveness. A battery of criteria should be developed to fit the specific requirements of a company, but basically they should focus on the following five factors:

(a) future demand and economic potential of the country in question;
(b) distribution of purchasing power by population groups or market segments;
(c) country/specific technical product standards;
(d) the spill-over from the national market, via standards, regulations norms or economic ties, to other markets;
(e) access to vital resources, such as qualified labour force, raw materials sources, suppliers.

There is no reason to expand the list since additional criteria are rarely significant enough to result in useful new insights. Rather, management should concentrate on developing truly meaningful and practical parameters for each of the five criteria listed above, so that the selection process does not become unnecessarily costly and the results are fully relevant to the company concerned.

6

Tax controls
Governments may impose excessive and unconventional taxes on foreign businesses. For example, a new form of excise tax for which there is no precedent may be placed on the output of a foreign company. Such taxes are imposed for three reasons. First, an out-of-the-way burden on foreign companies is an indirect way of warning them that they are not wanted in a country any longer. Second, when a country is in dire need of new revenues, an additional tax burden on foreign companies appears not only politically prudent, but economically convenient. Thirdly, taxes can be retaliatory if a government, for example, learns that foreign companies have abused differences in international taxation and have deprived the country of due revenue.

Taxes *per se* do not hinder foreign enterprise. But problems do arise over excessively discriminatory taxes or taxes imposed at variance with company's agreement with government. For example, the host government may have agreed to give a tax 'holiday' to a company, say for five years, to establish its operations in the country. Three years later, the government chooses to reverse its position for some reason, such as a new government refusing to abide by the agreement entered into by its predecessor.

Exchange controls

Countries having difficulties with the balance of trade often impose restrictions on the free use of foreign exchange. For example, import of luxuries from outside the country is restricted. Similarly, restrictions are placed on the remittances from the country involving hard currency. The exchange control may also be an effort to encourage domestic industry. One of the best examples available in the world today of this situation is Nigeria.

Exchange control measures affect foreign businesses in two ways. First, profits and capital cannot be returned to the parent company at will. Second, raw materials, machinery, spare parts, etc. cannot be liberally imported for operating purposes.

Most developing companies utilise exchange controls to regulate their hard currency balances. The need for such regulation is one important reason for restrictions on the imports of consumer goods in most emerging countries. Sometimes even developed countries may resort to exchange control. Indeed, in 1981 France did this following a take-over by the socialist government.

Import restrictions

Import restrictions are primarily for the support of native industries. Consider a foreign pharmaceutical company traditionally importing certain compounds and chemicals from the parent company. If the host country places restrictions on imports, it may be forced to depend on local sources of supply for these raw materials. This can bring two types of problem for the foreign company. First, the local product may be of inferior quality which will affect the quality of the finished product. Second, locally the product may be in such short supply that the pharmaceutical manufacturer cannot acquire it in adequate quantities.

Presumably, government legislate import restrictions with the total industry, not a particular company, in mind. Thus, the difficulties likely to be faced by a foreign company do not really figure in this discussion. Further, when a country wants to encourage domestic industry as a matter of industrial policy, import restrictions are adopted with the realisation that the local product will be inferior, at least initially. Strictly from the point of view of the government, import restrictions seem reasonable but they naturally jeopardise the functions of a foreign business.

7 The term Eurodollars refers to US dollars accumulated over the years by European banks and other banks outside the United States. Since these dollars are outside the jurisdiction of the United States government, the European banks are free to deal in them without any restriction.

In addition to the US dollars acquired by banks with their own or foreign currency, Eurodollars also come into existence when a domestic or foreign holder of dollar demand deposits in the United States places their own deposit in a bank outside the United States.

Usually banks are supposed to maintain certain reserves in some proportion to their deposits to protect their depositers. Eurodollar borrowing and lending can be done anywhere in the world without being subject to cost regulations imposed by the US authorities on banks in the United States, particularly in reserve requirements.

Eurodollars reached a substantial amount in the early 1970s. The total deposits were greater than the total gold reserves held by governments. It is estimated that in the 1980s Eurodollars will increase to over one trillion. How big this amount is can only be considered by relating it to the fact that the total gold reserves held by governments are about 40 billion.

While initially the offshore market was created in US dollars, today a number of other European currencies are freely deposited and borrowed outside their home bases. These are the German mark, the Swiss franc, the English pound sterling and the French franc. As time passes, monetary authorities see the problem related not to the Eurodollar alone, but to the Euro-currencies.

The prefix Euro in Eurodollars does not limit the dealings in them to Europe alone. It just happens that the market for expatriate US dollars grew up in Europe and that most of the dealing in Eurodollars was done by banks in London or other European financial centres. Thus, the term Eurodollar has been loosely applied to deposits in Toronto, Hong Kong, Kuala Lumpur, Rio de Janeiro and Singapore.

The market in Asian dollars is really only an offshoot of the Eurodollar market. The Asian market deals in US dollars and other leading currencies deposited in local banks, and then lends them to Asian borrowers.

8 Market agreements affect international marketing in a number of ways. First, the scope of the market is broadened. For example, after the formation of the Common Market, the French market ceased to be just a French market, rather it became a part of a larger common market. Such an expanded market provides a flexibility which would not be feasible dealing with individual countries. Under a free trade area agreement, internal trade barriers among member countries are abolished and a company may move products from one country to another freely.

This permits a company to achieve economies of scale not only in production, but also in promoting the product, in distribution, and in other aspects of business. For example, the establishment of the European Common Market made it feasible for the Ford Motor Company to integrate its operations in Germany and the United Kingdom.

Second, market agreements change the nature of competition. For example, before the formation of the Common Market, many American multi-national corporations found little local competition in Western Europe, but afterward, local companies were encouraged to expand quickly. They became factors in the market, through mergers, with the encouragement of member governments.

Third, market agreement firms expand through mergers and acquisitions and thereby become highly competitive outside their market area as well. For example, after the formation of the European Common Market, French and German companies were able to compete aggressively against both American and Japanese multi-nationals.

Finally, market agreement countries are able to make decisions favourable to all member country companies. It would not be feasible for an individual country to enforce such measures. For example, Common Market anti-trust policies could adversely effect an American company and its subsidiaries or licensees that previously had been given exclusive rights in, say, Italy and the Netherlands.

It is important to mention also that economic integration, while leading to a variety of benefits, can create some problems. Consider, for example, the potential for trouble with the free movement of labour within the European Community. With relatively poor countries like Spain and Turkey joining the Common Market, controversy over guest workers from these countries in Germany in particular, is likely. In the long run, the free movement of labour may become elusory. Another problem is the jeopardy into which existing agreements by a nation are thrown when it joins a market group. Entry into the EEC caused Great Britain's commitments to the Commonwealth to diminish. Agricultural overproduction and inefficiencies are always potentially controversial among member countries, since no nation wants its output outpriced by cheap imports. Agricultural exports are likely to be a chief issue of conflict between the EEC and the United States.

It should be noted that a market agreement does not create a homogeneous market, but simply broadens the market base. Within the enlarged heterogeneous market, segments ought to be identified for the development of the marketing strategy, each segment served by a unique marketing mix. Such an approach might not be possible for each individual country, however. Many marketers erroneously thought that with the establishment of the Common Market, Western Europe would present a single homogeneous market. Even the individual consumer was supposed to lose his individuality.

While there is not, apparently, a homogeneous market for consumers, there are homogeneous segments within the European Common Market that must be recognised and each segment served through a unique marketing programme.

9 Initial analysis may indicate an open space in the market for a possible entry. Nevertheless, competitors may follow right on the heels of your entry. Additional analysis is needed to figure out the competitive advantage the company has over its rivals, both existing and potential. The following questions should be raised to analyse the competition:

(a) Who are the competition now, and who will they be in the future?

(b) What are the key competitors' strategies, objectives and goals?

(c) How important is a specific market to a competitor, and is it committed enough to continue to invest?

(d) What unique strengths do the competitors have?

(e) Do they have any weaknesses that make them vulnerable?

(f) What changes are likely in the competitors' future strategies?

(g) What are the implications of competitors' strategies on the market, the industry and your own company?

While it may be relatively easy to pinpoint current competition in an international market, analysis of competition in the future is difficult because there is no way to figure out which companies from different parts of the world may become interested in the market in future. In any event, the best way to examine competition is to draw up a demographic profile of the industry. Markets dominated by small single-industry businesses or small national competitors differ from those dominated by multi-industry companies, and those in turn are different from those controlled by multi-national foreign companies.

Obviously, a major multi-national corporation with multi-industry interest would have certain inherent strengths which a single-industry foreign national company would not match. For example, multi-national corporations can often provide consumers with better and cheaper products or services, react faster to changing economic conditions, and more adroitly overcome or capitalise on market distortions created by governments than can national firms. These large companies have the resources to sacrifice profits in one country, in order to penetrate or gain position there, whilst using profits from another country to support this aggressiveness. They have the ability to work with governments, select the least costly source of supply, and even negotiate favourable trading concessions.

However, it is a mistake to believe that multi-national corporations always have superior leverage. Local foreign competitors may be small, but they can be helped by their governments. For example, governments can require that foreign competitors reduce profitability in order to increase local employment levels or maintain the balance of trade. Governments can also ban a multi-national company from obtaining supplies in low cost areas.

A simple listing of major competitors is not enough. It is also important to learn about their goals and aspirations. In fact, an attempt should be made to know competitors' total financial situations including their serious problems as well as their advantages and opportunities.

Further, the competitors' relative strengths and weaknesses should be examined. It is desirable to recognise the credible factors which could directly or indirectly bear on a product's performance in a given market. For example, adequate distribution may be critical in a developing country with inadequate means of transportation and communication, while research and development would be strategic to gain a competitive edge in Western Europe.

An example of strength is provided by the Japanese motor car companies. It is a known fact that the Japanese have captured a major share of both the European and the United States markets. Let us assume the Ford Motor Company decides to retaliate by exploring the possibility of entering the Japanese market. Despite all its strength and experience in international business, however, Ford may find itself greatly constrained in its endeavour by one weakness: cost structure. Because of wage price and managerial efficiency differentials, the Japanese companies can build and ship a car to Europe or the United States at a lower price than it costs America or Western Europe to produce the same vehicle. Thus, even if Ford were to assemble their cars in Japan, other things being equal, it would still be severely handicapped because of the cost advantage of the local companies. Of course, Ford might well pay lower wages in Japan, but this advantage would be wiped out by the experience that the Japanese have in Japan. In brief, despite the fact that Japan represents a viable market, analysis of the microeconomic environment paints a discouraging picture for a company such as Ford to enter into the Japanese market.

10 This statement is very true. All too frequently companies send technical men or engineers to make an appraisal of a situation in a particular country; and such men tend to overlook cultural problems. One company, when establishing a manufacturing plant in an overseas city, was surprised when it encountered vicious labour problems, and they were eventually forced to abandon the entire operation. A cultural anthropologist could have told them that for centuries the people in this city had been political agitators and strongly anti-business. They simply did not work for a living, but insisted that any business in the area contribute to their welfare, almost free of charge. Business cannot be carried on in such a cultural environment. Yet another example is where a manufacturer

attempting to do business among a certain group of nations discovered to his concern that he could not trust the word of associates. Their written contracts were worthless scraps of paper. Any anthropologist could have told this businessman that among these people sharp practices are badges of honour, and they only stick to their word when it is to their advantage to do so; they seldom honour their debts and would embezzle anything they could. How can you do business with such people? There are ways, but they pose limitations.

On the other hand, there are countries whose cultural code is such that there is little worry about their meeting obligations. The cultural patterns of a nation also affect its taste, preferences in goods, consumption habits, and the reactions to various stimuli.

It must be remembered by the international executive considering foreign marketing that many typical innovations in one country are not marketable in foreign cultures. The English reaction to the American Betty Crocker cake mixes is an example. The American General Mills Corporation spent nearly $1 million advertising four varieties of mixes, altered their formulae to try to please the British palate, and adjusted the volume to fit smaller English cake pans. The whole programme was a failure, because British women refused to accept the mix or the principle of the labour-saving convenience. They felt that they were not doing their duties properly as housewives. General Mills had previously had a similar experience in the breakfast food market.

3 World marketing infrastructures, and international and multi-national organisations

INTRODUCTION

The questions and answers in this chapter relate to that area of the syllabus concerned with world marketing infrastructures: local and international sources; banking, transport, insurance, communications, etc.; local and international research, advertising, media agencies, etc.; international monetary fund. The chapter also covers international and multi-national organisations: forms of organisation for international and multi-national operations; centralised and decentralised policies; setting objectives for international operations; monitoring and controlling overseas business; transfer of personnel and recruitment of nationals.

QUESTIONS

1 How does the factor of differing environments help distinguish domestic marketing from international marketing?

2 Explain the concept of 'production sharing' which is a new concept of international business and trade recently introduced by Peter Drucker.

3 Describe the activities of the International Monetary Fund.

4 In relation to the International Monetary System, what is a petrodollar?

5 Discuss the implications of the financial decisions of multi-national corporations on marketing.

6 In relation to the International Monetary System, explain the vulnerability of the international financial system as it is today.

7 What factors affect the design of a multi-national company organisation structure?

8 Why is the matrix structure of organisation proving popular with many multi-national corporations?

9 How best could you achieve the integration of multi-national marketing activities?

10 As a company's size increases, the distance between top management and marketing operations grows, making the control and analysis process more difficult. How would you attempt to overcome this?

ANSWERS

1 The environment within which decisions are made is unique to each country. It is this differential of environment that distinguishes international marketing from domestic marketing.

Typically, a company should make domestic marketing decisions having due consideration to internal and external environments. The internal environment factors primarily refer to corporate objectives, corporate organisation and structure, and some resource availability. External environment factors include competition, technological change, economic climate, political influences, social and cultural changes, legal requirements, ethical business standards, consumerism, and changes in marketing channels.

A company interested in doing business in a foreign country would face the same internal and external factors but from an entirely different environmental perspective. Economic conditions vary from one country to another. Certain laws in certain countries make it much tougher to do business than in other countries. Women have an important decision-making role as consumers in the Western world, but this is not the situation in Moslem and other Middle Eastern cultures. Business environments vary tremendously even among countries that are geographically in the same region, or that have the same cultural heritage. For instance, it would be wrong to assume that the United States and the United Kingdom have common marketing environments. There may be some similarities, but overall the two are very different.

The nature of decision-making in international business is essentially the same as in domestic business. Consideration of environment, however, is more philosophically abstract. In addition to the commercial internal and external environmental aspects, each individual country has a total environmental reality that the international marketer must perceive. The international marketer can define this reality using four large general categories: economic, cultural, political and legal environments. In addition, an understanding of international economic institutions, for example, the International Monetary Fund, and an understanding of agreements among nations is essential, even though it may not be strictly correct to label these as a part of a country's marketing environment.

Furthermore, an international marketer must be sensitive to aspects of his own domestic environment, such as competition and technological changes. Marketing decisions to serve the international customer also require consideration of the firm's domestic business — in objectives and strategies, commitments and resources, and organisation structure.

2 Peter Drucker describes production sharing as follows:

> It is the newest world economic trend. Although production sharing is neither export nor import in the traditional sense, this is how it is still shown in our

trade figures and treated in economic and political instructions. Yet it is actually economic integration by stages of the productive process.

The production sharing process describes and economic reality existing in developed countries where higher levels of education create higher levels of personal expectation. Then there follows a gradual disappearance of semi-skilled and unskilled labour, so necessary to labour-intensive manufacturing. Production sharing suggests that developed countries will turn to developing countries where the availability of labour is a major asset.

Production sharing enables companies in developed countries, possessing sophisticated management skills and high technology to combat successfully profit-threatening foreign imports. For example, a European company may utilise its skilled labour and technology to process a product partially, and then have the manufacturing stage, requiring more unskilled of semi-skilled labour, performed elsewhere. This enables a company to remain competitive against overseas imports. In essence, production sharing is an alternative to completely foreign imports.

It should be noted that the strategy of not charging duty on product exported from the United Kingdom and most Western European countries, has proved to be a tremendous advantage. By using production sharing techniques, companies can take advantage of this purely technological and sophisticated production capability. It encourages the retention of technology in one's own country and this in turn encourages technology with new benefits to one's own economy. The process also allows those industries which know how to use production sharing to continue employing thousands of their own nationals to perform skilled jobs in their own country, and still compete against foreign importers.

Production sharing, however, also benefits developing countries since they must find work for their surplus labour, which is qualified for only unskilled jobs. With only limited technology, capital and management available to develop their own integrated industries, developing countries have difficulties absorbing unskilled and semi-skilled people into the labour force. As a matter of fact, even if integrated industries could be established in developing countries, they would probably not have sufficient demand for the resultant product. Via production sharing, the developing nations find a mutually beneficial arrangement for solving their employment problems.

Currently, production sharing seems to be quite prevalent, and growing at a rapid pace. It is a new phenomenon for which there are no classic or neo-classic explanatory theories. Strictly speaking, production sharing is different from the traditional idea of international trade. It is a transnational business integration, a new relationship made possible by technological and business forces. Production sharing offers both the developed and developing countries of the world a chance to share their resources and strengths for their mutual benefit.

3 After the Bretton Woods conference in 1944, an institution called the International Monetary Fund (IMF) was established to oversee the newly agreed monetary system.

More and more nations joined the original 55 IMF signatories, so that today there are over 150 members. With the passage of time, various changes were made in the IMF system to ameliorate the difficulties that nations faced. For example, if a nation's fixed parity ceases to be realistic, it may therefore either revalue or devalue its currency. In such cases, the IMF agreed on orderly and reasonable changes in parity based upon the initiative of the country concerned. Such a system of alterable parity is often termed the adjustable peg.

There are several major accomplishments to the credit of the International Monetary Fund.

(a) rapidly increasing volume of trade in investment;

(b) flexibility in adapting to changes in international commerce;

(c) efficiency;

(d) hardiness;

(e) growing degree of international cooperation;

(f) capacity to accommodate reforms and improvements.

To an extent the Fund served as an international central bank to help countries during periods of temporary balance of payments difficulties, by protecting their rates of exchange. Because of that, countries did not need to resort to exchange controls and other barriers to restrict world trade.

As time passed, it became evident that the Fund's resources for providing short-term accommodation to countries in monetary difficulties were not sufficient. To resolve the situation, the Fund, after much debate, created special drawing rights, often referred to as paper gold, designed to provide additional liquidity to support growing world commerce.

Participant nations may use special drawing rights in a variety of ways: as a source of currency in a spot transaction, as a loan for clearing a financial obligation, as security for a loan, as a swap against currency, or in a forward exchange operation. A country with a balance of payments need may use its special drawing rights to obtain usable currency from another country designated by the Fund. A participant may also use special drawing rights to make payments to the Fund, such as repurchases. The Fund itself may transfer special drawing rights to a participant for various purposes including the transfer of special drawing rights instead of currency to a member using the Fund's resources.

4 The term 'petrodollars' refers to earnings from oil exports by the oil producing countries, often referred to as OPEC countries. These countries are Saudi Arabia, Iran, Iraq, Libya, Kuwait, Nigeria, Venezuela, Indonesia, The United Arab Emirates, Algeria, Qatar and Ecuador. The fourfold increase in the price of oil in 1973, and semi-annual increases thereafter, have led to the biggest shift of financial resources from one group nations to another in the economic and financial history of the world.

For world business and trade to run smoothly in the midst of such a resource shift, it is important that oil earnings be recycled into international capital markets. This is feasible in two ways:

(a) through the importation of goods from non-oil producing countries; and
(b) through depositing the surplus funds with multi-national banks.

Through this recycling process, the overall financial impact of petrodollars is reduced. Yet the existence and growth of petrodollars is a big issue confronting international economic policy-makers for two reasons. First, the oil exporters' long-term investments, purchases of imports, and short-term placement of funds, do not match the current account deficits of individual oil importing countries. Thus, the surplus earnings of oil exporters have to be transferred, or recycled, to the oil importing countries with inadequate foreign exchange to pay for their petrol imports. Secondly, the size of the financial holdings of oil exporters has altered the political and economic relationship between a sizeable part of the developing world and the industrialised nations.

The United States of America has so far received a large proportion of petrodollars in the form of export earnings, via different kinds of goods and services, and through foreign investments in US corporations, real estate, and direct deposits in US banks. However, the United States economy is deeply interrelated with other nations of the world. Thus, the impact of events elsewhere, such as recessions in other industrialised countries, as well as in Africa, Asia and Latin America, are keenly felt by the United States economy. Failure to reallocate financial resources to enable individual nations to meet their oil import requirements leads to restrictions on their non-oil imports. The developing countries could even resort to foreign exchange restrictions and exchange rate changes, as well as seeking renegotiation of overseas debt.

The OPEC nations are fully aware of their new power and have exploited the situation to their best advantage. At the same time, considering the susceptibility of their own fortunes to international disorder and their need to become fully acceptable members in world and Western nation financial circles, they have gone along with a variety of measures to recycle petrodollars to the benefit of both developed and developing countries.

5 An enterprise ultimately ventures across national boundaries for the enhancement of its long-term profitability. Therefore, financial commitments and their results deeply affect the marketing perspective of a business. While the relationship between finance and marketing functions is nothing new, in the realm of international business, financial considerations can bear on marketing decisions more heavily.

Marketing is affected by the international financial policies of the parent company, both directly and indirectly. Transfer pricing policy, for example, has significant direct impact on marketing. Transfer pricing means, in brief, setting prices for the transfer of goods, services, and technology between related affiliates in different countries. Such inter-firm transfer pricing is affected by many considerations, such as: fund positioning, income taxes, tariffs and quotas; managerial incentives and evaluations; anti-trust laws; the interests of joint venture partners; and corporate bargaining power with suppliers and financial institutions. Many of these conflicting considerations have financial underpinnings.

Eventually, all marketing decisions that involve captal and/or other types of long-term financial commitment on the part of the parent company must be viewed in the context of corporate international financial policy. For example, marketing wisdom might suggest improving the provision of after-sales services, which might entail manufacturing parts locally. But the latter could require substantial investment and transfer of technology. Considered in the context of overall financial goals, the parent company might find it undesirable to invest in manufacturing spare parts and suppliers in a host country. Or the parent company may learn that another affiliate recently expanded capacity to manufacture the same parts, or that the political situation in the host country is discouraging to additional investments, and so on. In the end, the decision, which based on marketing consideration appeared potentially desirable, may be postponed or dropped when viewed from the financial angle.

The financial strength of a company deeply affects marketing, particularly in the company's ability to maintain inventories. Making timely delivery to customers could provide important competitive leverage in international business, particularly if inventory replenishment involved great distances and time. Similarly, marketing is affected by the company's ability to make economic bulk purchases of merchandise.

The company's capacity to undertake promotion in the mass media to strengthen the brand image, to commit resources to research and development for the timely introduction of new and improved products, or to make investment in developing cordial relationships with channels of distribution, also affect marketing. It is this intimate relationship between the two functions of finance and marketing that requires basic knowledge of financial matters in order to conduct international marketing with expertise.

6 Since the first oil crisis in 1973, international banking has become a dominant force in the international monetary and financial structure. This evolution has occurred in the following way. The unspent surplus balances of the oil producers were mainly deposited in Western banks, while the banks played a crucial role in meeting the increased financial needs of non-oil developing countries. The volume of international bank loans more than trebled from 1953 to the end of 1979, standing in excess of $1,000 billion.

The vital role that private banks played in salvaging the developing countries in the 1970s has had the following consequences:

(a) The banks find it difficult to meet their normal obligations with short-term maturity funds.

(b) Inflation has caused their capital ratios to decline.

(c) They are rapidly running up against countries borrowing limits, which were legally imposed or internally set for the containment of risks.

(d) A large proportion of the loans are concentrated in potentially vulnerable countries, like Zaire, Peru and Turkey.

(e) Finally, the profitability of international lending is declining.

The people involved in international banking are aware of the problems of the international financial system and discussions have taken place on many occasions in recent years on how to reduce international lending and liquidity risks. For example, it has been proposed that a private safety net be organised for individual banks to resort to in case of an emergency in terms of liquidity. Such an arrangement would ensure the stability of the system by an injection of liquidity if, for some reason, the deposits were to dry up. The idea of a safety net, however, has been opposed by representatives of Third World countries. They fear such a measure would scare private banks that deal with developing countries. In the 1980s, however, under the umbrella of the IMF, some sort of multi-lateral agreement — a standby swap agreement between the IMF and each of the 20 or so major international banks could be worked out — should be effected. Since a liquidity crisis could be very profitable, and would very probably be accompanied by an exchange crisis in which many banks of different nationalities might be involved, an international swap network would offer an adequate degree of security.

7 A multi-national corporation must choose an organisational structure that maximises decentralisation while still providing for the coordination of independent activities. The structure is mainly determined by the following environmental factors.

Quality of management The decentralisation of authority to the local level can become quite a problem because of the quality of management varies from country to country. However, authoritative committees, either at the corporate or regional level with majority control, can be used to offset this potential problem.

Diversity of product lines Most companies with a high degree of product diversity decentralise on a product basis, rather than on an area basis. Companies producing a few similar product will not decentralise on a product basis because of the high degree of interdependence among these products. But complete standardisation is usually not practical or desirable for marketing decisions because of different market characteristics and consumers.

Size of firm Firms which derive a substantial portion of business from foreign operations usually drop the international division structure in favour of a product or geographic structure, which facilitates growth. As long as its international business is small, a firm can operate effectively with an international division structure.

Localisation of subsidiaries and their characteristics A company which emphasises local and regional variations will lean towards the geographic structure because specific geographic variation must be specifically catered for. On the other hand, a company whose subsidiaries are similar to those of the home country is unlikely to favour a geographical structure because a good degree of standardisation can be used in promoting products.

Economic blocks Companies operating within a regional economic block usually integrate their subsidiaries within the block area to deal better with trade barriers; they oversee these operations by establishing special regional organisational units. Such a design makes it feasible to provide adequate responses to the unique economic characteristics of the block arrangement.

The ultimate decision of a firm's international organisation structure is based on specific factors unique to that company's operating environment. Hence no two companies, even in the same industry, will exhibit exactly similar structures. In the computer industry, for example, IBM and Sperry Rand use different organisation structures. Sperry Rand operates with a product structure because of a diversified product line, while IBM, because of its large size, has an area organisation.

8 One of the recent developments in organisation design is the matrix structure. This structure, which first achieved prominence in the 1960s, has been adopted by many multi-national corporations. The matrix structure offers greater flexibility than the single line of command structure, and reconciles this flexibility with coordination and economies of scale, the strength of large organisations. The main identifying feature of a matrix organisation is that certain managers report to

bosses rather than the traditional single boss; there is a dual, rather than a single, chain of command. Companies tend to adopt matrix forms when it is absolutely essential to be highly responsive to two sectors, such as product and geography; when uncertainties generate very high information processing requirements; and when there are strong constraints on financial and/or human resources.

For the multi-national company, the matrix organisation is a solution to the problem of responding to economic and political environments. A matrix organisation can have both geographic and product management components. The product management component would have world-wide responsibility for a given product line; the geographic management component would be responsible for all product lines in a national setting. Because the responsibilities overlap at the national product/market level, both are brought into play for major decisions. A national subsidiary product division must be able to relate to both in order to operate adequately.

In the matrix organisation it is expected that managers in the geographic area will defend postions favouring responsiveness to the local environment, and product managers will defend positions favouring efficiency and overall economic competitiveness. Because their past experiences and their interests do not coincide, geographic and product managers tend to behave differently in a given situation. This creates a duality of focus.

Most matrix organisations adopt dual budgeting systems, whereby each arm of the matrix generates a complete budget. Parallel accounting systems provide independent controls. Dual personnel evaluation systems go hand-in-hand with dual budgeting to help sustain a power balance. If a person is to be directed by two superiors, both should take part in that person's evaluation. Employees with two bosses must know that both bosses have a part in each employee's evaluation. That way, a commitment to both orientations is encouraged. Many matrix organisations insist that both superiors 'sit in' when evaluation feedback is given to employers and both advise employees of salary changes so that the reward will not be thought of as coming from one side of the matrix only.

In designing a matrix system, one has to be aware of its typical problems. Power struggles are a constant problem when the system is first applied. These struggles result from a dual command system which has a tendency to create an inbalance of power as each side determines the limits of its influence.

Another problem is the mistaken belief that matrix management is group decision-making. It is not. Each matrix boss and his parallel in the other 'arm' have separate functions which should seldom conflict.

Matrix structures have a tendency to collapse during economic crises. In a crisis situation, matrix structures often become a convenient excuse for poor management.

In conclusion, the matrix system is a great benefit to companies that have to react quickly to the environment. Companies generally evolve into matrix forms rather than starting with them from scratch. Besides geographic and product matrix, systems there can be geographic and functional, or functional and product, matrix systems.

9 A key problem of multi-national corporations is how to tie the business activities of the subsidiaries together. There are different ways to integrate subsidiary operations, one of which is centralisation. But centralisation has limits. For example, there are products that are relatively culture-bound and require local adaptation. In such cases, the tailoring of marketing programmes to local conditions requires that authority be transferred to subsidiaries. When efficient centralisation is not feasible, there are three other methods for integrating corporate activities: corporate acculturation, systems transfer and people transfer.

The process of subsidiary acculturation involves assimilating corporate management's criteria for decision-making into subsidiary management thinking. Through this process, subsidiary managers can manage the company's overseas operation with relatively little interference from headquarters.

Systems transfer refers to the use of a uniform framework for marketing, planning and budgeting. This can serve to educate managers towards a disciplined analysis of business, provide head office with comparable data from all subsidiaries, standardise the process of decision-making throughout the organisation, and facilitate communication between head office and subsidiaries and amongst subsidiaries in different countries.

People transfer refers to the establishment of personal contact across borders among head office and subsidiary personnel. This includes long-term assignments of managers abroad and short-term meetings between head office and subsidiary executives and among personnel from different foreign subsidiaries. People transfer can help to smooth out the differences of viewpoint that exist in a multi-national organisation.

10 In a changing environment, information must come swiftly to ensure quick action in response to any success or failure. This timing factor alone has lead to a trend towards a much tighter control of foreign subsidiaries by multi-national corporations.

Another factor favouring stricter controls is the development and emergence of common markets. A common market eliminates taxes and tariffs among its member countries. As a consequence, firms attempting to do business in those markets have wisely relocated plants and reorganised distribution marketing functions to include these common market countries. But hand-in-hand with expansion must go control. Tight control should ensure consistency in product and marketing performance.

Yet another reason for the adoption of strict controls is the correction of unsatisfactory performance by subsidiaries. Frequently such failure is caused by a subsidiary manager's incompetence. But, for whatever reason, control over subsidiaries should improve, as well as provide, standards for achievement.

Further, since a multi-national organisation typically has several foreign subsidiaries in different parts of the world, a good control system is important to ensure that these subsidiaries move together toward a common goal, spelled out by the corporate strategic plan. On the other hand, a poor control system can make the task of evaluation and adjustment a very cumbersome one.

A good control system is also vital in evaluating the performance of top management in each subsidiary. Since the environmental conditions surrounding each subsidiary differ, it is impossible to use a completely standard system of evaluation. Some managers are forced to operate under far more severe conditions than others. A good control system allows for the consideration of varying factors in order to measure the true progress of an operation. Finally, a good control system permits better strategic planning and implementation of that planning. A management control system in a multi-national company should meet 10 basic requirements in order to ensure effective monitoring and evaluation of subsidiaries' performances:

(a) The control procedures and techniques to be used should be understandable and acceptable to the subsidiary heads involved.

(b) The subsidiary head should take an active part in formulating the control procedures and techniques to be used.

(c) The subsidiary head being evaluated should actively participate in the appraisal process.

(d) Each subsidiary should be given realistic objectives. These objectives should take into account each individual subsidiary's internal and external environments.

(e) Financial as well as non-financial data should be utilised to evaluate subsidiary performance.

(f) The control system should detect and report deviations from subsidiary plans as soon as, or before, they occur.

(g) The subsidiary head should be evaluated on the basis of performance only in those areas under direct control. The evaluation should take into account those factors which influence subsidiary performance but over which the subsidiary has little or no control.

(h) Control techniques should be tailored to the internal and external environments of the specific subsidiary.

(i) The control system should not stagnate, but should be revised and improved as required by changes in the subsidiary's environment.

(j) Top management must tie compensation to results achieved and outstanding performance must be tangibly rewarded.

4 Marketing planning and control

INTRODUCTION

This chapter deals with that part of the syllabus covering marketing planning and control: formulating plans for international and multi-national marketing; the marketing mix; product, price, promotional, distribution and competitive strategies; product development and multiplication; standardisation of elements of the marketing mix in international trade.

QUESTIONS

1 How would you attempt to seek planning effectiveness at subsidiary level in a multi-national environment?

2 Given the nature of the changing international corporate environment and the need for more sophisticated management, how would you approach the task of obtaining more effective management of international business?

3 Describe marketing planning at the corporate level.

4 How and why would you introduce additional products to the international product line?

5 Discuss the role of 'service' in international markets.

6 Describe the strategic significance of pricing in international markets.

7 What factors can affect transfer pricing in international markets?

8 What criteria could be employed to identify suitable intermediaries in international markets?

9 Describe the importance of international physical distribution.

10 What specific considerations would you give to international media planning?

ANSWERS

1 Effective planning at the subsidiary level should be encouraged through: the setting of objectives; the training of planning professionals; the development of planning and communication systems; and a cordial, collaborative attitude between all the people involved. The core of these measures is cooperation between the subsidiary and the parent company.

Objective setting
It is most essential that the subsidiary's objectives are neither directives from the head office, nor solely defined by the subsidiary itself in isolation from corporate direction. Rather, the objectives should be jointly set so that both corporate-wide perspectives and conditions peculiar to the subsidiary's environment are weighed in arriving at the subsidiary's objectives.

A cadre of planning professionals
The company should develop a cadre of international strategic planning professionals. Such professionals should have an awareness and insight into the country or region whose planning they coordinate. In other words, marketing planning should not be entrusted to a finance department which examines strictly in terms of set formulae and cut-off points. The planners at headquarters should be sensitive to the varying environment of each subsidiary before passing judgement on its financial performance.

Planning and communication systems
Traditionally, multi-national corporations have pursued standardised strategies world-wide. For example, if a corporate decision is made to increase market share for a particular product, that decision must be carried out globally. Standardisation, however, ignores the realities of the market-place for subsidiaries. The problem may be solved in two ways:

(a) by overhauling the planning system to take into account the marketing environment of each subsidiary; and
(b) by developing appropriate data bases through effective communication between the subsidiary and the head office.

Collaborative attitudes
Both the subsidiary and the parent corporation should develop an attitude of cordiality towards each other. Neither can do an adequate job of marketing planning on its own. They should collaborate with each other, the parent playing the staff role with the subsidiary assuming the line responsibility for maketing planning. In this way headquarters would be able to bring its systems capability to the planning while the subsidiary would contribute its deep knowledge of the market-place.

2 The effectiveness of international business management can be enhanced by adopting the following approach.

Emphasis should be placed on the fundamental nature of each of the various businesses to be managed internationally. This is the key to strategic management, rather than basing it on the nature of the many geographic units in which those businesses must function.

The essential step in determining how best to manage international operations is the 'unbundling' of existing activities. Unbundling will identify the individual natural businesses which exist. Such analysis helps to determine the functions to be carried out with regard to each natural business among corporate head offices, overseas regional offices, and local offices.

The natural business of any multi-national corporation falls into one of five categories of business:

(a) domestic business;
(b) domestic business with export;
(c) international business;
(d) overseas national business; and
(e) an *ad hoc* business.

This categorisation of business activities offers a number of advantages. It ensures that the corporation fully understands the nature, extent of involvement, risk, and contribution of its offshore activities, and thus encourages greater rigour in the articulation of its international strategies. Further, it applies the widely accepted modern concept of managing by strategy to international, as well as to domestic, operations and thereby provides much needed integration of global operations. Disfunctional conflicts are eliminated from the traditional artificial barriers that are erected organisationally around products and markets, and thus strategic issues are allowed to arise.

It identifies more clearly the specific types of information needed to manage different businesses internationally. The location and functions of different organisational units are defined: for example, resource allocation and information input responsibilities will be assigned between corporate, regional and local units. Also, the qualifications required of managers at various levels of the international corporate structure will be established.

Domestic business A domestic business produces and sells its products only domestically, whether by choice or as a result of various economic, technological, tariff, or non-tariff barriers.

Domestic business which exports A domestic business which exports is one that produces and sells basically the same product abroad and domestically, and provides the major link between each of the relevant domestic and overseas units. The fact that the corporation may establish an assembly or manufacturing facility abroad, in order to expand or retain a market for its products, is merely a part of its export strategy and does not change the basic nature of the business. Neither does the fact that modest changes in the product may be required to satisfy local requirements change the basic nature of such a business.

International business International businesses compete globally, usually on the basis of price. For the most part, such businesses consist of a few large companies that produce and distribute goods or services through units strategically located around the world. There appear to be three sub-groupings of international businesses:

(a) commodity products businesses, including wheat, tea, many base metals, oil, petro-chemical products and money;

(b) manufactured products businesses including watches and pocket calculators;

(c) international bid businesses, which involve the sale of international consulting, engineering, and construction services on a bid basis, and also include the sale of large, highly priced machinery, such as mainframe computers and generators, and large telecommunication systems.

Increasing internationalisation of standards is likely to expand the number of products that will be appropriately considered as international businesses.

Overseas national business The focus of an overseas national business is the products being offered by a geographically defined market area, which may include only one country or a number of countries. The products or services sold by the corporation in that area may bear little relation to those being sold domestically.

Ad hoc businesses An *ad hoc* business is an isolated business focused around a product or service activity which bears little or no relation to any of the other activities of the corporation, domestically or in a geographical region. It may have arisen as a result of unique business conditions; for example, a corporation may need to reinvest profits locally because of foreign exchange controls, or may need to take back foreign goods in barter.

3 Corporate management mainly plays two planning-related roles:

(a) It provides various information input to the subsidiaries and reviews and approves their plans.

(b) It develops a corporate-wide strategic plan. The corporate strategic plan may be either one global strategic plan covering both domestic and international markets, or two separate strategic plans, one each for domestic and international business. Presumably, companies with an ethnocentric or polycentric orientation would follow the latter course. Geocentrically oriented firms, however, would consider global markets as one market and would not make a distinction between domestic and international business.

A corporate head office's role in the planning efforts of subsidiaries has been examined on many occasions. Strategic planning among corporations is a new phenomenon which became popular in the 1970s. The initial efforts of strategic planning, as might be expected, were limited to domestic business. Strategic planning in international business is still in the developmental stage. Thus, overall experience in strategic planning for world-wide business is limited, and the following is therefore based on theory rather than practice.

Strategic marketing planning constitutes only a part of the strategic plan. The true role of planning is to articulate the means of implementing strategy. Strategy is the course of direction, and the intention is to influence the behaviour of competitors and the evolution of the market to the advantage of the company. Stated differently, business strategy is the concept of changing the competitive environment. Thus, a strategic statement includes a description of the new competitive equilibrium to be created, the cause and effect relationships that will bring it about, and the logical steps to support the course direction. A strategic plan specifies the sequence and timing of steps that will alter competitive status.

Strategy and the strategic plan are different things. But they succeed or fail together. A strategy may be brilliant in content and logic, but fail because the sequence and timing of the plan are inadequate. A plan may be a laudable implementation of a worthless strategy. Against today's background of mounting labour costs, sluggish growth in home markets, shifting exchange rates, and rising import barriers abroad, international strategy becomes increasingly significant. Shrinking profit margins from domestic operations impel multi-national corporations more strongly than ever to make explicit strategy statements.

Two related developments appear to signal the continued importance of strategic planning for international business:

(a) companies that derive a major portion of their sales and profit from overseas activities and look to markets abroad for future growth, must depend on a well-prepared strategy to pursue appropriate paths.

(b) Given the changing patterns of competition since the 1970s, stratgic planning is a critical factor in maintaining leverage in overseas markets.

4 Products may be added to the line for two reasons:

(a) to serve an unfulfilled customer need in a particular market overseas; or

(b) to use optimally the existing marketing capacity.

For example, a chemical company selling fertilizer and pesticides overseas in developing countries may discover a dire need for quality seeds. It may, therefore, add seeds to its line. Alternatively, the same company may feel it has established a good distribution network to serve rural customers and that it is not being fully utilised. The company may, therefore, consider products which could be successfully distributed to their rural customers. Such products may or may not be related to the company's business.

The implementation of this strategy alternative can be illustrated with reference to Colgate's Palmolive experience. They distribute internationally a variety of products which belong to other companies. For example, Colgate sold Wilkinson razor blades for their British manufacturer before it was acquired by somebody else. Colgate did the same for Henkel, a German company, selling Pritt gluestick.

It is important to note that multi-national corporations often do not add products to their parent country market in the same way as to the international market, where product line strategy alternatives are pursued in response to the needs and opportunities of world markets. The products for addition to the line are determined according to inputs or product specifications received from markets abroad. In so far as possible, attempts are made to develop one standardised product to serve customers world-wide.

The decision to add a product to a line is influenced by such considerations as marketing compatibility, finances, organisation and environment. Marketing compatibility involves the match between the new edition and the current one, and potential marketing compatibilities of the parent company and its foreign subsidiary in matters such as product, price, promotion and distribution. The closer the proposed product is to current marketing perspectives, the easier it would be to market the product successfully. A low compatibility, however, may affect profitable marketing. Thus, in the earlier example, the chemical company may find adding seeds to its line more compatible than offering leased agricultural machinery.

A sound business judgement requires a full examination of the financial risks and opportunities relative to the product addition under consideration. The common criteria for use in determining the financial compatibility of the proposed addition are profitability and cash flow implications.

The environmental compatibility includes concern for the customer, competitive action and legal/political problems. The inclusion of a product in the line should not pose any problem for either existing or potential customers. At the same time, the competitive reactions to the company's product addition should be projected and evaluated. If the political/legal problems are likely to become a big stumbling block, it might be best to call the whole thing off.

5 Service constitutes an offer to maintain the original product through overhauling, replacement of parts, adjustments and the like. Most industrial products and many consumer durables require servicing on a regular basis. Provision of service on an international basis is important on two accounts:

(a) Service must be provided to comply with the warranty policy. For example, if a piece of equipment carries a year's warranty on certain parts and functions, the manufacturer should make arrangements to ensure that the terms of the warranty are adequately fulfilled by providing appropriate service facilities.

(b) Service ranks as a promotional tool. When a product, by its very nature, periodically requires after-sales service, the company which provides such a service has an edge over the competitor who does not offer service.

The formulation of a service policy requires an objective assessment of needs. The needs may vary by country, depending on such factors as intensity of use, climatic conditions, and the technical skills of the people using the product. For example, in Western countries high labour costs mean that varous industrial machine tools are used much more intensively than in other countries. In an extreme climate, a product is very likely to require greater care. Also, when the people using the product have marginal skills, the need for service escalates.

A prerequisite of an offer of service is an adequate supply of spare parts. Companies often fail in this regard, and thereby earn a bad reputation among their customers. The problem in supplying parts is that many products come in different models and parts frequently vary from model to model. Furthermore, a product may have a large number of parts, some of which are exorbitantly expensive, and a service facility has to carry all of them. There is no easy solution to this problem. Usually companies consult their own past experience to work out a list of parts which often need replacing and then carry these parts in the inventory.

Providing service also necessitates training personnel to perform the servicing. Most companies handle the training process in one of two ways: the native service personnel are either trained in their own country by one or more technicians flown in from the home country, or, conversely, they are brought to the home country for training. Usually training involves on-the-job experience as well as classroom instruction. Training on high technology products is rendered on an ongoing basis. Many companies have teams of trainers who visit country after country in order to update local personnel on new materials/parts/processes etc. related to the product.

Finally, a good service programme is helpful, directly and indirectly, in getting feedback from customers on various aspects of the marketing mix. The service organisation, based on customer inputs, can serve as a catalyst to generate ideas on product improvement. Similarly, this information can shed light on other aspects of the marketing mix.

6 The role assigned to the pricing variable in developing the marketing mix depends on its strategic significance. Traditionally, many companies have relied more on non-price competition than on pricing. For example, Terpstra found that many companies generally avoid price competition in the Common Market and more often go after competition leverage through advertising, selling and product differentiation. This sort of behaviour can be attributed to the fact that American manufacturing costs are usually particularly high, which makes it difficult to compete price-wise. Further, the quality of American and European goods is considered high, which permits targeting the product for a segment for which price does not matter.

In the last few years, however, price competition has been stressed more than before. Sales promotion, pre-sale and post-sale service, advertising and product differentiation, and product quality are no longer depended upon exclusively. This change has been necessitated partly by the importance of focusing on mass markets overseas, particularly those markets in Western Europe. A small decrease in price can be an effective way of increasing penetration in many foreign markets, especially wherever there is considerable price consciousness and where products are not highly differentiated. For example, the Italian domestic appliance industry in the 1960s made significant inroads in Western European markets through price competition. By the mid-1960s, Italian-made refrigerators accounted for over 30% of the total French market, and over 40% in Belgium, the Netherlands and Luxemburg. Furthermore, costs in many countries (Germany for example), had been rising faster than in many others. Thus, price competition is feasible in some cases.

Leff makes an interesting case for penetrating Third World markets through judicious use of pricing. The high elasticity of demand for consumer products and the highly skewed income distributions in developing countries lead him to recommend making changes in the pricing/output strategy. In this way, mass markets can be developed, enabling the multi-national corporation to achieve higher profits and larger growth, and enabling the host country to enhance the rate of economic development.

Marketing executives in the less developed countries frequently complain of the small and narrow markets for many consumer products. The relatively small size of markets for non-agricultural consumer products is not surprising in the light of the economic and demographic conditions in the less developed countries. Faced with this situation, marketing executives have tried to enlarge the markets for their products with advertising, promotion, and other techniques of modern marketing. The scope for using such techniques effectively is not always great, however. The following is an alternative approach to the marketing of many consumer products in the less developed countries. This approach would seek to expand markets and optimise returns by implementing a pricing policy to reduce the real relative price of a company's products in order to bring them within the reach of the broader population. Such a pricing policy generally receives relatively little attention as compared with the other elements of the marketing mix. There are special reasons why a strategic pricing policy along these lines might be expected to have particularly fruitful effects in the conditions of the less developed countries. A good example is, that by lowering a price in a particular country, although it may affect the profitability in that country, it is feasible to expect that the increased volume of sales that result from the lower price will more than offset the lower profit margin. Furthermore, apart from its relevance for marketing *per se,* pricing policy also has important implications for top level corporate strategy in developing-country markets.

7 Economic theory holds that price reflects demand and supply. In the case of intra-company transactions, however, the parent company can control transfer price because the exchange is little more than an accounting entry between units of the same company. The principal objective of the parent company in setting intra-firm prices is to maximise the long-term economic interests of the total organisation. In this endeavour, one or more affiliates of the company may often end up losing, which leads to conflicts which must be resolved. Essentially, transfer pricing decisions are affected by the following factors:

(a) income tax liability within the host country;
(b) income tax liability within the home country;
(c) tariffs and/or customs duties within the host country;
(d) exchange controls within the host country;
(e) profit repatriation restrictions within the host country;
(f) quota restrictions within the domestic economy;
(g) credit status of the parent company;
(h) credit status of the foreign subsidiary or affiliate;
(i) joint venture constraints within the host country.

The importance of these factors varies from company to company and according to the location of affiliates, but research indicates that income tax liability is the most important variable influencing transfer pricing. This conclusion, however, is based mainly on research conducted to investigate multi-national corporations' experiences viz-a-viz industrialised countries. In the case of developing countries, profit repatriation restrictions, exchange control constraints within the host country are often regarded as the three most important factors affecting the pricing decision. Despite the importance of different factors in different parts of the world, the motivation behind transfer pricing is the same — to maximise overall corporate performance.

To illustrate the point, consider the ramifications of no international rules on the allocation of costs and income for tax, or other, purposes. In the absence of uniformly enforced standards of tax base division, the multi-national corporations can set their transfer prices to minimise tax liability. This may require discretionary transfer pricing and profit shifting to affiliates in low tax jurisdictions. Tax rate differentials, import duties, and foreign exchange restrictions may all influence the pattern of profit sharing. The profits may be shifted from a parent to an affiliate or between affiliates in various ways, such as by creating interdivision costs, fees for contracted services, salaries, interests, rent, purchase premiums, discounts and royalties.

8 Finding reliable distributors is a major challenge for companies entering markets in other countries. There are a number of potential sources for finding overseas distributors — local trade associations, banks, chambers of commerce, and embassy offices (both domestic and in various overseas countries). In the United Kingdom there is also the British Overseas Trade Board. Of all these, in the United Kingdom it is the British Overseas Trade Board that provides the most thorough information. Exporters or potential exporters may seek the names of agents and/or distributors abroad who have indicated an interest in handling specific products.

The following criteria should be employed to identify suitable intermediaries: financial strengths; good connections; the number and kinds of other companies represented; and the quality of local personnel, facilities and equipment.

Financial strength
Sales in foreign markets take time to mature. Yet the distributor must invest in personnel and equipment ahead of the actual business activity if the organisation is to have an effective beginning. Thus, the prospective distributor must be financially sound and should have the strength and will to take the risks involved. Financial strength involves both credit standing and cash flow position.

Good connections
In a large number of countries, business is conducted on a personal basis. In many cases, the government is deeply involved in business. Thus, for agents and distributors to be effective, they should be well connected both in private and in government circles. They should be regarded as respectable business persons by all concerned and follow established traditions and practices.

Other business commitments
Information should be gathered on other commitments that the potential intermediary is involved in. For example, someone currently dealing in non-competing goods and enjoying a good reputation for providing service, handling complaints and problems, and carrying inventory might be a viable candidate. Information on performance can be sought from the companies he has been representing. In addition to an encouraging reputation, any experience gained through handling complementary goods would be advantageous in representing the firm's products. However, sound business practice prohibits distributors handling competing lines.

Personnel, facilities and equipment
The number and quality of the representatives, employees, equipment and facilities should be thoroughly examined. After all, the reputation of the foreign firm in the host country depends on the activities and behaviour of the people representing it. Not only should their people be skilled and qualified in their trade, but also have good public relations. Furthermore, the distributor's facilities and equipment should be adequate as well as properly located. If certain equipment is lacking, the distributor should be willing to make additions. Often potential representatives are willing to hire more people and purchase additional facilities and equipment, if selected. To ensure that the distributor is up to such promises, it is best to specify such provisons in the original agreement.

9 The importance of international physical distribution is illustrated by Japan. Two large city areas in Japan, Tokyo and Osaka, consume approximately 85% of all petrol sold in Japan. The physical distribution system for a particular oil company serving Japan is made up of four different levels of intermediary agents: national wholesaler, regional wholesaler, local wholesaler and retailer. The petrol is physically delivered to the national wholesaler, who then has it delivered to the regional one, then on to the local one, and finally to the retailer. There is nothing odd about this distribution system until one stops to consider that all channel members are located within the same city area. It would be considerably more convenient and far cheaper to deliver the petrol directly from the oil company's tanks to the retailer. Because of the cultural environment in Japan, it would not be entirely feasible to streamline this distribution system. Nevertheless, the example serves to indicated that, by evaluating and implementing an alternative system, the delivery cost of the petrol could be lowered. For example, a British manufacturer trying to penetrate the Japanese consumer goods market, satisfied the cultural requirement by routing the paperwork through various levels of appropriately compensated intermediaries while distributing the product itself directly.

Distribution is one area in marketing where management might have a tendency to view the distribution function as a so-called 'cost loss' without realising that considerable savings can be achieved by proper analysis and revision of distribution systems. The physical distribution of goods is usually accepted as it is. It is rarely realised that this is one area that offers great potential for increasing efficiency. In no other function is there as much waste, duplication, and indifference as there is in the moving of goods from one country to another.

Even in a strictly domestic business with many production plants, warehouses and markets, physical distribution is considered to be a difficult function. Added to this, in the international context, are the complexities of national borders, customs of trade, tariffs and duties, carrier performances, nationalism, monetary exchange, and the necessity of filing numerous documents.

10 The decision on media should be made simultaneously with the decision on copy. It is influenced by media availability, media coverage and media cost.

Availability
Media availability in the world is more restricted than in countries such as the United Kingdom. Even in developed countries like Switzerland, commercial advertising is permitted only during certain hours. Many countries ban the advertising of certain products. For example, Venezuela bans foreign cigarette and alcoholic beverage advertising. In the United Kingdom, the government once questioned the high expenditures budgeted by Unilever and Procter & Gamble for advertising detergents. In brief, in media planning careful analysis is necessary to figure out what media are practical before making the actual selection.

Coverage
Media coverage varies from country to country. It is affected by the range of exposure and ownership of receivers. Ownership is a problem in the developing countries where only a small percentage of the population own radios and/or televisions. Printed media present similar problems. The masses may be illiterate, or cannot afford to subscribe to newspapers or magazines, or live beyond circulating centres. In addition, the heterogeneity of a country with different languages or cultural or religious groups may make it difficult to reach many people through a single advertising campaign. A related problem here is the availability of coverage statistics. In many countries the sole source of such information is the government, whose figures may be overstated for political reasons, besides being haphazardly gathered and probably outdated. In other countries, absolutely no information may be available on the coverage of different media, except the 'best guess' of bureaucrats. In any event, subsidiary management should gather as much information on media coverage as possible in order to select the media focus.

Cost
The final consideration is cost. In many countries media prices are subject to negotiation. Thus the cost could be affected by the bargaining abilities of the subsidiary management. On the other hand, in some countries media rates are arbitrarily set and increased without any market justification. This often happens when media are government controlled and do not depend solely on advertising revenues to operate. Further, in less developed countries media costs are relatively high compared with those in advanced nations.

The real cost of reaching potential buyers with advertising messages may also be high because the media are not readily available, and a large proportion of the population is scattered in rural areas. After considering all the problems, subsidiary management must judicially choose the best media available for its purpose.

5 Information collection, analysis and interpretation

INTRODUCTION

This chapter covers that area of the syllabus relating to information collection, analysis and interpretation: marketing information systems for international business; sources of information; analytical techniques; researching overseas markets; monitoring overseas operations for feedback and control; market segmentation.

QUESTIONS

1 Why might you need to segment overseas markets by religion?

2 What is the 'portfolio approach' to segmenting and classifying countries.

3 Describe some of the problems relating to foreign secondary data.

4 How would you resolve the problems of collecting primary data overseas?

5 What steps would you follow in establishing an international marketing information system?

6 One of the problems of international research is to identify alternative information sources overseas. How would you attempt this?

7 Describe the types of information you would need to obtain from overseas markets in respect of product, promotion and distribution.

8 What sort of sampling and questionnaire problems might occur in international research?

9 How does international marketing research differ from domestic marketing research?

10 Defining the problem in international marketing research is often a problem in itself. Why?

ANSWERS

1 Religion constitutes an important element in society in many cultures. It can greatly influence lifestyle, which in turn affects marketing. Following this logic, religion could work out to be a viable criterion for grouping countries.

Religion can be defined as the quest for the values of the ideal life, and involves three phases: the ideal, the practices for attaining the value of the ideal, and the theology or world view relating the quest to the surrounding universe. This definition covers virtually all aspects of a country's life — its aesthetics, its material culture, its social organisation, its language, even its politics and economics. Religion as an aspect of culture is very important.

Animism, Hinduism, Buddhism, Judaism, Islam, and the Christian religions are the major religions of the world. Briefly, Animism is a prehistoric form of religion — ancient religion without religious texts and specific words but with some magic. Animism today is found all over the world but is practised most obviously in African countries. Some Latin American countries have animistic tendencies as well.

Hinduism, defined more as a way of life than a religion, is practised mostly in India. Considered to be 4,000 years old, it reflects a complex set of tenets and beliefs, but lacks a common creed or dogma.

Buddhism sprang from Hinduism in India and Buddhists are found mainly in south-east Asia and Japan.

Judaism is the name given to the religion and institutions of the Jewish people. It is chiefly centred in the cult of the word of God, preserved in the scriptures and in particular in the 'Torah' (law) and in prayer. The centre of Judaism is Israel.

Islam is practised by over 500 million people living in about 30 countries. The Islamic countries are located mainly in the Middle East, North Africa, and south-east Asia. Islam tends to define a total way of life that its adherents should follow. It includes legislation which organises all the relationships of mankind.

Christianity, sometimes referred to as the religion of the western world, is found all over the world. Christianity began to emphasise individuality more than other religions. Although there are marked differences between the two major divisions of Christianity, Roman Catholicism and Protestantism, basically it stresses similar values, such as achievement and thrift. Interestingly, the Protestant countries in particular, rank economically amongst the highest in the world in terms of GNP per capita.

The effect of religion on lifestyle makes it a relevant criterion for grouping countries. Yet the formulation of common marketing strategy for a group of countries following Islam, or any one religion, may not in itself suffice. Both Pakistan and Saudi Arabia are strong adherents of Islam, but the economic differences between the two countries would invalidate lumping them together for marketing decision-making. Saudi Arabia, with a per capita GNP of approximately £6,000, is a customer for a variety of consumer and industrial products. On the other hand, Pakistan, with a per capita GNP of only £220, offers a very low potential for international marketers. Similarly, France and the Phillipines, both primarily Catholic countries, cannot be served by following the same marketing perspective. In brief, while religion, via culture, plays an important role in determining lifestyle, by itself it may not serve as a viable cirterion for grouping countries.

2 This new approach, based on strategic planning frameworks for classifying countries, was recommended by Rizkallah. The 'portfolio approach', as illustrated in Figure 1, proposes dividing countries on a three-dimensional basis: country potential, competitive strength, and risk. Following this method, 18 country segments are obtained.

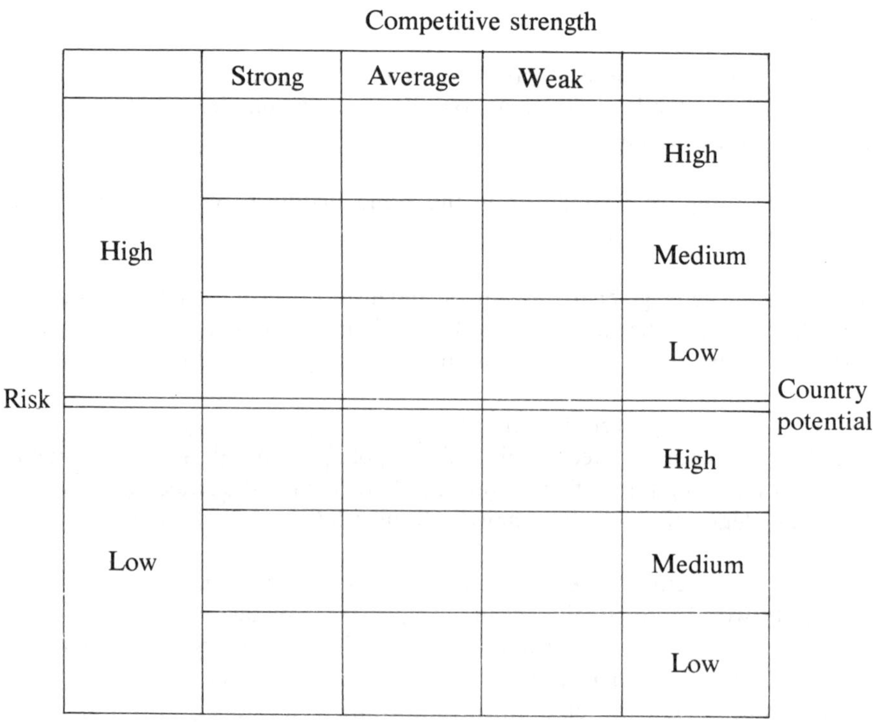

Figure 1 The portfolio approach

Country potential in the portfolio approach refers to the market potential for a firm's products/service in a given country, and is based on such factors as population size, rate of economic growth, real gross national product, per capita national income, distribution of population, industrial production/consumption patterns, and the like. Both internal and external factors determine competitive strength. In a given country, the internal factors include: the firm's market share; its resources; and facilities, including knowledge of the unique features of that country, and the skills and facilities it owns to match these features. External factors include: strength of competitors in the same industry; competition from industries producing substitute products; and the structure of the industry locally and internationally. Risk (that is, political risk, financial risk and business risk) is any factor that causes variation in profit, cash flow or other outcomes generated by involvement in a country. Rizkallah claims the following advantages for the portfolio approach:

(a) It is three-dimensional, and that implies greater representativeness of the multi-national environment.

(b) Its dimensions are relevant to marketing.

(c) It treats risk as a separate dimension, which makes it closer to the real world situation since many countries of the world could be of high potential and very attractive, but of different degrees of risk.

(d) Each of the preceding dimensions is a composite measure of a variety of sub-factors. For example, neither GNP nor income level, each by itself, is adequate as a descriptor of overall country potential.

(e) It uses 18-cell matrix with three levels of each country potential and competitive strength dimensions, and two levels of risk. This is important because the world contains not only highs and lows, but also middle positions as well.

This approach represents an interesting method for achieving the segmentation of countries. It requires, however, an abundance of information, both internal and external to the company, which may not be easy to collect and analyse. Additionally, this approach is more relevant for use at a product/market level than at head office level. Thus, a company involved in marketing a number of products/services abroad will have to work out a number of segmentation schemes. The scheme, however, makes strategic sense and provides an important framework for analysing opportunities for chosen products in selected markets which appear to be potentially viable.

3 Secondary data available in the foreign country suffer in comparison with similar information available from home sources. The researcher must be aware of problems and deficiences when interpreting information. Some of the difficulties which may be encountered with secondary data from overseas countries are as follows:

The underlying purpose of data collection The single most important source of marketing related secondary data in a country is the government. The government as a political institution may not approach data collection with the same objectivity as a business researcher. This problem is particulaly difficult in developing countries where governments may enhance or even change the information content in order to paint a rosy picture of the economy in that country. Often, therefore, political considerations overshadow the reliability of the information.

In western countries it is worth noting that, as a society, we are more open than other countries. Often, no matter how embarrassing information may appear to be for the government of the country concerned, the free flow of information is considered essential. This, however, is not true elsewhere. It is not surprising, therefore, that the plight of the poor in many western countries seems exaggerated when measured by standards of poverty in many developing countries. The researcher must ascertain that the data available are accurate within the limits of its source, and that there are no hidden assumptions which might distort the information from the researcher's point of view.

The currency of information Information gathering is an expensive activity. When the government has limited resources, the gathering of data becomes unimportant. Thus, information may not be gathered as frequently as is needed. The researcher needs to be very careful that the information available overseas has not become outdated.

The reliability of data We have already mentioned the political considerations and how they may affect reliability of data. Additionally, the reliability of data may be affected by data collection procedures. For example, the sample may not be random, so that the results cannot be assessed to reflect the behaviour of the total population. Even when a good sampling plan has been laid out, it may not be properly adhered to.

It may be difficult for the researchers to judge the reliability of secondary data available in a country, and it would be disfunctional to try to test that reliability. If the researchers are, indeed, very concerned with reliability, they would be better off undertaking the gathering of primary data. Researchers should judge for themselves how far to accept the data on the basis of inputs from different contacts in the country about their own experiences with secondary data in that country.

Data classification Yet another problem has to do with the classification scheme of the available data. In many countries, data reported are too broadly classified for use at the micro level. For example, in Thailand in the category construction equipment, machinery, and tools, they include large bulldozers as well as hand-operated drills. Consequently, a company interested in manufacturing heavy construction machinery in Thailand cannot get a clear idea about the current availability of such equipment in that country from the information given under that category.

Comparability of data Multi-national executives often like to compare information on the host countries for such matters as review of market performance, strategy effectiveness in different environments, etc. Unfortunately, the secondary data obtainable from different countries are not readily comparable. Cateora reports, for example, that in Germany purchases of televisions are considered expenditures for recreation and entertainment, while in the United Kingdom television purchases are in the category of furniture, furnishing and household equipment. These discrepancies make brand share comparisons almost impossible.

The availability of data In many developing nations, secondary data are very scarce. Information on the retail and wholesale trade is especially difficult to obtain. In such cases, primary data collection becomes vital.

4 In attempting to resolve the problems of the collection of primary data overseas, there are certainly no fool-proof methods. However, the following steps may help to eliminate some of the problems.

The international marketing research operation should be undertaken in conjunction with a reputable market research company within that country. Such a company may be a foreign office of a major advertising or market research company, or a locally owned company belonging to a third country, like a Japanese advertising agency in France. The resources of the cooperating firm will be invaluable; for example, its knowledge of local customs, including things like the feasibility of interviewing housewives while husbands are at work; the familiarity with local environments, including modes of transportation available for personal interviews in smaller towns; and its contacts in different parts of the country as a source for drawing samples.

From the very beginning, a person fully conversant with both sound marketing research procedures and the local culture should be involved in all phases of the design and research. Such a person can recommend in how many languages to draw up a questionnaire, and what sort of cultural traits, habits, customs, to keep in mind in different phases of the research.

The questionnaire may first be written in English, and then a native, fluent in English, can translate it into a local language or languages. A third person should re-translate it into English. This re-translated version can then be compared to the original English version. The three people involved should work together to eliminate the differences in the three versions of the questionnaire by changing phrases and words. Ultimately, the questionnaire in the local language should accurately reflect the questions in the original English questionnaire.

If feasible, the person hired to conduct the interview should have prior experience. The local cooperating firm may be helpful here. In any event, complete instructions and training should be given before the work starts and the conducting of interviews should be practiced again and again. Ways to ensure that the interviews follow the instructions must be found for proper sampling controls. For example, the researcher might accompany the interviewer sporadically.

Finally, the researcher should draw the best possible sample. If the sample is not random, the researcher should employ appropriate quantitative techniques in analysing the collected information so that the results reflect the reality of the situation.

5 Figure 2 shows the essential steps for developing and maintaining an international marketing information system. As indicated, there are five essential components to be considered: information needs, identifying information sources, gathering information, analysing information and disseminating information.

The information will be needed at a group head office, regional offices and different country locations. Another way of looking at information needs is to differentiate between strategic and operational information. Still another way of categorising information was suggested by Keegan. His framework suggested that information may be grouped into the following broad areas:

(a) Market information: this consists of market potential; consumer/customer attitude and behaviour; channels of distribution; communications media; market sources; new products; competitive sales; competitive marketing programmes and plans; competitive products; competitive operations; and competitive investments.

(b) Prescriptive information: this consists of foreign exchanges; foreign taxes; other foreign prescriptions; and one's own governmental controls.

(c) Resource information: this should consist of information in respect of manpower; money; raw materials; and acquisitions and mergers.

(d) General conditions: this area should cover economic factors; social factors; political factors; scientific and technological factors; management and administrative practices; and any other information not given in any other category.

It is difficult to suggest a general framework for classifying the information needs of all companies or any particular company. Every company should work out its own information categories, which may be based on different schemes. Which kind a company will establish is influenced by the marketing information needs of

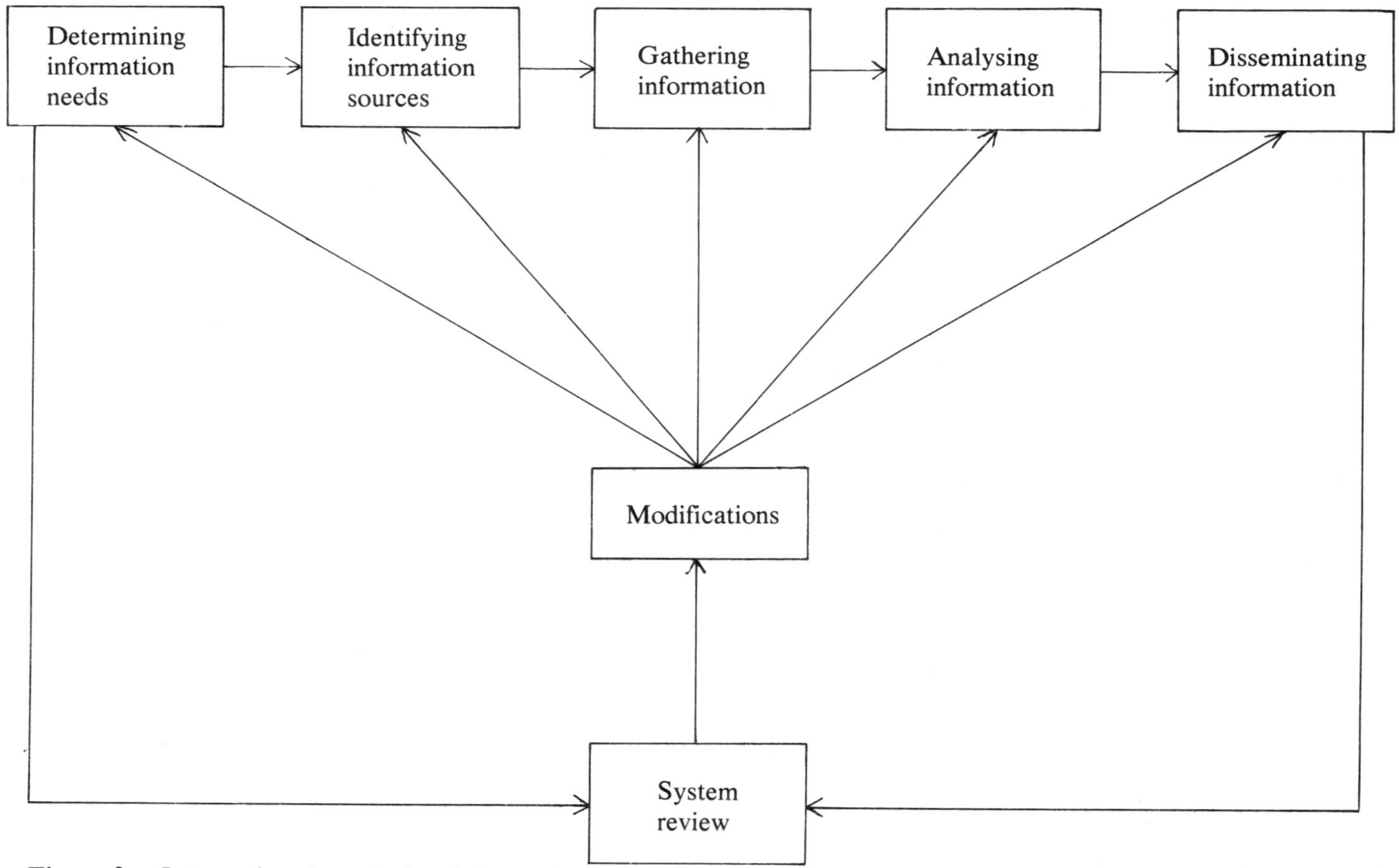

Figure 2 International marketing information system

the company, and the attitude of its top managment towards an integrated management system. Whatever the ultimate system is (highly structured and/or computerised, or unstructured and manual), it must meet in sophistication and range the anticipated information uses it will be called upon to meet.

6 In international research, once the problem has been defined, one must determine where the necessary information can be found and how it can be obtained. In some cases, the survey may be confined entirely to secondary data, that is, published information that has been collected elsewhere. It may be available free (for example, in the United Kingdom government statistics are, in the main, free of charge), or for a price (from syndicated research suppliers, for example), or through restricted distribution sources (such as trade associations' statistics).

Let us assume that a company such as the Ford Motor Company is interested in establishing its new world car in India in collaboration with a government of India enterprise, a state-owned company. Before committing itself to the joint venture, the Ford Motor Company would like, naturally, to study the car's market potential in India over, say, a ten-year period. Fortunately, the Indian government collects a variety of socio-economic and demographic information on a regular basis. This information is conveniently available. Ford Motor Company, therefore, can use with confidence such secondary information as population projections, data on income, consumer expenditure patterns, and rural/urban population shifts, to assess the market potential.

Sometimes internal data are also useful. Existing files, in fact, can often provide important insights into the question in hand. In the example of the Ford Motor Company, it might have found that it had already gathered sufficient information on population trends in India when it had earlier negotiated for the assembly of tractors. Thus, there would be no need for another source of information.

In cases where no amount of investigation of secondary sources or internal data provides the required information, primary data would have to be compiled from scratch, through interviews and other direct collection of information. Primary data may be gathered in various ways, e.g. from trade association representatives, government experts, managerial personnel, and/or the buying public.

If, for example, a company is interested in introducing its prefabricated houses into South America, it well have to study house-buying behaviour in the various target countries. Since this target information may not be convieniently available from secondary sources, primary data gathering may be essential. The importance of such information for decision-making is revealed in the study on the subject carried out in the United Kingdom.

Home ownership in different countries could also have completely different implications. In the United Kingdom the proverb that 'a man's home is his castle' is far more applicable than in West Germany, France or the United States, where the geographic and social mobility of the population means that the regular exchange of homes is a common place experience during the life cycle of most families. Therefore, the decision-making patterns of husband and wife, and the amount of effort spent in making a home-buying decision, should be quite different between these countries.

Thus, before entering the market with prefabricated houses in South America, the company has to learn through primary research in which ways 'house' might mean 'home' in various locations.

7

Product research
Product research means both product line research and individual product research. This kind of research indicates when to add, delete, or change the product.

The company operating overseas must often decide which product line it should add, which it should drop, and which needs rejuvenation. These decisions require a variety of information. For example, a large paper products company manufactured an expensive line of writing paper, as well as other kinds of paper products. The company had about 30% market share in Latin America, but the demand had been constant for a number of years. As part of a programme for centrification of product lines, the company wondered if there had been changes in the office environment in Latin American countries which made the use of expensive paper obsolete. In other words, should the product line be abandoned? The company then undertook marketing research to find an answer to this question.

A manager may also require marketing research information on each individual product. As a product passes through its life cycle, different marketing programmes must be developed for every stage. Thus, it is important to trace the product on its life cycle curve in order to choose the appropriate marketing programme, and marketing research can be of real value in plotting a product's life cycle in different countries.

Promotion information
Promotion research is concerned with research for advertising and personal selling. Companies consult the findings of objective research before spending money on advertising campaigns, in order to choose appropriate copy and appeals, and make the best media selection. A trading stamp company, operating in Europe, for example, redeems stamps that are saved by consumers in two ways, either in merchandise or in travel. Over the years, it was found that more and more customers preferred overseas travel rather than merchandise. For the company, however, merchandise was more profitable, so the company

considered starting an advertising campaign to entice consumers into redeeming their stamps in merchandise. The company wondered if a merchandise catalogue, which emphasised the virtue of material acquisitions as status symbols, would be persuasive in Europe. The production of the catalogue would cost about £500,000, so the catalogue's market effectiveness had to be tested beforehand.

A pattern of selling, just as advertising, must produce profits. Consider the complaint of a sales manager of a major pharmaceutical company: '. . . my sales people are not productive enough, although we pay them a lot more than the industry average in Italy'. Marketing research can provide insights into problems related to personal selling, which involves questions about how many sales people to hire, and how much to pay them, how to form sales territories, how much time to spend on retaining existing customers and how much on developing new accounts.

Distribution information
Distribution research consists of channel research and location research. Channel research can help a company decide which channels to use for distribution of its products. Marketing rsearch can provide information on the availability of channels and their relative desirability.

A water system manufacturer traditionally, for example, used manufacturers' representatives for the distribution of its water pumps in an overseas market. The company, however, was becoming dissatisfied with manufacturers' representatives and wanted to use its own sales force. A marketing research company was asked for a study of the effects on sales of making such a change.

Location research concerns decisions about warehousing, stock and inventory, and physical transport. For example deciding whether to own a warehouse in Germany or to use a public warehouse there requires marketing research.

8 In respect of sampling problems, any good piece of research should reflect the perspectives of the entire population. This is feasible, however, only when the sample is randomly drawn. Unfortunately, in many countries it is difficult to get completely representative information on the socio-economic characteristics of the population, because such information is lacking or, at best, is inadequate. Most samples in the end are biased. Cateora says:

> In many countries, telephone directories, cross index street directories, census and block data, and detailed social and economic characteristics of the universe are not available on a current basis, if at all. The researcher then has to estimate characteristics of population for analysis, sometimes with little basic data on which to build an accurate estimate. To add to the confusion, in some cities in South America, Mexico, and Asia, street maps are unavailable; and in some large metropolitan areas of the Near East and Asia, streets are not identified, houses not numbered.

Even if a workable random sample is drawn, inadequate means of transportation may prevent interviewing people as planned. For example, in developing countries, many areas, especially rural ones, are quite inaccessible. Thus, data collection may have to be confined to urban areas only. Further, only a small percentage of the population in many developing countries have telephones. The World Bank statistics indicate, for example, that there are only 3 telephones per 1,000 people in Egypt, 4 in Turkey, and 29 in Argentina. In many countries, the postal system is inefficient, so that letters may not be delivered at all, or may reach the addressee only after a long delay. In brief, it may be extremely difficult to obtain a proper random sample, especially in developing countries.

In respect of questionnaire problems, in many countries different languages are spoken in different areas. A questionnaire, then, has to be in different languages for use within the same country. In India, for example, there are 14 official languages spoken in different parts of the country, while most government and business affairs are conducted in English. Similarly, in Switzerland, German is used in some areas, and French in others. In the Republic of Congo, the official language is French, but only a small part of the population is fluent in French.

Unfortunately, translating a questionnaire from one language to another is very difficult. In the translating process many points are entirely mispresented, as many idioms, phrases, and statements mean different things in different cultures. A Danish executive observed:

> Check this out by having a different translator. Put back into English what you have translated from the English. You will get the shock of your life. I remember, 'out of sight, out of mind', had become 'invisible things are insane'.

9 The procedures and methods of conducting marketing reseach are conceptually the same for both domestic marketing and international marketing. For example, before collecting data, the researcher must have a clear idea of the research problem. Likewise, only an appropriate sample will yield valuable results. Procedural similarities aside, international marketing research differs from domestic marketing in three major ways.

(a) The effects of the international environment on the whole company as a profit-oriented unit are considered. For example, the marketing research project concerned with the ramifications of a substantial price increase in a particular foreign country must consider questions that do not apply to the domestic market. For example, will the company's subsidiary be nationalised if prices are increased beyond a certain level?

(b) Many concepts and frameworks, such as market segmentation, which constitute the core of market decision-making in domestic marketing, may be unusable in international marketing. It is not because the concept cannot be transferred, but because the information necessary to make such a transfer is not available. For example, if there is a lack of current income distribution data on a country, any analysis of the demand for a product will assume incorrect income categories and, therefore, cannot mean much for practical purposes.

(c) Finally, the ethnocentric nature of marketing makes cultural differences among nations a significant factor. Thus, culture in a domestic market can be considered to be naturally understood, but in international marketing culture must be fully investigated.

It appears that risk is a less important determinant of purchase behaviour in Mexico than in the United States. In a survey the Mexican sample varied in the amount of risk it perceived in the three purchase situations (i.e. bath soap, toothpaste, instant coffee), but the mean level of risk in all three cases was significantly lower than in the United States sample. The findings suggest that marketers will have to make adjustments in their strategies when entering Mexico. On a more general level, the findings raised the question of the applicability of employing other concepts of consumer behaviour in overseas markets. Considerable international research is necessary to answer this question.

10 The first task, of defining the problem, which sounds very simple, may be the pivot task in the entire research study. In defining the problem, two important considerations are market structure and product concept.

Market structure refers to the size of the market, its stage of development, the number of competitors and their market shares, and the channels through which the market is approached. The importance of market structure in problem definition is shown by a Reader's Digest study which reported that French and German consumers ate significantly more spaghetti than Italians. This finding was wrong. The study had concerned itself only with packaged, branded spaghetti, and not total spaghetti consumption. Because much of the spaghetti sold in Italy is unpackaged and unbranded, the results of the study were totally invalid. The Reader's Digest researchers should have clearly defined the kind of spaghetti consumption to be studied in the countries concerned.

Additionally, a product may be viewed differently in different cultures. Thus, even before attempting to define the marketing research problem for study, exploratory research may be necessary to understand the product concept, that is, the meaning of the product in a particular environment. In this way, problem definition will be appropriate to the concept of the product held in the particular country of interest.

The researcher Berent pointed out that milk-based products are viewed very differently in the United Kingdom and Thailand. In the United Kingdom, they are usually consumed at meals and at bedtime for their sleep-inducing, soothing, relaxing properties. In Thailand, the same products are consumed on the way to work, and often away from home, for they are considered to have invigorating, energising and stimulating properties.

Let us assume a multi-national marketer is interested in finding out the potential market for his brand of yoghurt in the United Kingdom and Thailand. The problem definition in the two countries will have to be stated differently. In the United Kingdom, the yoghurt might be primarily perceived by the consumers as a healthful and relaxing product to be used prior to retiring. In Thailand, the research problem would determine if yoghurt would be considered mainly as energy food to start the day with.

6 International selling and distribution

INTRODUCTION

The questions and answers in this chapter cover that part of the syllabus dealing with international selling and distribution, including: franchising, licencing, agencies, overseas sales force organisation; trading and exchange institutions; joint ventures, costs and control of sales and distribution; logistics, financing goods in distribution.

QUESTIONS

1 What orientation, training and compensation package would you offer to an expatriate going overseas?

2 Describe how the role of personal selling and sales personnel might differ in overseas situations.

3 Recently, a new trend has emerged to assign employees at all levels from one host country to another. Why has this happened and what are the pitfalls?

4 Describe the different methods available for direct distribution through agents overseas.

5 How would you control and measure performance of your overseas intermediaries?

6 What are the major problems that companies face in franchising in overseas countries?

7 What factors must you consider in order to establish feasible overseas channel alternatives?

8 'It has long been held that the channels of distribution available in a country depend on its stage of economic development.' Discuss.

9 Discuss the role of public relations in international marketing.

10 Why can companies no longer afford to transfer people from nation to nation without having an appropriate policy?

ANSWERS

1

Orientation and training

Sales personnel involved in overseas assignments should be orientated to the new job and provided with relevant training. Essentially, orientation and training should cover the terms and conditions of the assignment, language training, and cultural training.

The terms and conditions of the assignment
The employee should be provided with a clear and concise overview of the company's expatriate policies and procedures and compensation system. They should be given information on housing, transportation, and schools in the host country, and on arrangements for moving house.

Language training
This is perhaps the most basic type of knowledge that a foreigner needs for a productive life in a host country. Language is the key to a country's culture. It permits understanding of the subtleties of the country and the reasons why certain things are done differently. Language can be learned in different ways: in a language school with regular programmes lasting several months; through an intensive programme of a few weeks' duration offered by a commercial school or university; or at home through correspondence and tape cassettes. Do-it-yourself kits are available for home study programmes in the form of records, cassette recordings, books, telephone conversations with language instructors, and different combinations of these alternatives. Regardless of the method, the one central ingredient in learning a language is proper motivation on the part of the employee and the family. It is incumbent upon the multi-national employer to emphasise the need for language training.

Cultural training
Both academic and interpersonal cultural training should be given. Academic training includes the provision of things like books, maps, brochures, films and slides. The interpersonal training consists of making arrangements for the candidate and the family to make a trip to the host country, in addition to meeting host country natives in their home country and people who have lived in the host country.

Compensation

In respect of compensation, sales people away from their home base cost more because they must be paid extra compensation. The extra compensation covers primarily three factors. Firstly, it is a premium for climatic conditions in the host country, separation from friends and relatives, cultural shock, and subjection to situations of political instability and economic risk in conditions of unstable currencies. Secondly, it is an allowance for housing, childrens' education, return trip home on a regular basis, income tax and the overall costs of living expenses. Thirdly, there are certain prerequisites common in host countries for particular positions, like a car and driver, servants, and membership of certain clubs. The elements of compensation and the amount paid under each heading differ from country to country.

Considering the expenses involved in transferring non-natives to host countries, the company should make a careful study of the conditions in each country and undertake regular reviews of any changes. Overheads must be monitored; changes in costs, taxation, facilities and currency values are by no means negligible. Experts in the field are highly priced and their travel budgets are extremely large. Nevertheless, the cost is a sound investment if, as a result, the company's team of expatriates and/or third country nationals is fairly compensated and has confidence in head office policy towards them.

2 Sales personnel in international business can be classified in two ways — either by the task they perform, or by their nationality. Principally, there are three categories of selling task: sales generation, sales support and pioneering work. Sales generation is the creative task of helping the customer to make a purchase decision. Sales support is concerned with the after-sales service. Pioneering work is undertaken by a manufacturer's salesperson to stimulate demand to help the distributors. When classifying sales personnel by nationality, there are also three categories: expatriates, natives and third-country nationals. Expatriates are home country employees on assignments in the host country. For example, a sales manager from the United Kingdom assigned to launch the sales effort in Spain would be considered an expatriate. Natives are employees belonging to the host country. A Spanish national working for a company as a salesperson in Spain is a native. Third-country nationals are employees transferred from one host country to another. For example, a French national transferred to Spain would be defined as a third-country national.

For the most part, companies do not transfer selling personnel abroad. There are two main reasons for this. Firstly, selling requires deep familiarity with the local culture, which an expatriate cannot be expected to have; and secondly, it is extremely expensive to assign expatriates to selling positions. Such reasons lead companies (IBM for example), to depend mainly on nationals for selling jobs. There are occasions, however, when companies may assign expatriates to work, usually for short periods, in the selling area. Such a practice is more commonly followed in the marketing of high-volume items. The expatriate, who has a proven track record at home, can be quite helpful in resolving difficult foreign situations, and/or in serving as a catalyst for the natives. For example, the elevator company, Otis, had to assign a sales engineer from the home office to provide after-sales service for its lifts in a large office complex in Singapore for a year. This became necessary because the native salesforce had failed to ensure smooth functioning of the lifts. Likewise, many companies use expatriates to provide on-the-job training to the natives. In fact, many companies have a group of seasoned sales people who travel from country to country assisting native salesforces in selling the company's products. Numerous goods require selling directly from the home office, which usually involves expatriates. For example, Boeing bids to sell aeroplanes to foreign airlines from its headquarters in America. Its sales people, mainly expatriates, travel extensively world-wide to call on its customers.

The management of the native salesforce is a local matter to be handled according to business practices in the host country. From the viewpoint of parent companies, therefore, the major concern is with expatriates and third-country nationals.

3 It is certainly true that in recent years a new trend has been to assign employees at all levels from one host country to another. This trend has arisen for two reasons. Firstly, in many countries of the world there is a surplus of workers while other countries lack adequate workforces. For example, Saudi Arabia's population is about 6 million. If a company is developing fast, it may need a large salesforce and may find it difficult to find suitable Saudi Arabians to fill such postions. Saudi Arabia is, therefore, forced into accepting sales people from other developing countries, like Pakistan, India or Korea. Secondly, a company often needs a salesperson with certain requisite experience for a subsidiary. Looking around, the company discovers the most appropriate person for the job is a third-country national.

Third-country individuals face unique organisational problems. For example, third-country employees naturally want to know to which organisation, the parent company or the host country company, they belong in regard to promotion benefits and their feeling of identity. To manage third-country employees effectively, both head office and host country management should study their special problems. An appreciation of their needs enhances performance for the benefit of the whole organisation.

The particular problems faced by third-country nationals, which an organisation should seek to minimise, are as follows:

(a) blocked promotions;
(b) transfer anxieties;
(c) income gaps;
(d) unfamiliarity and adaptability difficulties;
(e) avoidance of long-range projects;
(f) inappropriate leadership style;
(g) non-participative decision-making and screening of information;
(h) insufficient authority in industrial relations;
(i) lack of commitment of top ranking third-country managers to the perpetuation of the host country organisation.

4 A company may deal with different types of agent intermediary overseas. These agents do not take title to the goods and usually work on commission only. The product involved and the way it is marketed in the home country would indicate who might be employed to undertake overseas distribution such as sales representatives, purchasing agents, or export brokers.

Sales representatives
These agents resemble a manufacturer's representative in the home country. A manufacturer supplies the sales representatives with literature and samples to conduct sales in a pre-arranged territory. These sales representatives usually work on a commission basis, assume no risk or responsibility, and are under contract for a definite period of time. They may operate on either an exclusive or non-exclusive basis, and do not handle competing lines. They serve as a good source of market information.

Purchasing agents
Purchasing agents are also referred to as buyers for export, export commission houses, or export confirming houses. They are very active in many European and American markets, seeking goods of interest to their foreign principals. Their product quality and price demands stem from the requirements of the principals.

Usually, foreign purchasing agents represent governments or big contractors, either for a specified time or for a particular task. In any event, they do not provide continual service and stable volume to the vendors. For example, a foreign government might authorise a purchasing agent to buy designated goods in the United Kingdom for the completion of a large production plant. Once the plant is constructed, the purchasing agent ceases to be active.

Purchasing agents receive commission from their principals. A transaction with a purchasing agent is completed, as in domestic marketing, with the agent handling all packing and shipping details. A purchasing agent may represent several principals requiring the same goods and may deal with different competing vendors.

Export brokers
An export broker brings the foreign buyer and the domestic seller together. Usually, export brokers receive a commission fee from the seller for their services. They neither take title to nor possession of goods, and assume no financial responsibility relative to the export transaction. Export brokers are generally used in the export of commodities such as grain and cotton. Only rarely is the export broker involved in the export of manufactured goods.

5 Distribution in foreign countries through intermediaries always entails some degree of compromise. This compromise involves the loss of control over a multi-

national corporation's foreign marketing operations in exchange for relatively low-cost representation. While some controls must be relinquished to intermediaries, even in domestic markets, in overseas markets it is more significant because the company has no permanent presence abroad. A distributor (the only means of accomplishing all of the related tasks such as selling, servicing, providing market research), often falls short of the expectations of a producer. The independent distributor represents an entity separate from the exporter and their goals may not match exactly. Despite the fact that the exporter/manufacturer lacks full control of foreign distribution, he still wants adequate information, and wants to encourage high performance by channel distributors which are not a part of his own network.

From any viewpoint, companies using independent distributors will have great difficulty in controlling them. It is difficult for the exporters to make sales forecasts, assess sales targets, and develop customer contact plans when there is no access to the distributors' administration, sales reports, or other records. Thus, the manufacturer should not depend on controls to optimise distributive performance, but should instead use motivational methods.

A distributor wants to do the best possible job for each of its manufacturers, but he really cannot. So he concentrates on products for which: (a) he makes the most money; and (b) he has the least aggravation or the greatest personal pull. The following are some of the ways in which one can build loyalty:

(a) Build your distributor into your company: bring him into your picture, discuss future plans as they affect his area with him, often seek his advice.

(b) Give your distributor an attractive profit margin; try to keep in mind that you want to be in business with him for several years; make him want to continue the relationship.

(c) Be sure he has credit terms which make him competitive or more so, in amount and length of time for payment.

(d) Maintain regular correspondence, and make sure that he can clearly understand what you have to say.

(e) Make a point of commenting on successful distributors in whatever communication you use in his area.

(f) Keep your obvious control to a minimum; as his performance improves, your supervision can be reduced.

(g) If financing is needed locally and you have the ability to help, do so if his situation justifies this.

(h) Bring the distributor to the home country on occasions, and let him see what goes on.

(i) Offer a scholarship to the children of the successful distributor.

(j) Establish a recognition system: presentation certificates, cash prizes, overseas trips and so on.

(k) Make available remembrance items, give-aways with your company name and if warranted, with his name too.

Research on this subject notes that the performance of an overseas distributor is affected by such relational factors as formalisation, standardisation, reciprocity, intensity and conflict. Formalisation refers to the extent to which the relationship is agreed upon and made explicit. Standardisation indicates the extent to which the established roles and trading routines are adhered to. Reciprocity means the extent to which the manufacturer and distributor are both involved in decision-making, despite the traditional domains of each party. Intensity is the level of contact and the exchange of resources between the parties. Finally, conflict refers to the level of tension and disagreement between the two parties. The findings of much of this research strongly indicate that high performance is associated with certain relational characteristics. It requires that the two parties:

(a) adapt their roles and routines;
(b) display a commitment to developing business in the market in question;
(c) exhibit lower levels of intercompany tension and disagreement.

Formalisation, however, does not seem to affect performance significantly.

6 Companies face a variety of problems in their efforts to engage in international franchising. Some are similar to those faced in domestic markets, but differ in intensity and severity. The biggest problem is host government interference and red tape.

The problems can be classified as follows:

(a) *Government and legal restrictions* The tax structure, barriers against foreign ownership, and limitation of profit repatriation are some of the problems causing trouble for a major proportion of international franchising companies.

(b) *Selection and method of operation* The method of operation depends largely on the business practice of the host nation, the availability of qualified franchisees and the availability of capital.

(c) *Choice of location* The selection of a proper site is a crucial factor in the success of a franchise.

(d) *Availability of supplies* Two business inputs — qualified personnel and food materials — face scarcity problems in both Japan and Europe.

(e) *Adjustment to local taste and customs* Recognising local traditions and tastes is of the utmost importance. Culture, habits, consumer behaviour and desires vary widely from nation to nation.

(f) *Operational problems* After the outlet is open, it faces problems which threaten its continued existence. The two prevalent challenges facing international franchising have been competition and the ability to adapt to local conditions while maintaining one's uniqueness. Monitoring the customs and habits of a host country is always necessary in order to discover or anticipate changing trends.

(g) *Limited expansion opportunities* The international franchising industry has been a relatively recent development. Progress, however, has been rapid, and presently the large American and European franchises all have outlets in foreign nations, with plans for yet further expanison. Analyses indicate that although there are difficulties which must be overcome, expansion opportunities do exist and there appears to be cause for optimism on the future of international franchising.

The international franchisor must ascertain the basic practicability of transporting his business system to a foreign country; he must engage in a thorough market research study before attempting to expand internationally. Success in international franchising will probably depend upon the ability to adjust to a culture with different attitudes, values and beliefs.

7 The characteristics of customers, products, intermediaries, competitors, marketing environment, and company strengths and weaknesses, determine the various possible alternatives to the distribution of a line of products. If the number of customers is large and geographically widespread rather than concentrated, and if they make their purchases in small quantities at frequent intervals, the company will have to opt for intensive distribution, that is, a large number of outlets. Another factor to be considered here is the desire of the customer to deal with a particular type of channel. For example, the customer in a country may dislike the idea of buying groceries from large supermarkets. In other words, the cutomer's susceptibility to different selling methods is an important factor to be considered.

A variety of product characteristics have an effect on the selection of channels of distribution. If the goods happen to be of a perishable nature, direct channels are desirable. Channels for products that are voluminous in relation to their prices would be long. Shorter channels are employed when the unit value of the product is high, as in the case of computers, or when the product has to be custom-made, like air-conditioning equipment for a large building. Proximity to the customer helps in cutting down costs as well as in rendering good service. Also, products requiring installation and regular maintenance would call for shorter channels of distribution. Most capital equipment falls into this category.

The kinds of channels available can restrict the selection. The company should consider the terms demanded by different channel constituents and evaluate them in comparison with services and benefits provided, including factors such as channel location, credit granted, the quality of the salesforce, warehousing facilities, reputation within the market, the outlay on advertising and overall experience. Consideration must also be given to the demands of the intermediaries that the company uses. Depending on other factors such as customer and product characteristics, the company will choose those channels that make the maximum impact in the market at minimum cost.

Host country trade practices concerning the distribution of a particular product is another influential variable. It is not necessary, however, to follow competition. But innovations may not be easily accepted in all countries. Even today, many Swiss homemakers prefer buying groceries from local 'momma and poppa' type corner shops.

The environment of the host country constitutes another variable to weigh in making a channel selection decision. For example, the economic structure affects the suitability of a particular channel. In free economies, it is common practice to use private agents or distributors who buy and sell at a mark-up. Most agents or distributors function as part of local companies, which deal in a large number of product lines ranging from sweets to sophisticated machine tools. However, in state-controlled markets like Iraq, Libya, South Yemen and Syria, international marketers must do business with state-owned trading companies operating on very low margins which cover physical distribution costs but not usually any other necessary marketing activities. In such countries, international marketers often retain the services of private agencies to promote their products to the final consumers. Poor economic conditions may not justify committing the company to excessive fixed costs, and thus distribution through wholesalers may be deemed the best alternative. A depressed economy may also demand cutting down on non-essential services.

Cultural conditions might also militate against the utilisation of a particular type of channel.

The final factor in evaluating channel alternatives is the company's own strengths and weaknesses in the overseas market. A well-known company of long standing in the market will tap channels more easily than a new entrant. A financially strong company need not necessarily opt for channels that absorb a part of the distribution costs of inventory, transport, advertising and training. Similarly, a company with a large number of products for the same market could deal with the customers directly.

All these factors serve as a basis for determining the feasible alternative channels of distribution. Generally, a company would have three channel alternatives: selling direct to the customers; selling through intermediaries based in the home country; and selling through foreign distributors. In practice, however, channels in international marketing can be a labyrinth of conglutinative relationships. For example, the company might well sell directly in some countries, while employing UK based distributors in another country, and utilising overseas distributors in still other cases.

8 The channels of distribution available in a country do depend on its stage of economic development, which is reflected in the per capita income and the socio-psychological, cultural or anthropological environment. On this basis, we can conclude that:

(a) The more developed countries have more levels of distribution, more speciality stores and supermarkets, more department stores and more stores in rural areas.

(b) The influence of foreign import agents declines with economic development.

(c) Manufacturer/wholesaler/retailer functions become separate as the economy develops.

(d) Wholesaler functions approximate to those in America and Western Europe with increasing economic development.

(e) The financing function of wholesalers declines and wholesale mark-ups increase with the development of the economy.

(f) The number of small stores declines and the size of the average store increases as a country's economy develops.

(g) The role of the pedlar and the individual trader, and the importance of the local markets, decline as the economy grows.

(h) Retail margins improve with increasing economic development.

According to this theory, changes in the channel structure of a country can be introduced only in response to changes in its economic and other environments; channel changes cannot be brought about by outside influences. At the cost of oversimplificiation, for example, supermarket distribution would not work in poor countries such as Egypt, Kenya and Pakistan because the economic and other environments operating in those countries are not conducive to such a form of distribution. Research on this subject, however, casts doubts on the viability of the theory. Some results showed little evidence to support the idea that the development of a marketing system in a country is determined by the limits of its social, economic, technological and cultural environments. It was found that channel structure and relationships mainly depend on the relative size of the companies at different channel stages, rather than on a country's level of development.

Apparently, the relationship between a country's channel structure and its environment remains undefined. All one can really say, given the current state of the art, is that distribution channels, like any other socio-economic phenomenon, evolve slowly from a multitude of factors, some direct and some indirect. It is very difficult to know precisely what these factors are, let alone their relationships.

9 Public relations serves as a useful device for establishing a foothold or strengthening an existing position in an overseas market. The public relations activity is directed towards an influential, but relatively small, target audience of editors and journalists who work for publications (or in broadcasting) aimed at a firm's customers and prospects. Since the target audience is small, it is relatively inexpensive to reach.

To do an effective public relations job overseas, an international marketer needs to hire an established public relations company. It is desirable to look for a firm that has relevant experience and adequate resources. If a company's UK public relations firm has an office in the host country, it may be retained there too. Alternatively, one may have to choose from among the local public relations firms available. After the firm is recruited, the company should develop a dossier, that is, a package of information that editors may file for future reference. A typical dossier runs to a number of pages and includes information on the company's capabilities, its technologies, its pre-eminence, and why it operates in the host country. The dossier may be supplemented with a corporate brochure, preferably in the host country's language or languages, identifying world-wide manufacturing, research and development, and sales service locations. Usually, the dossier is accompanied by a letter inviting editors to contact a designated person for further information. This letter may also state that articles and releases will be regularly issued by the company in the future.

The company should decide, in consultation with the public relations company, how an initial contact should be made with the target audience — editors and journalists. At this stage, the public relations firm is better known to the audience than its client. In fact, some public relations companies are so well accepted in a country that a release by them on the company's behalf signals to editors that the story is newsworthy, factual and worth publishing. Thus, the public relations firm should play a leading role in establishing initial contact for the company.

Future announcements and releases may either be custom-developed for the host country, or extracted from those prepared for the domestic market. In other words, a company entering an overseas market may re-use some of its UK news releases, application case histories, technical and feature articles, and the like. The appropriateness of domestic material in an overseas market may be judged by the host country marketing management and the public relations company. Where necessary, however, original releases must be produced and issued as appropriate.

Once the story or article on the company appears in print, it will be read by only a small fraction of customers. But it is important to get all the promotional value one can from a good placement. One way of doing this is to send story and article reprints in quantity to the company's sales people and distributor sales people for use in their sales calls and mailings. The reprints support sales training too. New sales people can learn much about the company's products and applications from a file of articles.

The activities outlined above help in establishing a group name for the company and its product during the start-up period. To continue to generate news and be visible in the long run, a variety of techniques can be used. These include interviews and the publicising of talks by area executives, publicity for new product designs or services developed in or for the overseas area, case histories from customers' experiences in the area, special activities for media, invitations to the press to cover company-sponsored seminars, meetings, and workshops, and photographs to meet an editor's expressed needs. These techniques assist in localising the company. Beyond that, as the company becomes fully established, the public relations activites may include sponsored speeches at seminars, and management leadership in professional associations.

10 It is true that companies can no longer afford to transfer people from nation to nation without having an appropriate policy as a guide. Too many people and too much money are involved. While the common practice is to hire nationals for sales positions, the number of short-term specific assignments for solving *ad hoc* problems is on the increase, which requires bringing in expatriates or third-country nationals.

Theoretically, the appropriate company policy would deal with such matters for non-national sales persons. The policy would cover the determination of the most appropriate nationality, the selection of the non-national sales person, plans for repatriation and reassignment, work assignments, and the development of national sales persons by the non-national selected. In reality, companies may not have a thoroughly articulated policy for expatriates and third-country employees that covers all these points. But increasingly companies attach importance to the problems that occur when people work in different cultures. As an example, one company has defined the following corporate procedure for assignment, repatriation, and reassignment of international employees.

Background
The long-term interest of the company is best served by limiting international assignments to those management and professional employees who have an

established record of confidence. International assignments can be a valuable supplement to the normal training and development programmes for the high potential employee. Management and professional people with international experience are an invaluable corporate asset, and every effort should be made to ensure that experience gained by employees through such assignments is retained and properly utilised.

Consequently, all organisation units assigning personnel internationally should develop specific plans for the selection, assignment and repatriation of management and professional employees. Consistent with the needs for international staffing, organisation units should identify confident employees who have the desire and potential to undertake successfully an assignment abroad.

Guidelines

In the first place a pre-assignment orientation programme should be planned and implemented on a timely basis to ensure that candidates and their dependants are fully prepared to undertake international assignments. Organisation units assigning personnel internationally will define in writing all known conditions of assignment, including (but not limited to) the employee's salary, allowances, duration of the assignment, etc. The employee should be provided with copies of all applicable policies and procedures. In respect of repatriation and reassignment, the organisation unit should periodically review the status of their international assignees, and develop specific repatriation plans for each employee. Where performance continues to be satisfactory, it is the responsibility of these units to ensure that personnel selected for international assignments will have, on their return, positions at least equivalent to those held by them prior to accepting international assignments. For coordination reasons, it is also the responsibility of these units to keep key personnel services advised of the repatriation plans or problems.

Application

This procedure applies to all organisation units assigning personnel internationally, as well as to all management and professional personnel who accept an international assignment, with the exception of those engaged in service or other activities which normally require international travel, or who are assigned for a limited time to specific international customer contracts abroad.

Abroad, as domestically, poor supervision and inappropiate policies produce negative results. Deficiencies in management away from home can be costly. More and more attention, therefore, is likely to be given to recruiting, selecting, developing, and motivating managers for overseas assignments, however brief the assignment may be.

7 Exporting and importing

INTRODUCTION

This chapter covers that part of the syllabus relating to exporting and importing, and includes: a comparison between export selling and export marketing; an appreciation of the procedure and documentation for exporting and importing; the role of government and international bodies in relation to exports and imports; visibles and invisibles; balance of payments.

QUESTIONS

1 Explain the difference between exporting, joint venture and direct ownership, in international business.

2 Describe the different types of contractual agreement that can be entered into in international markets.

3 In the UK a major source of aid to exporters is the British Overseas Trade Board. Many countries have similar institutions. Using either the United Kingdom, or a stated country of your choice, explain the types of aid that are normally available.

4 What do you understand the term 'balance of payments' to mean?

5 What are 'invisible' earnings?

ANSWERS

1

Exporting

With exporting, a company reaches international markets by selling directly through its own salesforce or indirectly through foreign merchants or agents. In direct selling, a company situates its salesforce in a home office or a foreign branch office. This technique is prominent when customers are easy to locate or come to the seller. In indirect selling, a company hires outside specialists to search out and contact customers. These specialists are based in the home or foreign country. Indirect selling is applied in situations where customers are hard to locate, the exporting company has limited resources, or local customs are unique.

An exporting structure requires minimal investment in foreign facilities. There is no foreign production by the company. The exporter may modify its packages, labels or catalogues at its domestic facilities in response to foreign market needs. Exporting represents the lowest level of commitment to international marketing. As an example, Paul Masson Wines are made in California and exported to many European countries. Foreign wholesalers market the wines through grocery stores and off-licences.

Joint venture

In a joint venture the company agrees to combine some aspects of its manufacturing or marketing efforts with those of a foreign company in order to share expertise, costs and connections with important persons. For example, Philips, a large, Netherlands-based manufacturer of electronic products, electrical appliances, etc. has recently entered into a number of joint ventures.

A joint venture may also result in reduced costs and favourable trade terms from a foreign government if products are produced locally, and foreign ownership is established. For example, the number of joint ventures between Japanese and British companies is growing, because Japanese firms see them as reducing the possibility of UK trade restrictions as a method of easing political tension. United Kingdom companies view these ventures as a means of establishing operations in the Japanese market and as a way to restrict the operations of potential competitors.

A joint venture can take the form of licensing, contract manufacturing, management contracting or joint ownership. Licensing gives a foreign company the rights to a manufacturing process, trademark, or patent, in exchange for a commission, fee, or royalty. Coca-Cola license their products. Under contract manufacturing, the company agrees to have a foreign company make its products locally. In these situations companies market the product itself and provide management expertise. This arrangement is very common in publishing.

Direct ownership
Direct ownership involves the full undertaking and control of all international operations. The company owns production, marketing, and other facilities in foreign countries without any partners.

In some cases, international operations are organised into wholly owned subsidiaries; for example, Atari operates wholly owned subsidiaries for its video games in the United Kingdom, France, Germany and the Netherlands. The company has all the benefits and risks associated with ownership. There are savings in labour, and marketing plans are more sensitive to local needs. Profit potential is high, although costs are also high. The possibility of nationalistic acts is present, and government restrictions are likely to be more stringent. This is the riskiest form of organisation.

Frequently, companies combine organisational formats. For example, a firm could use an exporting organisation in a country that has a history of the state taking over the assets of foreign firms, and a direct ownership organisation in a country that provides tax advantages for plant construction. In the case of McDonald's, internatinal expansion is carried out by opening company-operated stores, and affiliate-operated stores. With affiliate-operated stores, McDonald's usually own 50% or less of their assets the rest being owned by resident nationals.

2 There are several types of contractual agreements:

(a) Patent licensing agreements, which are based on either a fixed fee or royalty basis, and usually include managerial training.

(b) Turn-key operations, which are based on a fixed fee or cost-plus arrangement, and include plant construction, personnel training, and initial production runs.

(c) Co-production agreements, which are most common in the socialist countries, where plants are built and then paid for with part of the output.

(d) Management contracts, which are currently widely used in the Middle East and require that a multi-national corporation provide key personnel to operate the foreign enterprise for a fee, until local people acquire the ability to manage the business independently.

In some contractural agreement situations, where risk of expropriation and resistance to foreign investments create uncertainty, licensing works as a viable alternative. Licensing encompasses a variety of contractual agreements whereby a multi-national marketer makes available intangible assets — such as patents, trade secrets, know-how, trademarks, and company name — to foreign companies in return for royalties or other forms of payment. Transfer of these assets is usually accompanied by technical services to ensure proper use. Licensing, however, has both advantages and disadvantages.

Some of the advantages are:

(a) Licensing requires little capital and serves as a quick and easy method of entry into foreign markets.

(b) In some countries, notably the developed communist countries, licensing is the only way to tap the market.

(c) It provides life extension for products in the maturity stage of their life cycles.

(d) It is a good alternative to foreign production and marketing in an environment where there is world-wide inflation, skilled labour shortages, increasing domestic and foreign governmental regulation and restriction, and tough international competition.

(e) Licensing royalties are guaranteed and periodic, whereas shared income from investment fluctuates and is risky.

(f) Domestically based companies can benefit from product development abroad without research expense, through technical feedback arrangements.

(g) When exports are no longer profitable because of intense competition, licensing provides an alternative.

(h) Licensing can overcome high transportation costs, which make some exports non-competitive in the target markets; and it is also immune to expropriation.

(i) Finally, in some countries, manufactures of military equipment or any product deemed critical to the national interest may be compelled to enter licensing agreements.

On the other hand, there are certain disadvantages:

(a) To attract licensees, a company must possess a distinctive technology or trademark, and a company or brand name that is attractive to potential foreign users.

(b) The licensor has no control over production and marketing by the licensee.

(c) Licensing royalties are negligible compared with equity investment potential. Royalty rates seldom exceed 5% of gross sales because of host government restrictions.

(d) The licensee may lose interest in renewing the contract unless the licensor holds his interest through innovation and technology.

(e) Finally, there is a danger of creating competition in third, or even home, markets if the licensee violates territorial agreements. Going to court in these situations is expensive and time-consuming, and no international adjudicatory body exists.

3 The British Overseas Trade Board started its work in 1972 to help British exporters. The members of this Board are drawn from government and industry, and its role is to provide information, advice and help for the exporter. It does this by directing the gathering, storing and dissemination of overseas market research, by the provision of advice and help to individual companies, by the organisation of collective trade promotions, and by the stimulation of export promotions' publicity.

More specifically, the services offered by the Board include the following:

(a) world-wide counselling service;
(b) market research data bank on overseas tariffs and import regulations;
(c) free initial market research assessing market potential in overseas markets;
(d) an export intelligence service to subscribers; and
(e) assistance in finding an agent or distributor.

It keeps an overseas traders' list, will assist in establishing status reports, and gives free information on regulations affecting manufacture under licence. Additionally, it has a full export marketing research scheme.

The Board also helps the coordination of government assistance at home and abroad to companies pursuing large overseas projects. It provides updated market statistics which can be used in conjunction with the statistics of market intelligence library. It is responsible for carrying out overseas seminars, trade fairs and exhibitions, and store promotions.

Additionally, it runs the market entry guarantee scheme for use by exporting companies. Finally, at all times it liases with the appropriate division of the Department of Industry in the United Kingdom, and additionally provides information services from overseas embassies, high commissions and consulates.

The British Overseas Trade Board provides a major service to exporters and may be seen as the export marketing department for many British companies. For some of the services it provided it is possible for funding to be arrange, so that costs to exporters are minimised. Where charges have to be made, they tend to be nominal.

4 The balance of payments of a country summarises all the transactions that have taken place between its residents and foreigners in a given period, usually a year. The word 'transactions' refers to: exports and imports of goods and services; the lending and borrowing of funds; remittances; and government aid and military expenditures. The term 'residents' means all individuals and business enterprises, including financial institutions, that are permanently residing within a country's borders, as well as government agencies at all levels. In other words, the balance of payments reflects the totality of a country's economic relations with the rest of the world: its trade in goods, its exchange of services, and purchase and sale of financial assets; and such important governmental transactions as foreign aid, military expenditures abroad, and the payment of reparation. Certain forces determine the volume of these transactions, how they are brought into balance, what problems arise when they fail to balance, and what policies are available to deal with those problems. The balance of payments record is made on the basis of rules of debiting and crediting, similar to those used in business accounting. For example, receipts are entered as credits, and payments as debits. Thus exports, like sales, are entered as credits; imports, like purchases, are debits. All transactions effecting increases in assets, like direct investment abroad, or decreases in indebtedness, like the repayment of external debt, are recorded as credits. However, decreases in assets, like liquidation of foreign securities, and increases in liabilities, like borrowing abroad, are treated as debits.

5 If a country imports more goods than it exports, it incurs an adverse balance of trade, and if it exports more than it imports, it is said to have a favourable balance of trade. On the face of it, an adverse balance of trade would appear to be a serious matter for the country that incurs it, because somehow or other it has got to pay for this deficit and strive very hard to avoid such deficits in future years. However, actual physical goods are not the only items that enter into international trade, for there are 'invisible' items, such as banking and insurance services, tourism, and profits and dividends of overseas investments. The net total of these 'invisibles', i.e. the difference between the total of such services sold abroad and the total purchase from abroad, has to be added to the balance of trade to arrive at the balance of payment on current account, and it is the latter balance that is of particular importance to the country concerned.

To a considerable extent, the invisible earnings are dependent in the United Kingdom upon the pound sterling being used as a reserve currency, i.e. overseas countries, especially in the Commonwealth, keeping pound sterling balances in London as reserves to be used in financing their trade with the rest of the world. They consequently use the banking, shipping and other services of the City of

London, which they would be less inclined to do if they switched to using some other currency for trading and reserve purposes. If one carries out a closer examination of invisible earnings in the United Kingdom, the information tends to show that the earnings abroad of the financial sector (such as banks and insurance companies) and the earnings from investments abroad in the form of interest, profits and dividends, account for much of the favourable total; but this total is greatly affected by the colossal amount of government expenditure overseas to maintain military bases and embassies, etc. And also to service government debt held overseas.

8 Multi-national marketing strategy

INTRODUCTION

This chapter covers that area of the syllabus concerned with multi-national marketing strategy, and includes: objectives of the multi-national corporation; attitudes towards multi-nationals; development of multi-national marketing strategies and marketing mix strategies.

QUESTIONS

1 What is the difference between objective and goals?

2 What steps would you take in attempting to predict the profitability of an international marketing venture?

3 What factors would you need to consider in establishing an international marketing strategy?

4 The numerous attitudes towards multi-national corporations have resulted in tremendous challenges for the multi-national corporations to overcome in the future. What would you regard as the key challenges?

5 Once a marketing strategy has been established, the marketing plan must be developed. How would you set about this?

6 When a company moves from domestic to multi-national marketing, two important considerations are:

(a) the possible need to adapt the basic product characteristics;
(b) determining what price should be charged for the product.

How would you set about these tasks?

7 An overseas subsidiary of a multi-national would normally undertake both short-term marketing planning as well as strategic planning. What problems do you consider it might face in strategic market planning?

8 How would you attempt to establish market entry objectives?

9 Describe the different strategies that a company can adopt for international growth.

10 Promotional standardisation in international markets is not as common as product standardisation, but is often as important. How would you attempt to establish a standardised promotional campaign?

ANSWERS

1 The two words 'objectives' and 'goals', often used interchangeably by businessmen, can be differentiated to convey two quite different concepts, as implied in the definition of strategy. The distinction between these two concepts is important because a statement of strategy needs them both. Delineation of objectives and goals serves two different management purposes.

An objective is an aspiration to be worked toward in the future. A goal is an achievement to be attained at some future date. However, these short definitions fail to convey the essence of the difference between these two concepts — that is, the distinction between reaching and grasping.

The difference between objectives and goals may be drawn in terms of the following four dimensions:

(a) *Time frame* An objective is timeless, enduring, and unending; a goal is temporal, time-phased and intended to be superseded by subsequent goals. President Kennedy's goals in the United States for the 1960s were achieved, and *did* contribute towards his objective, but new goals for the 1970s were needed for the maintenance of leadership objective.

(b) *Specificity* Objectives are stated in broad, general terms, dealing with matters of image, style, and self perception; goals are much more specific, stated in terms of a particular result to be accomplished by a specified date. It is because of their open-endedness that objectives can never be achieved, while goals can. We may believe that landing the first man on the moon did re-establish scientific leadership, but that perception may not be universally shared. To shift the analogy, we clearly won the battle, but not necessarily the war.

(c) *Focus* Objectives are usually stated in terms of some relative environment which is external to the organisation; goals are more internally focused and carry important implications about how the resources of the organisation will be utilised in the future. Objectives are frequently stated in terms of achieving leadership or recognition in a certain field. A goal implies a resource commitment, challenging the organisation to use those resources in order to achieve the desired result.

(d) *Measurement* Both objectives and goals can frequently be stated in terms that are quantifiable, but the character of the measurement is different. Quantified objectives are stated in relative terms. For example, the managers of one growth company have stated that their objective is: 'To achieve a compound rate of growth in earnings per share sufficient to place its performance in the top 10% of all companies'. This objective may be achieved in any one year, but it is timeless and externally focused, combining a continuing challenge for the management of that company. A quantified goal is expressed in absolute terms. Several years ago, a chairman of a diversified aircraft company stated that the company would 'achieve 50% of its sales revenue from non-government customers by 1980'. The achievement of that goal can be measured irrespective of the environmental conditions and competitors' actions.

In order to prepare an affective statement of strategy in a complex organisation, the distinction between objectives and goals must be recognised. Objectives are the first element in a statement of strategy; goals are the last. In the time that elapses between the delineation of two statements, there must be a great deal of interplay between the managers at various levels in the organisation's hierarchy. The above discussion has allowed only the basic delineations in this complex process of starting with a statement of objectives and working towards the development of more specific goals.

2 The process of predicting the profitability of an international venture should follow this sequence of steps:

(a) *Estimating existing markets* Whereas market research data are ususally plentiful in developed countries, that is seldom the case in other countries. Particularly in underdeveloped countries, market research data are very scarce, often unreliable and/or out of date. If these statistics are gathered, they are not normally made public. Market research facilities are available in some countries but not in others, and it is often necessary to start from scratch to obtain such basic information.

(b) *Forecasting markets* In many foreign countries, forecasting is more than usually hazardous. Most Western countries are used to stability in government, currency, and legal framework. Instability is a way of life in many countries. With a constant danger of reversals in political direction, inflation of currency, or dramatic changes in laws governing the conduct of business, it is very difficult indeed to make medium- or long-term predictions for foreign markets.

(c) *Estimating market shares* Not only are total markets difficult to predict, estimating brand shares is also often subject to a wide range of error. The products of a foreign based company may not be well received by consumers. Product features or sales techniques that make a substantial difference to Western consumers may mean little or nothing to foreigners at a different stage of market development. Governments and other local organisations may discriminate in many ways against foreign companies and their products, through purchase preferences, taxes, tariffs, quotas, or outright boycott.

(d) *Forecasting costs and profits* Not only are sales revenues difficult to forecast, but cost estimating in foreign investments is complicated by a lack of knowledge of local practices, legal restrictions, and trade practices. It may be difficult, for example, to obtain residents' or work permits for key employees, and others may then have to be brought in from elsewhere at substantial increases in cost.

(e) *Estimating cash requirements* Cash flow forecasts are often difficult to make. It is usually difficult to estimate foreign practices in the payment of bills, for example. Financial insititutions are normally less well developed than in the Western world, and funds are less readily available on short notice. In addition, remission of funds to the United Kingdom parent company may be blocked or otherwise restricted.

(f) *Discounting future income* The discount rate chosen is a measure of risk and uncerntainty in the future. As such, it is one of the key judgements to be made in foreign investment decisions. Normally, a substantially greater discount rate would have to be taken on foreign investments to take into account the relative lack of knowledge, foreign exchange risk, and other areas of uncertainty regarding future income flows.

The net result is that the foreign investment decision process involves significant differences from the domestic investment decision. Wide ranges of error in estimates are common, and unforeseen factors generally loom very large in the final outcome.

3 Successful export marketing, like domestic marketing, rests upon the willingness of top management to search out market opportunity, appraise it objectively on its merits, and then support a marketing effort with the necessary resources. Figure 1 shows the principle elements of an international marketing strategy.

Identifying and measuring foreign market opportunity

The key contribution of international market research is the identification and measurement of foreign target markets that offer the most profitable sales potential to the manufacturer. Sales potential is the sales volume the manufacturer can reasonably plan to achieve in a particular foreign target market over a period of, say, three to five years. But this sales potential estimate presupposes a given marketing effort, and the final estimate also constitutes a yardstick against which to measure the effectiveness of marketing operations. The more the manufacturer knows about the identity and behaviour of his final buyers — Who buys the product? Why do they buy it? How do they buy it? When do they buy it? Where do they buy it? — the more precisely he can define his foreign market target and design a marketing strategy that matches it. For these and other reasons, international market research is an indispensible foundation of international marketing strategy.

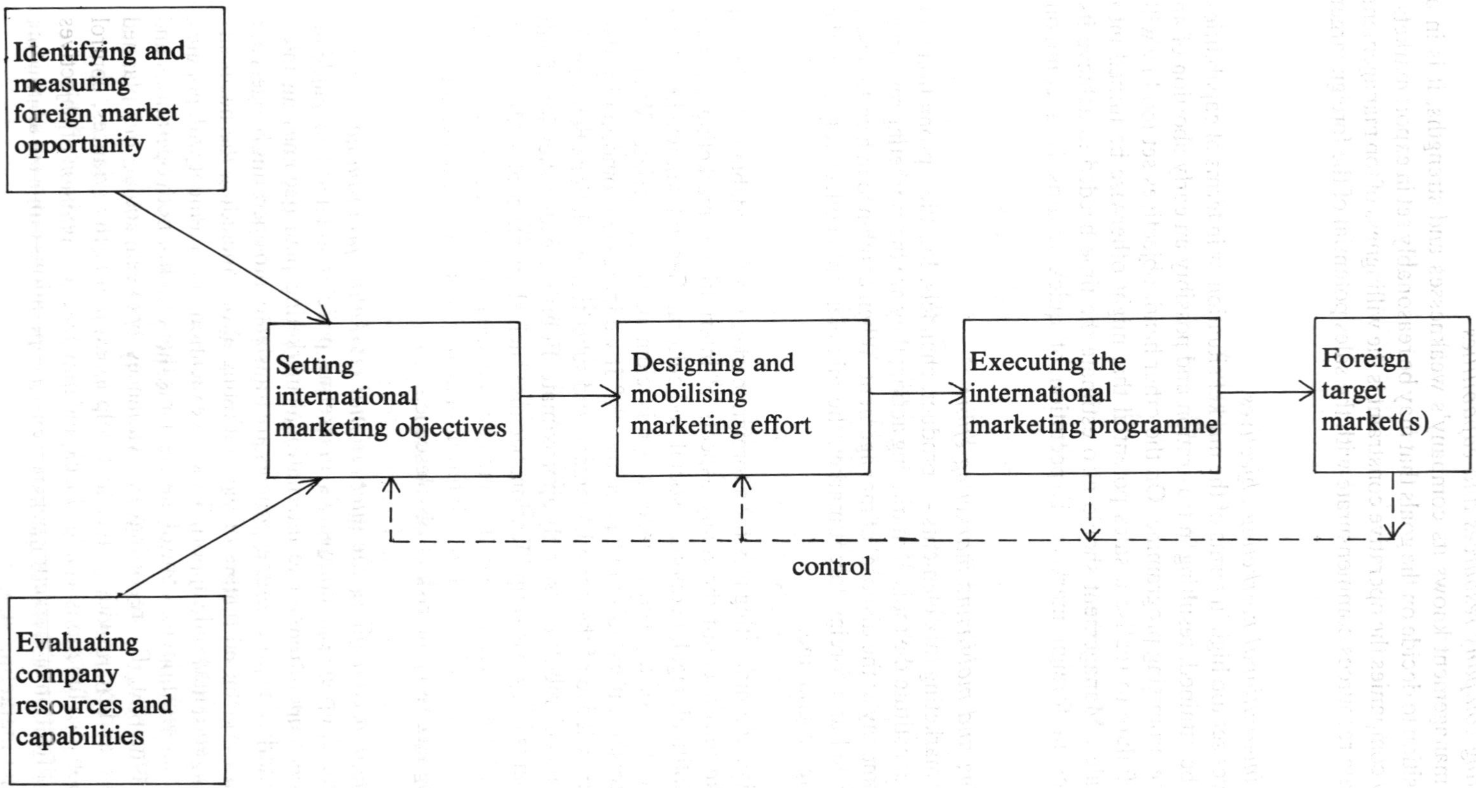

Figure 1 Elements of an international marketing strategy

Evaluating company resources and capabilities
Unless management knows its company's weaknesses and strengths, it is in a poor position to decide on the goals that may be reasonably set in export markets. In many companies the operative constraint is the willingness of top management to allocate resources commensurate with the sales potential of the foreign target market.

Setting international marketing objectives
Objectives set too high in terms of the market situation or in terms of capabilities will not be attained, resulting in frustration and possibly an early abortion of an otherwise promising programme. On the other hand, objectives set too low will mean a failure to realise a sales potential that might otherwise be turned into actual sales. Management should also estimate the time needed to achieve its objectives in foreign markets. Expectation of quick returns is a common mistake.

Designing and mobilising marketing effort
The five marketing mix elements — product, channels, logistics, promotion and price — constitute the tools of marketing action; they are the marketing resources of the company at the disposal of management. When combined in a certain way and directed at a foreign target market, the mix elements collectively form the marketing programme.

The design of a marketing mix for a foreign market is a formidable task. First, it must take into account the many aspects of international marketing environments: political, legal, economic, social and cultural. Second, knowledge of the effect on sales of a given change in a mix element is appropriate. What will happen to sales if we raise our price by x%? If we increase promotion by x%? Third, knowledge of the complementary and substitutive relations between the different mix elements is also only approximate. Fourth, the identification of only five elements is a gross simplification, because such elements contain many sub-elements; for example, promotion includes personal selling, advertising, sales promotion and publicity. Fifth, international markets are dynamic; and any marketing mix runs the risk of obsolescence.

Executing and controlling the international marketing programme
Once agreed upon, the company's marketing policies are used to guide its international operations. The international marketing plan becomes an international marketing programme; policies are translated into operating budgets and directives covering all phases of the marketing effort, including the necessary production and financial support. To keep execution in agreement with policies, management must devise control mechanisms that monitor both operations and the target market. By reporting any variances between actual and planned operations, and by providing data that help to explain such variances, control information also functions as a feedback and may lead to a revision of objectives and a modification of marketing policies. Just as operations represent an ongoing

effort, so should the planning of objectives and the international marketing mix. Control is the link between the two.

4 The key challenges to be overcome by multi-national corporations in the future are:

(a) the management of foreign-dominated liquid assets;
(b) expansion of growth policies;
(c) decentralisation of the production process;
(d) automation of assembly lines;
(e) corporate labour relationships;
(f) globalisation of consumer tastes.

In the management of foreign-dominated liquid assets, multi-national corporations conduct business in a number of foreign currencies. The exchange rates of these currencies are subjected to great upheavals with far-reaching consequences for earnings. These changes result from disturbances in international, social, political, and economic environment. Thus, in addition to protecting their business from competitive inroads, the management of foreign funds affects for example, the decision on the best currency mix to maintain on a short-term basis.

In respect of expansion of growth policies, traditionally, multi-national corporations have pursued expansion of growth overseas as an important corporate objective. Growth *per se,* however, may be problematic. The trade deficits of many countries, both among industrialised and third-world nations, and a common desire among nations for self-sufficiency, may render achievement of perpetual growth in foreign markets difficult. Even where opportunities are plentiful, an entry should be clearly earmarked with a possiblity of retrenchment or exit forced through economic nationalism or other political reasons. For example, it may become virtually impossible to raise capital in a host country, the traditional source of long-term funding, and that would certainly block growth.

As regards the decentralisation of the production process, both for political and economic reasons, more and more industries may follow the strategic lead of the electronics industry and seek component specialisation rather than product specialisation. If all components of a product cannot be efficiently manufactured by a multi-national corporation in one host country, the organisation may opt for specialisation in a few components whilst depending on other sources for the others. The decentralisation of the production process can serve as a protection against expropriation of foreign operations by a host country. In fact, arrangements that involve more than one host country business should be attractive to host nations because local involvement in the manufacture of the product would be encouraged.

In the automation of assembly lines, in advanced countries especially, many routine tasks might be performed by robots. Japan is way ahead in this area, and the United States will probably move in the same direction in the coming years. Such automation of assembly lines ought to result in substantial cost reductions and uniformity in quality, which in turn, could affect favourably the competitive positions of both the United States and Japan in world markets.

In the area of corporate labour relationships, the third-world multi-national corporations, with the abundance of cheap labour in their factories, may emerge as a newly significant competitive force. This is likely to have a far-reaching impact on corporate labour relationships in the Western world. A new form of understanding and harmony between the traditional adversaries will become necessary for mutual survival. The changes in labour management agreements in the automoble industry in Western Europe and America bear testimony to the emergence of this trend.

Finally, in the area of the globalisation of consumer taste, interesting phenomenon concerns the development of a common world-wide preference for a variety of consumer goods. The global crazes for designer jeans and fast food illustrate the point. But the commonality of demand does not mean that the same marketing mix strategies would be effective in every overseas market. The marketing strategies must be appropriately customised to adapt them to local customs and traditions.

The world market-place, as the end of this century approaches, will be quite different from what it was in, say, the 1960s and the 1970s. While opportunities should abound, international marketers will need new strategic perspectives to capitalise successfully on these opportunities. The big growth and profits may not come from traditional policies and strategies. Major corporations may need to develop new marketing strategies that will not only enhance their competitiveness but also fit the needs of the future.

5 Before the marketing plan can be developed, one has, initially, to select national markets, and then determine marketing strategy. The marketing plan itself can then be developed.

This three-step approach is important. In developing detailed marketing plans, it is first necessary to determine which product lines fit in with local markets, as well as the appropriate allocation of resources. A rough analysis of the potential international business, global sales, and profit targets based upon the estimates worked out in the first phase of selecting national markets, will help in assigning product lines. A framework for resource allocation can then be mapped out according to rough comparative figures for investment quotas, management needs and skilled labour requirements. This framework should be supplemented by companies' specific examples of standard marketing strategies for each group of countries.

Different product lines can then be assigned to different country groups, and for each country category different strategic approaches can be specified; for example, support on large-scale products, establishment of local production facilities, cooperation of the local manufacturers.

The level of detail in this resource allocation decision framework will depend on a number of factors: company history and philosophy, business policy objective, scope and variety of product lines, and the number of countries to be served. Working within this decision framework, each product division should analyse its own market in terms of size, growth and competitive situation; assess its profitability prospects, opportunities and risks; and identify its own current strategic position on the basis of market share, profit situation, and vulnerability to local risks. Each product division will then be in a position to develop country-specific marketing alternatives for servicing each national market. Top management's role throughout is to coordinate the marketing strategy development efforts in the various divisions and constantly monitor the strategic decision framework.

This three-phase approach shows a number of advantages:

(a) It allows management to set up, with a minimum of planning effort, a strategic framework that gives clear priority to market selection decisions, thus making it much easier for the divisions to work out effective product line strategies, unhampered by the usual 'chicken or egg' problem.

(b) Division managers can foresee, at a fairly early stage, what reallocations of labour, management and capital resources are likely to be called for, and what adjustments may have to be imposed from the top as a consequence of inadequate resources.

(c) The company's future risk profile can be worked out in terms of resource commitment by country group and type of investment.

Briefly, this approach enables management to concentrate profitably resources and attention on a handful of really attractive countries, instead of dissipating its efforts in vain attempts to serve every possible country.

6

Adaptation of product

When a company shifts from domestic to multi-national marketing, it may certainly need to alter basic product characteristics. These changes may be minor in nature, or more fundamental.

The five product strategy alternatives that are available to international marketing planners are:

(a) Standard strategy, or product extention — this is often the most profitable and the easiest option. When customer need and use conditions are the same around the world for the product, the marketer can sell a standardised product with standardised promotional messages.

(b) Communication redesign — this strategy is appropriate when use conditions are identical to those in the domestic market, but the product serves a different function overseas. An example is the bicycle, which is mainly used for recreation in the United Kingdom, but provides basic transporations in many parts of the world. The marketer will maintain a standardised product, but will adjust all marketing communication to local needs and customs.

(c) Product redesign — this strategy is used by marketers when a product fills the same need around the world, but use conditions vary. The marketer will maintain the standard promotional appeal, but will vary the product to local use conditions. For example, petrol companies change the contents of fuel to suit weather conditions in foreign markets, but the Esso sales promotional campaign 'Put a tiger in your tank', was a standard message in every country in the world.

(d) Dual adaptation — dual adaptation strategy represents both communications and product redesign. It is applied when a marketer wants to reach overseas markets in which both environmental use conditions and basic production functions differ from the home country. An example is clothing. The marketer must alter both the product characteristics and the standard marketing appeal.

(e) Product invention — the first four strategies depend on the ability of the overseas consumer to buy the product. But if the target market's segments cannot afford the price, the company must invent a new, cheaper product to fulfil the need. The marketing theme must also be changed to fit the new product. A very good example is the hand-powered washing machine which was literally invented for this reason.

Pricing
In respect of what price should be charged for a product when it is sold in the international markets, these guidelines may be followed:

(a) a periodic review of prices;
(b) the setting of prices on a one-country basis;
(c) consideration of price discounts.

One study of multi-national marketing executives found that 45% considered pricing to the most important marketing strategy factor. Among price-setting considerations, production costs and the prices set by multi-national competitors were ranked as most influential. The prices of local firms in the host country scored third among price considerations, and consumer demand was ranked fourth. Marketers may not have absolute (if indeed, any) freedom to set prices abroad. Some governments in developing countries legislate low retail prices in order to promote a higher standard of living, especially on such necessities as food.

'Dumping' of products is a common practice in international marketing. A manufacturer of television sets may have an oversupply of last year's models in his warehouses. He dumps these goods by selling them at a lower price than consumers in the domestic market are being charged. This practice has become unpopular in many nations, and import duties may be raised when there is a suspicion of dumping.

7 A variety of problems can hinder a subsidiary's strategic market planning process. The first problem concerns the availability of adequate information. Both the subsidiary and the parent company can be blamed for this problem. Subsidiaries often lack the knowledge and resources to scan the environment systematically and gather adequate information from the external environment. Furthermore, internal information may not be adequately organised. Not the least problem is that available information on national trends and so on is often outdated, particularly in emerging countries such as Brazil, Nigeria and South Korea, which are changing quickly.

As far as head office is concerned, there may not even be a world-wide marketing information system in operation. Thus, information at head office from different subsidiaries from different groups is not adequately collected, nor is the information properly disseminated. Furthermore, sometimes information is poorly coordinated, or their might be an abundance of information but the right information may be nowhere to be found. It is quite conceivable that head office could request the information from a subsidiary that it had *itself* made available.

Lack of an established planning system is another problem. Emphasis on day-to-day matters by head office discourages strategic planning at the subsidiary level. In some cases, the planning system is too complex and unnecessarily cumbersome. Thus, a major portion of marketing managers' time in subsidiary companies is spent on responding to the needs of the parent company.

Yet another problem concerns the scarcity of trained managers. Subsidiaries often lack trained personnel to undertake planning. This problem can, however, be mitigated through training arranged by the parent company. Finally, if the plan is adhered to as a rigid instrument of control, it could lead to intra-company fighting and manipulations to ensure meeting cost and revenue projections. Such fighting leads to rivalries, which are obviously counter-productive. Manipulations result in a distorted picture of performance.

8 The first consideration in establishing market entry objectives is the degree of commitment to foreign operations. The company that views foreign operations as an integral element of its overall growth plan will establish a very different set of objectives from the company that considers foreign operations as a mere extension of its domestic goals.

One team of researchers identified companies that are committed to developing world-wide marketing strategies as geocentric, and firms that view foreign operations as an export of domestic strategies as ethnocentric.

Geocentric objectives

For this type of company the primary objective is determining whether to enter a foreign market in order to identify unmet consumer needs and to meet them. But allocating resouces to foreign operations is complicated by barriers, political regulations, differences in customs and business practices. Thus multi-national companies must take environmental constraints into account when evaluating foreign opportunites. Objectives to establish market entry could be based on: minimum market size; market growth potential; acceptable tariff barriers; acceptable price controls; attainable product standards; and political stability.

Management should rate countries on such criteria and determine whether market entry would meet international objectives. A poor rating on any criterion could mean a decision against entry, even if an opportunity exists to meet a defined set of consumer needs.

Ethnocentric objectives

The ethnocentric firm could base its decision on market entry more on domestic than foreign markets conditions; it might want to use, for example, excess capacity to drive down unit costs. The following international marketing objectives are motivated primarily by domestic operational considerations:

(a) To flee recessions — during the deep recession of the early 1980s several international companies increased their efforts in areas with greater economic growth.

(b) To counter demographic trends — the decrease in the birth rate in the Western world caused a company called Gerber, who produced baby foods, to establish operations in Costa Rica, where the birth rate was increasing, to escape domestic competition.

(c) To lower unit costs — this objective is particularly important for capital-intensive industries such as steel and motor cars. Japanese steelmakers rely on their domestic market for only 40% of production. Exports allow them to increase production and lower costs. Exports also help to make Japanese steelmakers move along the experience curve, thus increasing their productivity more than most other steelworkers in the world.

(d) To revitalise the product life cycle — when British and American filmmakers found that domestic sales were declining, they often exported films to foreign countries.

(e) Finally, to dispose of excess inventories — some companies seek to dispose of inventories overseas by dumping the products at lower prices. Many countries have anti-dumping laws that preclude such actions, however.

9 In domestic marketing, corporate growth strategies can be categorised according to whether the company was relying for growth on existing or new products in existing or new markets. The result of this would be to establish four general approaches to growth. The same framework can be used in examining multi-national growth alternatives except that: (a) instead of markets, we will refer to countries; and (b) instead of existing or new products, we will refer to a narrow versus a broad international product mix. This results in a model that presents four general growth strategies for multi-national companies.

Market concentration

Many companies direct single products to one or a few markets. A general food company sells chewing gum in France, ice cream in Brazil, and pasta in Italy. None of these businesses is large enough to justify sales on a global basis. Therefore, market concentration is a logical strategy if a product can be sold profitably to a limited market.

Another motive for pursuing a strategy of market concentration is the belief that the product appeals to a fairly homogeneous group in a few countries. Playtex is marketing its hair care line in highly industrialised countries, where women's hair care needs are relatively homogeneous. The company may feel that extending the line to other markets is too risky.

Market extension

A strategy of market extension is suitable for companies with a unique product line that can appeal to the needs of different customers in many countries. Such a strategy requires a company to have a competitive advantage in order to permit it to sell a narrow product line on a global basis. Coca-Cola and Pepsi-Cola are examples. These companies seek to create a competitive advantage so that their product line will be regarded as superior on a world-wide basis. The Japanese company, Honda, have successfully pursued a strategy of market extension by developing an inexpensive, reliable and easy-to-use motor cycle. Before they established a mass market, motor cycles were regarded as big, expensive machines, targeted to a small segment. The combination of a good, inexpensive product, a world-wide message, and a superior distributor network, permitted Honda to outflank its major competitors, and expand rapidly into foreign markets.

Product extension
This involves selling a broad product mix in a limited number of foreign markets. This strategy is logical if the multi-national firm:

(a) is well entrenched in these markets and views further expansion as risky; and
(b) can achieve economies of scale in advertising and distribution.

Economies of scale in advertising might involve a family brand strategy in which many brands are advertised under the corporate name. The General Electric Company uses a family brand advertising strategy in the international market as well as the domestic American market. Economies of scale can also be achieved in distribution. By marketing a broad product mix in a few countries, a company can distribute many of its products through the same intermediaries, achieving economies in transport, storage and direct sales.

Diversification
This is an aggressive growth strategy which involves expansion of both the product mix and foreign markets. Such a strategy can be employed by companies with sufficient resources to accomplish fast entry into many markets on a multi-product basis. The strategy also requires a broader product mix to appeal to many segments in different markets.

A company that is currently pursuing a diversification strategy is Johnson & Johnson. The company markets a broad range of household and personal care products in foreign markets. It currently sells in overs 40 countries and is expanding its operations at about two countries per year.

10 Although promotional standardisation in international markets is not as common as product standardisation, several companies have attempted to establish standardised campaigns because they believe their products can be sold through global appeals. Most companies have either adapted campaigns to local markets or followed a pattern standardisation strategy, developing a basic theme and allowing local variations.

The argument has frequently been made that good promotional themes have universal appeal. One advertising executive provided the rationale for a standardised promotional strategy:

> Different peoples are basically the same . . . An international campaign with a truly universal appeal can be effective in any market . . . The desire to be beautiful is universal . . . Such appeals as 'mother and child', 'freedom from pain', 'glow of health', know no boundaries.

Another reason to use standardised appeals is the proximity of many foreign countries and the consequent overlap in media outreach. For example, German television broadcasts are received by 40% of Dutch homes with TV sets; 4 million French housewives tune into Radio Luxemburg; and Paris Match magazine has a substantial circulation in most Western European countries. If campaigns for a product are differentiated, media overlap could cause confusion in regional markets. The growth of cable and satellite transmissions will also encourage marketers to address target markets that stretch across a number of countries, rather than market on a country-by-country basis.

Promotional standardisation creates the same risk as product standardisation, i.e. the possiblity of ignoring significant differences in local consumer needs. This danger led one executive to comment: 'You probably sacrifice a lot in effectiveness in the process. My recommendation is to challenge the local agency to improve upon the domestic campaign.'

As a result of these misgivings, many multi-nationals adapt promotional campaigns to local markets. Until 1981, Levi Strauss used an adaptive strategy to sell jeans around the world. The appeals differed as follows:

— In Europe, television commercials had a super sexy appeal.

— In the United Kingdom, advertisements showed Levi's as an American brand, and used a Wild West setting.

— In Japan, the brand was positioned as legendary, with the theme 'Heroes wear Levi's'.

— In Australia, commercials counted product benefits such as tight fit with comfort.

The cost and fragmentation of adaptation and the dangers of standardisation have caused many companies to move to a patterned promotional standardisation strategy. Using the same example, Levi's changed in 1981 from a localised approach to one in which the 'broad outlines of the campaign are given, but the details are not'. The company's director of advertising said that the home office develops basic building blocks for a campaign by using core values like honesty, credibility and social responsibility. The implication around the core is left to local agencies.

Differences in media availability between countries increases the likelihood of patterned standardisation; for example, commercial television time is available for one hour in Germany and is not available at all in Sweden; magazines are a major medium in Italy but a minor one in Austria; newspapers are national in the United Kingdom, but local in Spain. A patterned standardisation strategy can adapt to differences in media availability between countries.

9 International trade regulations

INTRODUCTION

The questions and answers in this chapter relate to that part of the syllabus covering international trade regulations, including: barriers to international trade, customs, quotas, tariffs, etc.; customs, economic and political unions; free trade areas; consumer and environmental protection; protection of indigenous industry, trade, etc.; nationalisation of foreign investment.

QUESTIONS

1 Discuss the fact that over the past 20 years there have been attempts to ease trade barriers and encourage international trade.

2 What are the effects of market agreements on international marketing?

3 Apart from the established market agreements between national, there are a variety of other arrangements that various nations can and have made for their economic benefit. Give examples of such arrangements.

4 What effect does the overall macroeconomic environment of the host country have upon marketing strategies for a multi-national corporation?

5 How can political conflict affect international business activities?

6 'Marketing decisions in the international context are deeply affected by the political perspectives of both home and host countries.' Discuss.

7 What form might a host country use in adopting measures that restrict imports or artificially stimulate exports ignoring the use of tariff barriers?

8 Describe the role played by the United Nations in trying to encourage economic cooperation and prosperity.

9 In the past two decades, important influences on European business have been: the increase of controls over monopolies and over competition-inhibiting practices and an increase in anti-trust legislation. Describe how this has taken place.

10 Describe the major trends in international business that affect competition in existing global industries, and the creation of new global industries.

ANSWERS

1 International marketers must understand the various regulations and barriers that operate in foreign countries, although certainly since the Second World War there have been attempts to ease trade barriers and encourage international trade.

Countries impose trade barriers to protect domestic industries and to raise money. The most common is the tariff, a tax on imported goods. Sometimes tariffs are so high that they effectively prohibit imports. For example, in Mexico the tariff on foreign-fabricated motor car parts ranges from 60 to 80% of the item's value. Some countries also set import quotas, a limit on the import value of certain product categories. Recently, the European Economic Community set import quotas on Japanese motor cycles and motor cars to protect domestic manufacturers.

Countries can also establish non-tariff barriers. One type is monetary restrictions. Countries have sometimes blocked foreign currencies to cut off or reduce imports as a means of bringing their balance of payments into line. Some countries also require an exchange permit to export goods. This permits a country to regulate trade through the approval of such permits, and to stipulate low or high rates depending on whether it wants to encourage imports or not. Another non-tariff barrier is product standards. Japan has a variety of product standards that restrict exports to Japan from both America and Europe. To sell an American or European car in Japan, one must go through volumes of documents on standards plus local testing of almost every vehicle, which can add as much as £500 to the price of a car.

In 1947 the United States of America, the United Kingdom and 21 other countries signed the General Agreement of Tariffs and Trade (GATT) to reduce tariffs and create a watchdog agency to monitor them. Since 1947, the GATT agreement has reduced tariffs seven times, the most recent being 'the Tokyo round', in 1979. The average tariff today is 8.3% in the USA, 9.8% in Western Europe, and 10.9% in Japan, a marked reduction from pre-World War Two levels of 50 to 60%. When the Tokyo round of tariff reductions becomes fully effective in 1988, the average tariff will be 4.3% in the USA and 2.5% in Japan.

Trade barriers have also been reduced through the formation of economic communities. The best known is the European Economic Community, better known as the Common Market, formed in 1958. It seeks to eliminate trade barriers between members and to encourage economic union. Other economic communities are the European Free Trade Association, the Latin American Free Trade Association, and the Council for Mutual Economic Assistance, commonly known as COMECON.

2 Market agreements affect international marketing in a variety of ways. First, the scope of the market is broadened. For example, after the formation of the Common Market, the French market ceased to be just a French market — rather it became a part of the larger Common Market. Such an expanded market provides a flexibility that would not be feasible dealing with individual countries. Under a free trade area agreement, internal trade barriers among member countries are abolished, and a company may move products from one country to another with complete freedom. This permits a company to achieve economies of scale, not only in production, but also in promoting the product, in distribution, and in other aspects of business. For example, the establishment of the Common Market made it feasible for the Ford Motor Company to integrate its operations in Germany and the United Kingdom.

Second, market agreements change the nature of competition. For example, before the formation of the Common Market, many American multi-national corporations found little or no competition in Western Europe, but afterwards, local companies were encouraged to expand quickly. They became factors in the market, through mergers and suchlike, with the encouragement of member governments. In the computer area, Siemens, CIL and Philips entered into a joint venture to compete effectively against IBM. Such cooperation among businesses need not necessarily be between companies of different nations. In Italy, for example, Montecatini and Edison Companies merged to form Montedison.

Third, market agreement firms expand through mergers and acquisitions and thereby become highly competitive outside their market area as well. For example, after the formation of the Common Market, French and German companies were able to compete aggressively against US and Japanese multi-nationals.

Finally, market agreement countries are able to make decisions favourable to all member country companies. It would not be feasible for an individual country to enforce such measures. For example, Common Market anti-trust policies could adversely affect an American company and its subsidiaries or licencees, which previously had been given exclusive rights in, say, Italy and the Netherlands.

3 In addition to the normal types of market agreements that extend among nations in different regions of the world, there are a variety of other arrangements that various nations have made for their economic benefit. For example, two different forms of agreement are the Commonwealth of Nations, and the commodity agreements and producer cartels. Although the Commonwealth of Nations is usually mentioned in relation to political unions, it is not strictly speaking a political union. The only political bond among the Commonwealth nations existed in the past when they constituted part of the British Empire. In addition, commonality is not fostered by the fact that the nations are geographically dispersed and represent different economic, political and cultural perspectives. Yet the group survives. On the economic front, the member nations

accord one another preferential treament by agreement to import from each other on a selective basis. Nevertheless, this situation has changed greatly since its beginnings in the post-World War Two period, partially on political ground and partially in response to individual economic interests. In particular, the UK's entry into the Common Market caused a decline in the economic role of the Commonwealth. By and large, the Commonwealth of Nations mainly provides member countries with the opportunity to gather around a table on an annual basis in order to review matters of mutual concern. This format enables members to become acquainted with particular issues and later arrange mutually beneficial agreements if they desire.

Another significant type of market agreement is the commodity agreement. Some have been entered into under the auspices of GATT to stabilise the prices of commodities such as textiles, sugar, tea, cocoa, olive oil, coffee and wheat. The underlying purpose of commodity agreements, which are made between producing and consuming countries, has been to prevent excessive fluctuations in prices for the benefit of the developing countries. Many of these countries are economically dependent on one commodity or another for economic health. This dependence does not fluctuate, as prices can, because of supply and demand conditions. For example, poor weather conditions in a producing country might spoil its crop and thus limit supply. Demand goes up and down in response to economic conditions in the consuming countries. Commodity agreements help producing countries receive stable earnings from the export of their commodities, while consuming countries are assured of adequate supplies of particular commodities.

The term 'producer cartel' refers to a unilateral agreement among producers of a commodity, or suppliers of a natural resource, to deal collectively as a group for the purpose of trading the commodity. The producer cartel became a popular mode of economic cooperation among producers of strategic commodities after the success of the OPEC petrol cartel. Since 1975, a number of producer cartels have been organised by countries exporting chromium, copper and rubber. However, it is unrealistic to expect other producer cartels to duplicate OPEC's record.

4 One of the best examples to use is Brazil. As Brazil is one of the few countries with rapidly developing economies, it would seem likely that there would be ample opportunities for international marketers. Yet, during 1980 and 1981, the Brazilian economy was beset by a variety of problems which restricted the realisation of opportunities there. By the end of 1981, the country had accumulated a huge external debt, attributed to oil imports, so that despite severe import restrictions, a record soya bean crop, an excellent performance by manufactured exports, inflation ran at about 80% during 1981, while the economy maintained its approximate 5% annual growth rate, Brazil had severe problems. Additionally, strict import restrictions limited the opportunity for exports to Brazil, whose soaring inflation required caution in establishing

manufacturing there, since new plant construction would be costly. Furthermore, Brazilian exports to foreign countries were less competitive in price. Thus, the short-run outlet for Brazil in 1982 appeared less than promising.

Additionally, the health of an economy affects consumer confidence, which is then reflected in consumer buying plans. A favourable economic climate generates a spirit of optimism among consumers who are then more willing to go out and spend money. But the reverse occurs when economic conditions are unfavourable. In Brazil's case, 1981 was not an exciting year from the viewpoint of consumers. With high inflation and emphasis on exports to balance the trade deficit, Brazilian consumers had to 'tighten their belts'.

While economic climate affects all businesses, some businesses are affected more deeply. International marketers should figure out the extent to which their business is susceptible to economic conditions. For example, in a depressed economy consumers tend to postpone buying durable goods. Thus, the economic environment in Brazil during 1981 seemed gloomy to television manufacturers overseas who were interested in entering the market. It should be cautioned, however, that the current economic environment is just one variable. Despite the fact that the short-run economic environment is less than conducive to profits, a company may enter an overseas market because of good long-term economic prospects in that economy, or other such favourable factors as growing political stability or the existence of low wage scales. The long-run perspective is the most important one if a company has sufficient resources to endure waiting for the future favourable environment.

5 Many countries in different parts of the world undergo political conflict of various sorts. Political conflict can be irregular, revolutionary, or discontinuous, and basically may be categorised as turmoil, internal war, and conspiracy. Turmoil refers to instant upheaval on a massive scale against an established regime, for example, the Islamic fundamentalists mass protest against Iran. Internal war means large-scale, organised violence against a government, such as guerilla warfare, for example, North Vietnam's actions in South Vietnam. Conspiracy represents an instant, planned act of violence against those in power, for example, the fatal attack against Egyptian President, Anwar Sadat. Political conflict may or may not have an impact on business; while the ousting of the Shah of Iran led to heavy losses by international business there, the murder of Sadat made no difference to international business in Egypt at that time.

It is possible that political change may lead to a more favourable business climate. For example, in Argentina after the Peronist regime was overthrown the new government's policy was so favourable towards multi-nationals that the previously nationalised firms were returned to their owners. Similarly, Sukarno's departure from the Indonesian scene improved the business climate there, as did Nkrumah's absence from Ghana.

It is important to make a distinction between political risk and political conflict. Political conflict in a country may lead to unstable conditions, but those conditions may or may not affect business. Therefore, political risk may or may not result from political unrest. Firms must analyse each occurrence of political conflict and assess the likelihood of its impact on business.

The effect of political conflict on business may be direct or indirect. Direct effects would be violence against the company involved, such as the kidnapping of an executive, damage to company property, or a strike. Overall, direct effects are usually temporary and do not result in huge losses. Indirect effects occur because of changes in government policy. In other words, political conflict leads to some change in a government's economic perspective. Such a change may come from a new attitude on the part of an existing government or through a new government. Further, the change may be motivated by a sincere desire to straighten things out or simply to divert public attention from other domestic problems plaguing the country.

In many developing countries, for example, a variety of expectations have been raised which could not be fulfilled, either economically or politically. Such a situation can lead to discontent and conflict. In Western societies discontent also occurs, but it has an outlet through the ballot box. In traditional societies, such an outlet is usually not available and the other main alternative is political conflict and unrest. Often governments may dramatise their viability by sometimes rash nationalisation of foreign business. Such actions divert attention from pressing problems by giving the appearance of taking effective measures, and they may take advantage of anti-foreign bias.

From the viewpoint of foreign businesses, it is important to understand the nature of political conflict and the motivation behind government action. If a changing government policy is merely for symbolic purposes, it represents less risk to foreign businesses. Also, when new policy is expressed through the imposition of certain constraints, requirements and controls of foreign businesses, it is important to assess the host government's administrative ability. The government must have the capacity to promulgate and enforce the new policy. When such capabilities are lacking, the new policy will remain a well-intentioned effort but without any actual effects on foreign businesses.

6 It is certainly true that marketing decisions in the international context are deeply affected by the political perspectives of both home and host countries. For example, government decisions have significantly affected the UK motor car industry. Stringent requirements such as the fuel efficiency standards have burdened the industry in several ways.

Governments around the world help their domestic industries to strengthen their competitiveness through various fiscal and monetary measures. Such political support can play a key role in an industry's search for markets abroad. Without such assistance, an industry may face a difficult situation. The UK motor car industry would benefit from government concessions favouring UK motor car exports. Other European countries, for example, rely on value added taxes to help their industries. These apply to all levels of manufacturing transactions up to and including the final sale to the user. Further, if the final sale is for export, the value added tax is rebated, thus effectively reducing the price in international markets. Japan imposes commodity taxes on selected lines of products, including motor cars. In the event of export, the commodity tax is waived. The United States has no similar arrangement. When a new motor car, therefore, is shipped from the United States to Japan, it receives no rebate or relief of its United States taxes upon export, and in addition must bear the cost of a commodity tax, depending on the size of the vehicle, when it is sold in Japan.

The competition facing manufacturers, therefore, both at home and in international markets, can be potent and resourceful. Moreover, a number of overseas competitors are wholly or partly state-owned, and respond to the direction of their governments, which depend heavily on their export business for the maintenance of employment and the earning of foreign exchange. This shows how politics may influence the perspectives of international marketing.

Multi-national corporation operations are affected by government regulations in three areas:

(a) the pattern of ownership in the parent company of the affiliate;
(b) the direction and nature of growth of the affiliate; and
(c) the flow of product, technology and managerial skills within the companies of the group.

Take, for example, the case of India. The impact of regulations on the strategies adopted by multi-national corporations there lead to one important conclusion: the strategic choices made by multi-national corporations' affiliates are a response more to regulations than to the interaction of market forces or to technological innovation. In other words, government, particularly in a developing country, can substantially influence the strategy of multi-national corporations' affiliates in ways which were thought impossible even a few years ago. In India, many multi-national corporation affiliates had to diversify into areas where neither the parent company nor the affiliate had the core capabilities. Competence ceased to be an important factor in strategy formulation, when compared to the need to comply with government directions and regulations. In general, the transfer of products and technology from the parent company in order to exploit new markets in the host country met with obstruction from the government unless the technology was in the area specified by their regulations.

With regulations forcing multi-national corporations' affiliates, operating in controlled economies, to move into areas where the parent company may or may not have prior experience, the parent company will find increasing difficulties in developing world-wide strategies to maximise their corporate interests. The large multi-national corporations will have problems in achieving world-wide integration of resources — physical, human, and financial. Dilution of ownership will lead to erosion of the power of the parent company to control the management process in the affiliates. In short, the dissimilarity of business between the affiliates and the parent, along with reduced ownership by the parent, will make the latter primarily an investor. If this pattern continues, parent companies will soon find that they are no longer in a position to integrate their resources world-wide.

7 Usually such laws are referred to as non-tariff barriers to international trade. There are several major types of non-tariff barrier.

Specific limitations on trade
Quotas limit the quantity or value of goods that can be imported from a source during a given time period. Proportional restrictions of foreign to domestic goods restrict the total imports of a product as a predetermined proportion of the total domestic production of the product. Minimum import price limits spell out a procedure for price setting on imports *viz-à-viz* the price of domestic goods at the same time. Embargoes force the complete prohibition of imports for certain types of goods.

Customs and administrative entry procedures
Valuation of imports or assessing import duty is left to the discretion of custom officials who use highly arbitrary and discriminatory procedure. Tariff classification allows the arbitrary designation of products in high tariff categories for purposes of assessing higher taxes. Documentary requirements in force entail cumbersome system of documentation in order to complete a foreign trade transaction. Policies allow enormous fees to be charged in order to complete entry procedures.

Standards
Standards disparity allows the application of different health, safety, and quality standards for similar goods from different countries. Arbitrary choice of testing methods allows the use of different testing methods for goods from different destinations to judge if the national product standards are met. Packaging, labelling, and marking standards are applied in stringent and discriminatory ways.

Government participation in trade
Government procurement policies are designed to favour domestic goods. Countervailing duties are imposed on imported goods to counteract the export subsidies to that industry in the exporting country.

Charges on imports
Prior import deposits require the importer to make a deposit with the government which may amount to as much as 100% of import value. Broader tax adjustments are fiscal measures which impose all the taxes on imported goods that are charged to domestic products. Adminstrative fees, special supplementary duties, import credit discrimination, and variable levies are other curtailing non-tariff charges.

Finally, there are voluntary export restraints whereby agreement is made between two trading countries to limit the exports of a specific product to a particular level, such as the agreement between the European Economic Community and Japan to limit Japanese car exports to the EEC. Orderly marketing agreements are specific agreements between trading partners whereby they agree to negotiate trade restrictions.

8 The United Nations has established a number of autonomous bodies and agencies to encourage world-wide economic cooperation and prosperity. Firstly, the World Health Organisation: WHO's work concerns the improvement of health conditions, but deals with such matters as drug standardisation, epidemic control, health service systems, and related programmes.

The International Civil Aviation Organisation (ICAO) promotes safe and efficient air travel through regulating the flow of air traffic, air-worthiness standards, airport operations, and related communications.

The International Telecommunications Union (ITU) regulates international communications via radio, telephone and telegraph. For example ITU controls and allocates radio frequencies and facilitates inter-country telegraph and telephone communications.

The Universal Postal Union (UPU) facilitates postal communications. For example, it conducts settlements among nations related to revenue sharing.

The International Labour Organisations (ILO) protects workers' rights, promotes workers' welfare and enhances the effectiveness of their organisations.

The International Telecommunications Satellite Consortium is another organisation that deals with matters of telecommunications. Its work mainly concerns new satellite communications technology.

Finally, the international Standards Organisation (ISO) is another specialised UN agency. It is particularly important because its administration bears directly on marketing. ISO promotes standardisation of different products and processes. The ultimate purpose is to encourage world trade and business without hinderance from design/style/feature variations among nations. To this end, ISO has over 100 committees that are actively engaged in developing uniform international standards in various fields.

The impact of these agencies on international business varies. But the importance of the need for standardisation does not vary. For example, a grinding machine still usable in the United Kingdom would be unsuitable in America for such reasons as differences in electric current and weight measures. In order to sell a Bristish-made grinding machine, the tolerance measurement would have to be varied to conform with measurements commonly used in America. Similarly, the electrical wiring would require change for the machine to operate on a higher voltage.

The differences in standards are among the main hinderances to world trade and business development. These differences have led to market opportunity losses for UK companies in many countries. This is one area where international cooperation is overdue. Interestingly, American and European industry and government have played almost no role in seeking common standards worldwide. This may be attributed to the fact that overseas business is proportionatly small. In the future, however, this is likely to change.

9 Most European countries, recognising the need for inter-company arrangements in certain circumstances, permit the making of restrictive agreements and cartels but reserve the right to limit or eliminate those which they consider to be against public interest. In such countries, agreements between companies are registered and may then be subject to immediate scrutiny and interference. There are other countries, such as West Germany, which forbids cartels in general, but allows individual ones if they meet certain strict requirements and are duly registered. In France, while the philosophy is similar, practice differs. Restrictive agreements are banned in principle, but individual exceptions are permitted; these, however, are not registered and come under control only in retrospect if they are found to be undesirable.

There are two important features which are common to all European anti-trust legislation:

(a) The actual size of the party concerned, and the share of the business in a market they will secure, are not in themselves grounds for unacceptability.

(b) The control of practices which are deemed to offend is an administrative rather than a judicial affair which means that the enforcing authorities rely on negotiations and persuasion, not on force.

Although the European attitude to anti-trust legislation is perhaps less severe than in America, and although permitting some cartels, it invites legal prosecutions, as so many industrial mergers have taken place in recent years, and economic power has become concentrated in such a way that European governments may, at some future time, have to set limits to permissible corporate size, treating each case on its merits.

In the last 10 years, the most significant anti-trust event has been the introduction of the European Economic Community's rules of competition, which transcend the rules existing in each of its member countries. There remain anomalies to be resolved as a result of conflict between EEC laws and those of individual countries. Although, for example, the EEC does not allow exclusive agreements, under Belgium law, independent distributors are given strong protection if manufacturers cancel contracts which contain a clause of perfect exclusivity. On the other hand, conflict may go the other way, and it often happens that an EEC rule is less strict than the one in use in a certain country. In Italy, for example, the anti-trust laws prohibit cartels completely, whereas the EEC rules tolerate what are described as good restrictive arrangements and cartels.

There are, or course, two obvious views of the way in which these disparities between national and supernational laws should be solved. One view is that all international agreements must accord with the Treaty of Rome, and that no national laws can take precedence over the rules of the EEC. The other is that an individual state, although a member of the EEC, should have the right to prohibit a company from being a party to an international agreement if the latter is against its own national law. Subjects such as these are still under discussion by member countries of the EEC, and it is probably going to be many years before they are, in fact, rationalised, if at all.

10 There appear to be a number of trends that hold great importance for competition in existing global industries and for the creation of new ones.

The reduction in differences between countries is an example of one such trend. A number of observers have pointed out that the economic differences among developed and newly developed countries may be narrowing in areas like income, factor cost, energy cost, marketing practices, and distribution channels. Part of this reduction may be due to the aggressiveness of multi-national companies in spreading techniques around the world. Whatever the cause is, it works towards reducing impediments to world competition.

One must also consider the more aggressive industrial policy. The industrial policies of many countries are in flux. Having adopted passive or protective postures in the past, governments like those of Japan, South Korea, Singapore and West Germany are now taking aggressive postures to stimulate industry in carefully selected sectors. They are also facilitating the abandonment of sectors deemed less desirable. This new industrial policy is giving companies in such countries the support to make broad moves that would transform industries to global status, like the construction of massive plants and large upfront investments in breaking into new markets. Thus, although companies in sectors not favoured by their governments may drop out, those companies that remain in global industries may well behave differently. As the latter are increasingly backed by governments taking an aggressive stance, the resources available for competition and the stakes involved are increased. Non-economic objectives made central by government involvement come increasingly into play. There is the possibility that international rivalry will escalate as a result of these factors and the barriers to exit will also increase, which further increases rivalry.

Another trend involves national recognition and the protection of distinctive assets. Governments seem to be increasingly cognizant of which of their resources are distinctive from the point of view of economic competition, and they are increasingly prone to capture the economic benefit for possession of these assets. Natural resources such as oil, copper, tin and rubber are obvious examples of assets that have been controlled either directly by government ownership or indirectly through joint ventures of governments and producers. The presence of abundant, low-wage, semi-skilled and unskilled labour in South Korea, Taiwan and Hong Kong is another asset explicitly recognised in some countries. The pro-active exploitation of such distinctive assets by governments is a reflection of changing philosophy towards industrial policy.

This posture has potentially fundamental implications for world competition in industries where such protected assets are important strategically. Foreign companies may be cut out of effective control of key resources. In oil, for example, such a re-orientation of government has caused a re-orientation of oil companies' strategies away from saturation retailing and other activities designed to reap profits at the production stage, and towards making profits at each vertical stage. In other industries, it may give certain firms of the home country fundamental advantages in global competition.

One must also consider the freer flow of technology. This appears to be giving a wide variety of companies, including the newly developed companies' competitors, the ability to invest in modern, world-scale facilities. Some companies, notably the Japanese, have become quite aggressive in selling their technology abroad.

There is also the gradual emergence of new large-scale markets. Whereas the United States has long been the strategic market for global competition because of its unique size, China, Russia and possibly India may ultimately emerge as huge markets in the future. This possibility has a number of implications. First, if China and Russia control access to their markets, their companies may become major global powers. Second, gaining access to one or both of these markets may well become a crucial strategic variable in the future, because of the scale it will provide to the successful company.

Newly developed countries are increasingly prepared, for some of the reasons suggested above, to make major capital investments in large-scale facilities, aggressively to seek to buy or licence the latest technology and to take enormous risk.

10 Five case studies

INTRODUCTION

It is often found with students sitting the case study part of this examination, that they are not equipped, by training or ability, to undertake the intellectually more demanding task of analysing a business situation and making sensible recommendations, even when guidance is given in the form of questions dealing with some of the issues to be covered. The Institute of Marketing examiners find, unfortunately, that a significant number of candidates fail to identify any additional topics to be discussed. A majority of students settle for attempting the minimum required, and thereby fail to see the problems of the company in the round.

The examiners make a further point concerning the assumptions which it is necessary for the candidates to make in answering any form of case study question. They say, as examiners, that they are happy to accept any assumption so long as it is reasonable in the context of the case. But many candidates make such wild and unrealistic assumptions, especially on financial matters, that they doubt their competence as potential businessmen.

These are drastic statements, and without any doubt, from the author's own experience, are very true indeed. It is nevertheless felt that one of the biggest problems of students carrying out case study work is a psychological barrier. It appears that the majority of students, once the term 'case study' is mentioned, immediately 'close down.' There is, in fact, no reason for this; and this introduction will give students some assistance in how they should approach mini-case work.

What is a marketing case study?
It is purely a collection of facts about an organisation; it often contains opinions of management and the judgements of management relating to that business situation in which a problem exists. Many cases are very true situations, and often are based on real company situations and real company problems. The basis of

case study work means that initially the student has to analyse the case fully; he has to obtain all possible pieces of information that are available within it. It is only then that the student is in a position to make decisions.

To expand on this idea, imagine that you are a manager in a company and have been in that company for five years. After such a period, you will be fully aware of how the company operates, their style of management, what type of decisions are made and how they are made. You will understand the present position of the company for which you work. You will know the individuals involved, their strengths and their weaknesses. Therefore, when a problem arises, you will be in a knowledgeable position and able to make an attempt to solve that problem.

With case study work, you come in 'blind' to a business situation where it is obvious that at least one problem exists. You know nothing about this situation; it is therefore impossible for you to make decisions about solving the problem until you have fully understood and, indeed, feel part of that organisation as though you had been with it for five years. The first part of case study work is, therefore, a detailed analysis of the information contained within it, so that you have a complete picture of exactly what is happening.

Finding the basic problems

It follows that your first step must be to read the case very carefully and remember as much of the detail that is given as possible. The first time you read it, it is probably best to make *no* notes whatsoever. Most students find that they need to read the case a number of times. It is appreciated that in an examination situation, there is a limit to the amount of time you could spend on reading the case, but in most Institute of Marketing mini-case situations, there is ample time to read it through three or four times. After the first reading, you will begin to get a clearer picture of what is happening, and usually the problems that exist begin to emerge. The more you read the case, the more clearly these problems define themselves.

One problem that the student faces here is to learn how to identify problems. These can be incorrect information; personal disagreements; wrong decisions; lack of marketing expertise; bad management practice; poor leadership, etc. It is important that you find the basic problems.

Methods of problem solving

Once you have identified the basic problems, then from further reading of the case, you can begin to build up information surrounding those problems. One quite successful method, (there is naturally more than one method of approaching case study work), is to use a SWOT approach. This stands for Strengths/Weaknesses/Opportunities/Threats. In using this approach, students can take points from the information given in the case and list them under those four headings — the strength the organisation has, its weaknesses, opportunities and threats. This method helps the student to establish clearly, by writing under significant headings, the information given in the case.

It is important that you sort the facts in the case, as often there are very many of them. Once you have sorted the facts, under the SWOT headings, then it is useful to try to put these facts into an order of significance. It is also important to separate out objective facts from subjective opinions and assumptions. Your own opinion is also important.

Usually one finds that there is a human problem in most cases, and this can be particularly relevant in the area of low morale and lack of motivation, and usually results in bad leadership. Look at the background of the people involved: their lifestyles, their personalities. How would you expect those people to react to given situations?

The way cases are written, you can be assured (although many students do not believe this) that sufficient information is given within the case material for you to arrive at good quality solutions.

You are entitled to make assumptions, providing they are reasonable, but you must state clearly what the assumption is and give the reasons on which it is based.

Once this stage has been completed, you must then ask yourself what you need to do to solve the problem or problems that exist. What you are concerned in obtaining is the 'best' possible solution. For any manager or student to obtain the best possible solution, that manager or student must be able to identify every single possible alternative. Common sense tells you that it is impossible to choose the best until you know *all* of these alternatives.

Having in your own mind justified the best solution to the problem, you should compare that solution against the information that you have already established in your SWOT analysis.

Ensure that you clearly state why you have chosen the course of action that you intend to take, in preference to the other courses of action available to you.

Having made that decision, you can then establish: what needs to be done to carry it out; when it needs to be carried out; what new resources are required; what organisational changes are necessary; and, of course, how much it will cost.

Finally, a word of advice. When doing your first case, you will probably find that it is perplexing. This is because you will probably not have built up an ability to establish a framework for the analysis required in problem-solving, nor have built up the necessary background of knowledge. This is why it is so important to read the case a number of times. It seems to the author that many students who are capable of analysing cases successfully, fail their examination because they attempt to solve the problem before they have enough information to do so. The only way to overcome this defect is to spend as much time as possible in analysing the details given in the case study.

CASE STUDIES

1 HAWKINS MARKETING LTD

John Hawkins founded Hawkins Marketing whilst a lecturer in marketing in the state sector of education in the United Kingdom in the mid-1970s. His background prior to five years in the state sector of education had been in various sales management and marketing positions in the marketing of high-volume consumer goods, primarily food and drink. He decided at the age of 42 to opt out of this career, went back to university and polytechnic, and then went into the state sector of education to lecture in marketing. After two years in the state sector, he realised the constraints that were being imposed upon him — being unable to innovate and bring in new ideas. It was at this time that he was given the opportunity, with the permission of his college, to carry out external consultancy work. Over the next two years, this consultancy work increased considerably, so that John Hawkins found himself in a position of earning more as an independent consultant than he was as a principal lecturer in marketing.

In 1976, he therefore decided to break away from the state sector, and concentrate entirely upon his consultancy activity. He was able very quickly to commence running short courses in marketing development and management development in various overseas countries and regularly visited South East Asia and West Africa on these ventures. These proved very profitable indeed. He also found no difficulty in gaining short-term contracts for lecturing in the private sector of education in the United Kingdom. In addition to this, he also regularly carried out small consultancy projects, giving advice primarily to small- and medium-sized companies within the United Kingdom.

It was because of his overseas experience that the idea of learning cassettes occurred to him. He had found in South East Asia and West Africa that in respect of many professional and institutional examinations, many overseas students could not afford to come to the United Kingdom to study for these examinations; and in their own country, there was usually such a shortage of places in polytechnics, universities and colleges that the majority of students were unable to obtain a place. This left many thousands of students who had the basic educational qualifications but had no opportunity whatsoever of carrying out serious study to obtain a professional qualification.

Over the next three and a half years, John Hawkins developed a Distance Learning Division within his consultancy in order to develop complete learning packages on audio cassette.

He analysed the syllabuses of the seven or eight major professional qualifications, and found that there was a common stream in many subject areas, such as management, marketing and computing.

He then decided that he would rationalise these various syllabuses into one central syllabus that satisfied the requirements of all these professional examinations. He decided to contract with writers and lecturers who were not only experts in their field, but who also had a number of years of industrial experience, to write up the whole text for each subject. Because he wished to keep the cassettes as true to life as possible, he decided that he would let the authors do the recording for the cassettes. He was able over the next nine months to bring together a package on marketing, management, and an introduction to computers.

These consisted of seven or eight one-hour audio cassettes supplied with a booklet of necessary diagrams, charts, etc., so that an intending student could study anywhere, at any time, only requiring a simple audio cassette player.

He decided to produce these himself, being unable to get government assistance under the small businesses guarantee scheme. He was very quickly able to borrow the necessary capital from his bank, and was extremely confident that his product would be successful.

He designed his own cassette labels and his own boxes; he purchased supplies of boxes, labels, cassettes and machines for a high-volume copy from masters. He contacted the recording company to produce masters from the cassettes of the authors.

With his knowledge and experience of these overseas countries, he was extremely confident of success, and contacted the British Overseas Trade Board in order that they could make enquiries on his behalf as to the possibility of obtaining agents and/or distributors in key overseas areas. He obtained considerable help and information from the British Overseas Trade Board and was basically swamped with initial enquiries from various potential overseas agents and distributors.

In view of this reaction, he went into small-time production to build up an initial supply for use, possibly as samples and for initial sales.

He followed up immediately the enquiries that he had received from the British Overseas Trade Board and many potential agents and distributors from South East Asia, East Africa, the Middle East and West Africa replied, showing considerable interest. He drafted a normal agency contract and duly sent off these contracts for discussion. Obviously, he would have had to deal by post with the overseas agencies and distributors because he did not have the finance to visit the overseas territories himself.

After a few weeks nothing had happened, except that the potential agents and distributors in various parts of the world had all written to him requesting as quickly as possible, samples of the product. With the very large agents and distributors he duly sent them an edited sample of one or two of the cassettes, but not the complete units. The response was negative, apart from a few letters from potential agents and distributors stating that they did not feel that this product range was suitable for them. In fact, John Hawkins made no sales whatsoever.

You are an experienced management consultant who has been asked to advise John Hawkins on the following factors:

(a) What went wrong with this operation?

(b) How do you suggest that if this operation is to be successful, he should carry on in the future?

2 THE HI-LIGHT MANUFACTURING CO LTD

James Collins had been a very successful salesman with the Hi-Light Manufacturing Co in the United Kingdom selling good quality, but competitively priced, disposable and non-disposable cigarette lighters. Because of his success as a salesman, he was very quickly promoted to area manager for the southern area in the United Kingdom and proved extremely good at this job.

Some three years ago, the company had decided to export, and felt that a very successful market for such products could be the Middle East. In consequence of this, they had been selling to a distributor based in Riyadh in Saudi Arabia, and over the past three years had built up a very successful sales record. Six months ago, the company heard of the possibility that the Saudi Arabian government would be imposing import restrictions which would give obvious advantages to the local manufacture of products.

As the total overseas business for the company represented only five % of total turnover, the overseas business was still regarded as of secondary importance. Consequently, the company had no real knowledge or expertise in the area of international marketing.

James Collins received a memorandum from Harry Morgan, his managing director, asking him to come and see him as soon as possible. At the meeting Harry Morgan asked James Collins if he would undertake responsibility for overseas sales, concentrating initially on the Saudi Arabian market, and explained the concern that was being shown in view of possible legislation by the Saudi Arabian government.

James Collins immediately proceeded to Saudi Arabia, and had decided that, in view of possible legislation, they should turn over the business in Saudi Arabia to a company capable of local production. James spent no less than six weeks in Saudi Arabia in an attempt to convince the new distributors on how best to succeed, following local production and local marketing.

He had managed to sign up the Al-Fazir Co, who were a very large family of leading Saudi Arabian industrialists and who had themselves built a fortune in many fields but were interested in expanding into yet new fields. For the Al-Frazir group, the cigarette lighters proved to be but a minor interest, but useful as an expanding field.

In the contract, the Al-Fazir Co had agreed to promote actively the cigarette lighters in Saudi Arabia. Certainly Harry Morgan understood this to mean that they would aggressively promote in Saudi Arabia to build the sales even higher than they had been in the past. It was very quickly found, however, that the sales began to drop steadily. It was obvious that the Al-Fazir Co was not pushing sales, and consequently, upon his return to the United Kingdom, James Collins *and* Harry Morgan decided to pressurise the Al-Fazir Co into an increased level of activity.

Nothing happened. James Collins then went again to Saudi Arabia, and decided to stay until he could get the Al-Fazir Co to move positively towards more successful activity. He visited the Al-Fazir Co people in the field, and he worked on a detailed programme to re-establish Hi-Light's market position. He found that Hi-Light's products were being sold from the Al-Fazir warehouses with virtually no sales effort and the promotion was limited to a few newspaper advertisements and a scattering of posters distributed by the Al-Fazir family's industrial representatives. They had not appointed any sales people, and the selling activity fell far short of Hi-Light's previous programme, and also short of its leading competitor.

For the past week, James had been trying to convince Musa, the Al-Fazir managing director that his programme should be adopted, but he had argued in vain. James had pointed out the low sales volume and the Al-Frazer limited programme, and said that this did not meet the terms of their agreement. James had supported his proposals in great detail, arguing particularly that Hi-Light's previous success and present results achieved by the competition proved that strong promotion was worth while.

Musa appreciated James's interest and efforts, but agreed to nothing. He explained that the drop in sales was inevitable with the change-over to a Saudi manufacturer. Although sales were lower, the company was making a reasonable profit. He said that to fulfil the contract terms, he had undertaken newspaper advertising even though he did not believe in it. He felt its blatant character reflected on the prestige of the Al-Fazir family.

Musa believed that a good product was its own best advertisement, and on that basis the Al-Fazir family had built a great business. He also observed that the closest competitor sold a higher quality cigarette lighter than Hi-Light's and it was quite probable that this, rather than the promotion, accounted for the success.

James found it hard to counter these arguments. He was sure that he was right, and equally sure that Musa was a very competent businessman who should be able to see the logic of James's proposals. He had a great respect and liking for Musa, and he believed that once Musa grasped the value of promotion, he would do great things for Hi-Light in Saudi Arabia. How could he convince him?

Musa Al-Fazir settled down one evening to relax before his meal and reflected on the happenings of the past week. He had spent a lot of time with James Collins. He liked him; he was full of energy and ideas, and he wished he could do something to help him, but James drove so hard, and for what? His whole arrangement with the Hi-Light Manufacturing Co had turned out rather differently from what the Al-Fazirs had expected. The product was good, and if only Hi-Light would leave it to them, his family could develop it into a good business as they had done with all their other operations.

But they were not left alone. Instead, there had been constant pushing, pressure and argument. These people from the United Kingdom never seemed to be satisfied with anything, and now they had sent out the young James Collins who scarcely knew Saudi Arabia, to tell Musa and the Al-Fazir family how to run their business. It was very unpleasant, and he hoped the young man would soon give up.

There are many problems emerging from this case, and you are asked to identify the problems and suggest a plan which would be capable of overcoming such problems and formulating a successful business venture for the Hi-Light Manufacturing Co in Saudi Arabia.

3 PORTCARE PRODUCTS LTD

Charles Dupont was the managing director of this small company with a mere £2 million turnover. The company consisted of Charles Dupont, six salesmen, a sales administration manager and a dozen or so workshop employees on a very unsophisticated production line. Because Charles Dupont was not an innovator, he had over the past decade built up this turnover mainly by copying or adjusting other people's ideas, and had found that he could make some money in this way even if the products that he produced had a fairly short life, which was indeed the case.

However, in 1980 when he was visiting an exhibition in the United Kingdom, the idea came to him that there must be many thousands of people in the United Kingdom who do not have washing machines, and that if he could produce a very cheap, portable mangle, this could have a useful market.

He fairly quickly designed what became known as the Portcare Limpet. It was a small, hand-turned mangle on an aluminium frame with rubber rollers and appended to each of the four feet were four 3-inch rubber suction pads. The idea was that if the housewife had a smooth formica surface, she could easily, by suction, attach the Limpet to that surface and use it quite efficiently as a miniature mangle.

By a considerable amout of hard work, Portcare Products produced a good product, and the salesmen were reasonably successful in selling into various organisations within the United Kingdom, particularly departmental stores, hardware stores and, after approximately one year, mail order houses. It became apparent that the Portcare Limpet was being used primarily for leisure activities by such people as campers, caravanners and boating enthusiasts, who found it a useful asset and had plenty of formica bases on which to use it.

Nevertheless, as had happened many times in the past, sales peaked at 100,000 units and began to fall quite quickly. Charles Dupont was, therefore, faced with yet another short-term product and realised that he had to come up with yet another idea if he was going to continue successfully in business.

During this time, he had had a fairly high rate of turnover with his salesmen; and Charles was attending a national conference at which he met one former member of his salesforce, Gordon Frazer. In the course of general conversation, Charles told Gordon of the short life and failure of the Portcare Limpet, and Gordon Frazer made the following statement to him: 'You should think about selling overseas, because there are no less than 600 million women in South America that don't use washing machines.'

This stuck in the mind of Charles Dupont, who by nature was fairly impulsive. Within 10 days, he was on a first-class flight to Rio de Janeiro. Within three weeks, he had quickly signed up an agent based in Rio de Janeiro and had given him the South American agency for the Portcare Limpet. Charles felt very pleased with this achievement and within three weeks was back in the United Kingdom, increasing production of the Portcare Limpet in order to establish a basic stock in Rio de Janeiro for sale by the agent.

During his visit to Rio, Charles had rented a small warehouse suitable for such stock, and the agent had agreed to watch over the stock and account for it as sales were made. Charles also agreed that he would carry out an advertising promotional campaign on behalf of the agent.

Once Charles was happy that production was under way in the United Kingdom, he returned to Rio to ensure that every part of initial stocking and organisation was properly established. He also established a system of communication with the agent; he made contacts with local advertising agencies and promotional companies and agreed an advertising and promotional campaign.

He then returned to the United Kingdom, anticipating very large unit sales. Within the first two months, no less than 10,000 units had been delivered to Rio and sales were running at 5,000 to 6,000 units per month.

Shortly afterwards, he received a long letter from his agent informing him that the agent did not consider the product worth while and was, therefore, not intent upon pursuing the matter further. Under the laws of that particular country, it was possible for an agent to do such a thing to a principal.

This naturally created tremendous problems for Charles Dupont. Having purchased supplies of raw materials, having increased the number of employees in his factory, having committed himself to an advertising and promotional programme in South America within a very short period of time, Charles Dupont was very seriously considering going into liquidation.

As an experienced marketer, you are to establish why you consider this project failed, showing in your answer what you would have done in attempting to do business of this nature, with such a product, overseas.

4 KARL KRONER GmbH

Karl Kroner GmbH, based near Frankfurt in West Germany, is, like many German companies, still privately owned, although it is a multi-national corporation operating in 17 countries with no less than 19 production units. In 1980 it showed a highly profitable turnover slightly in excess of £820 million sterling equivalent.

The Kroner Company is a fifth generation German family company, which in 1980 was directed by Josef Kroner, the only fully operational family member still on the Board, although it was anticipated that within a year Josef's son, Franz, who was already training in various departments of the company, would join it as an executive director.

After the Second World War, Karl Kroner GmbH only had a turnover of approximately £200,000, but, mainly due to brilliant entrepreneurship, Josef Kroner has built it into one of the most successfully family-based multi-nationals in West Germany. Its market includes brand leaders in brandy, liqueurs, fruit juices, wines and cosmetics, as well as the production of by-products from brandy and the production of vegetable and fruit powders which are sold to food processing units throughout the world.

Josef Kroner was a prisoner of war in England, having been captured at the beginning of the war at Dunkirk. He had a great love of England, and had always wanted to do business in the United Kingdom. Quite amazingly, however, he had never attempted to enter the United Kingdom except through their Swiss company who were the producers of vegetable and fruit powders. As a result of the Swiss director visiting London, they had built up a small business through an agent, selling tomato and fruit powders to the United Kingdom food sector.

Now that the United Kingdom were firmly established as members of the European Economic Community, Josef Kroner felt that something had to be done in respect of the United Kingdom market.

In the head office organisation they employed a German export manager who was responsible, not for the overseas production units, but for selling excesses of production of locally produced products.

Josef Kroner called in the export manager, Gerhard Muller, asking him to begin the planning for an entry by the Kroner Group into the United Kingdom market. He asked Gerhard to take his son under his wing so that he could gain experience of the United Kingdom.

Gerhard duly broke down the activities of the Kroner Group into product categories, and then, on frequent visits to the United Kingdom, made numerous attempts to establish either agencies or distributive arrangements for the various products and categories produced by the West German company. In almost every instance, Gerhard found that in the markets in which they would be interested, the competition by firmly established international giants was so intense that he decided that it would be an impossible task to enter United Kingdom markets.

After a period of six months trying extremely hard to get an opportunity gap, he reported to Josef Kroner the results of his investigations. Gerhard felt that he could not recommend an attempted entry by the Kroner group into United Kingdom markets in view of the information that he had elicited during his enquiries.

This did not satisfy Josef Kroner, who, being a very strong personality and a very successful businessman, was convinced that there must be a method of entering the United Kingdom market.

Bearing in mind the power and strength of the West German Kroner group, if you were appointed the international marketing director of the Karl Kroner group, what plan would you establish to determine entry into the United Kingdom by part, or all, of the Karl Kroner group.

5 FLITCH & KEY LTD

Flitch & Key are a world renowned producer of the famous Flitch sweaters, and are based in the very fashionable Burlington Arcade in London. They export their sweaters to many overseas countries, one of which is France.

The product range is fairly small except for a very large colour range, and the products are naturally exclusive and of very high quality.

Jacques Boisson, the sales manager for the Flitch & Key importing company of Mode pour l'Homme, was in the process of analysing his company's marketing programme for the Flitch sweaters, for which Mode pour l'Homme had the exclusive distribution rights for France. The Flitch sweater was a useful selling line, being up-market as is most imported clothing in France. They retailed on average at 840 French francs, which gave Mode pour l'Homme a 120% mark-up. Mode pour l'Homme purchased direct from Flitch & Key on an FOB London basis. Flitch & Key shipped directly to Mode pour l'Homme by overland trunker, direct from their production unit in Stafford through to the offices and warehouse of Mode pour l'Homme in Paris.

Flitch & Key quoted all their prices in pounds sterling FOB London, and overseas distributors, such as Mode pour l'Homme in France, remitted the payments by buying pounds sterling from a French bank in Paris and sending them direct to Flitch & Key in London.

The arrangement was that Mode pour l'Homme would place orders six months in advance of the main selling season to allow time for Flitch & Key to produce and ship. It was not possible for any re-orders to take place during the main sale season. Neither Mode pour l'Homme or Flitch & Key carried any basic stock in inventory.

Mode pour l'Homme also sold another line of sweaters made locally, and handled many lines of popularly priced sports shirts. Jacques Boisson, in reviewing the performance of each of the product lines, suggested that they must consider dropping the Flitch & Key products because the volume had been declining. Paul Mode, the managing director of Mode pour l'Homme, suggested that the Flitch & Key sweaters were excellent products and still popular, and that they should review the marketing programme for the Flitch & Key range of products to see if they could put new life into it by backing it with a proper promotional campaign. In the past, Mode pour l'Homme had done very little advertising or sales promotional work for the Flitch & Key brand, but had allowed it to more or less sell itself on its reputation alone.

(a) *What basic principle of international marketing is Flitch & Key violating with its present policies?*

(b) *You are asked to outline a marketing programme which will revive the sales of Flitch & Key sweaters in France.*

11 Solutions to case studies

1 HAWKINS MARKETING LTD

Before commencing a suggested answer, it is always advisable to carry out a SWOT analysis, looking at the strengths, weaknesses, opportunities, and threats that exist within the framework of this case.

Strengths
What strengths does Hawkins Marketing Ltd have and, in particular, John Hawkins himself? He is an experienced marketer; a qualified marketer; he knows further education, and has a good understanding of professional syllabuses.

Weaknesses
He has little or no overseas experience, except from running short courses. He has no production experience. He did try to do everything himself. There is no mention of price and pricing policy within the case. There is no mention of promotional activity within the case. It could be that these end-products are expensive to distribute, and there is no mention of methods of distribution. One must ask how far he investigated possible agents. They are a completely unknown organisation. It would be relatively easy for competition to enter this market, particularly with large markets. One must ask, were the samples that he sent good and reliable recordings? Finally, another possible weakness is whether or not he researched markets properly.

Opportunities
It is feasible to accept that there was an opportunity for this particular type of product, and it was a certainly an innovative idea.

Threats
There are one or two major threats that would appear fairly obvious. Audio cassettes are extremely easy to 'pirate'. Many developing countries also have very strict import duties and tariffs which might either prohibit entry or make the price so high that it makes the product itself too expensive for the segments of the market to afford.

Generalising, one must also ask whether he was wise to let the authors record, as they might be good authors but not necessarily have good speaking voices. One could also mention that when John Hawkins decided to produce the cassettes himself, was he capable of a professional recording standard? Also, were any of the authors well known, as often products of this type require a well-known name to help the image, and integrity, of the product. It was also noted that every agent required samples, and that John Hawkins did not make available to them full sets of samples. Maybe this was due to his possible awareness of easy piracy.

(a) *What went wrong with this operation?*
The key factor may well be the possibility of piracy. There is no doubt that audio cassettes are easy to pirate, and in many developing countries, particularly in South East Asia, this is a major problem for any producer. Coupled with this, the quality of the recordings, linked to the fact that only short-length samples were provided and that the authors voices were not professional, may have resulted in possible agents and distributors questioning the authenticity, quality and reliability of the cassettes. Putting yourself in the position of a possible overseas agent or distributor, would you consider taking on such a range of products, knowing the dangers that exist in relation to copying in your own country?

Generally, it must be said that it appears that insufficient market research was carried out, not only into the market segments themselves within the countries, but also into the alternative channels of distribution that might be available to John Hawkins. The products were unknown; the organisation was unknown; the authors were probably not well known; there is no mention of a full marketing plan to include advertising and promotion; and there is no mention of price.

It is therefore suggested that the reason for the operation not succeeding was probably due to all of the aforementioned factors.

(b) *Future course of action*
John Hawkins should be advised to halt the operation at the present time. He should contact the British Overseas Trade Board, as it is an established part of their service to carry out initial market research for a maximum of six countries. This research consists of both desk research from their existing library of data, as well as primary research carried out by the commercial attachés in the various embassies and high commissions throughout the world. Dependent upon the outcome of this initial research, John Hawkins should then ask the British Overseas Trade Board to do an in-depth research study of one or two of the most promising countries that emerge from the intitial research. The Board will carry out investigative research for a fee of only £100 per country.

The British Overseas Trade Board will also research possible agents or distributors, and will do much of the checking of the reliability, authenticity and suitability of overseas agents and distributors.

However, it is considered that John Hawkins must look very carefully indeed at the various channels of distribution that might or might not be available to him. One of the biggest problems he faces with agents or distributors is that he will have to build up stocks for both agents and distributors to sell, and this can be an expensive process. Unless he has knowledgeable agents, it would be extremely difficult for him to forecast sales targets per country, and thus this will complicate the existing production facilities that we are told are available. If eventually an agent or distributor type of operation proves to be the most viable, the advice must be for John Hawkins to obtain professional recordings of these subjects, and that the copies of the cassettes are professionally produced.

Another problem he faces with many developing countries is their ability to pay if they are working on an agency distribution agreement. This factor also applies on exporting a finished product in view of the possible high tariff barriers that might exist on importation of this type of product to many overseas markets.

Bearing in mind all of the weaknesses and threats that exist to this operation, the primary recommendation to John Hawkins would be to investigate thoroughly the possiblity of licensing. By giving a right to make, and a right to sell in overseas countries, John Hawkins would eliminate all of the production problems, all of the stock-holding problems, and all of the forecast problems for overseas markets. It has already been mentioned that these are major problems in such an innovative area where nobody has direct experience of marketing such products. If John Hawkins had professionally recorded, professionally produced master tapes, he could make that into a licensing package for which a lump sum would be payable by the overseas licensee. Although this would naturally reduce the continuity of income to John Hawkins, unless royalty fees were included, it would get the products established in many markets and would give him an immediate capital return for the investment that he had made. Should this prove successful with the three subjects that he has at present produced, he could then enlarge the list of subjects available considerably, thus increasing his income through granting licenses, and it would also give him the opportunity of diversifying into other similar audio cassette situations. This would also minimise any further capital expenditure on this project which must have already cost John Hawkins a considerable amount of time and money.

2 THE HI-LIGHT MANUFACTURING CO LTD

The problems in this case should be fairly obvious to students. Often one finds in exporting and international marketing that a company has excess production, and therefore decides to sell it overseas. The overseas sales prove quite successful, but very little expertise is put behind those sales, as they usually represent, as in this case, a very small percentage of total turnover.

The first problem appears to be that, although they received information that the Saudi Arabian government was going to impose an import restriction, there is no confirmation that this restriction was imposed, and as is well known, many governments make these statements and often never introduce such legislation. In any case, here we are talking not of an expensive, high technology production unit, but of a very simple production unit, which is relatively inexpensive and could be installed in a very short space of time.

Over the past three years Hi-Light had built up a very successful sales record. Why suddenly cut out a successful agent without, apparently, any warning or investigation whatsoever? Could they not have joined together with their existing agent on a joint venture, or even have decided to invest money in a production unit themselves in Saudi Arabia?

One must ask at this stage whether the company are, in fact, serious about the Saudi Arabian market. James Collins did not prepare at all for his visit to Saudi Arabia; he went out there straight away. Additionally, he completely lacked training and experience; he did not speak the language, did not understand the culture or the methods of doing business in Saudi Arabia.

It appears, also, that they did not thoroughly investigate the Al-Fazir Co: they probably chose them because they were big and important. It would, therefore appear that an error was made in choosing Al-Fazir.

From these factors emerge the present situation, which in itself is a major problem. Hi-Light have committed themselves to a major Saudi Arabian company; it appears that it is not going to work, and if they try to get rid of Al-Fazir, the problems that this could cause in trying to obtain another agent or distributor could be tremendous. If Al-Fazir are as powerful as is suggested, they could no doubt influence any negotiations that might take place between the Hi-Light Manufacturing Co and another prospective agent or distributor.

Therefore, the following course of action should be taken by the Hi-Light Manufacturing Co Ltd. Firstly, they should withdraw James Collins from Saudi Arabia and allow the Al-Fazir Co to concentrate, using their own methods, on the development of the market in Saudi Arabia.

Whilst this is taking place, the company should thoroughly analyse its role in exporting and international marketing, and be able to establish clear objectives for such operations. In order to do this they will need the services of an expert marketer in international markets, with particular knowledge and experience in dealing with Arab countries. With this executive, the company could then thoroughly research not only various markets, but also the significance of choosing the correct channel of distribution in those particular markets. It may well emerge, as a result of this investigation, that the method being employed by the Al-Fazir family is, in fact, the best method to increase and develop the market for Hi-Light in Saudi Arabia.

If, on the other hand, the investigation shows that changes need to be made, then it is suggested that the Hi-Light Manufacturing Co openly discuss their problems with the Al-Fazir organisation so that possible changes could be made in their arrangements, without the Al-Fazir Co using its strength to stop any such changes.

It is vitally important that whatever the Hi-Light Manufacturing Co do, they do it with the knowledge and support of the Al-Fazir organisation.

3 PORTCARE PRODUCTS LTD

Charles Dupont has broken almost every rule in the international marketer's book. He carried out absolutely no desk research. He took no advice from anyone, not even the British Overseas Trade Board. He allowed his impulsive nature to control all decisions that he took. He did not research channels. He did not follow any serious selection procedure in choosing an agent.

If he had sought advice in the initial stages from the British Overseas Trade Board, they would have provided him with ample secondary data on each South American country, which would probably have enabled him to give priority to one particular country. By using the same organisation, he could have obtained a short list of reliable agents; he could have had them vetted, and all this would have taken but a few weeks, and would have cost him nothing apart from the time involved.

If the initial data showed one country more prominent or inviting than another, he could, again, have asked the British Overseas Trade Board to carry out in-depth market research on that particular country. This would only have cost him £100. He completely ignored the legal implications of using agents in certain overseas countries, and obviously took for granted that the laws appertaining to agents and distributors were the same in South America as in the United Kingdom. This, of course, is not the case.

Not only has Dupont put himself in a situation where he will problably have to go into liquidation, but he has also put the agent in South America into a position where he can easily produce the Limpets locally and establish a successful marketing operation of his own in his own country.

What, therefore, can be done about it?

If Dupont is able to avoid liquidation for the next few months, the following course of action would be recommended.

He should immediately obtain the services of an experienced international marketing consultant, or indeed, employ such a person. He should also freeze any stocks that are either in transit or already in store in South America. He should also legally stop any activities, as far as this is possible, being carried out by the agent in South America.

The consultant and Charles Dupont should then carry out desk research to try to select the most suitable South American country in which to commence operations of this type. Here the use of a standard international marketing checklist would be invaluable.

All the following information, under various categories, is obtainable from the British Overseas Trade Board: in respect of the country itself, factors like the economy; the balance of payments situation; foreign exchange restrictions; the type of government and its stability; attitude to the United Kingdom; government controls; taxation systems; languages; incomes; occupational patterns; domestic structures; living patterns; culinary habits; as well as such things as the general level of prices. The Board could also give information on the markets themselves — their accessibility and size.

The company also needs information on the conditions of entry into particular South American markets. Are there import tariffs? What is their tax system? Are there import quotas and licences? Are there any statutory requirements? What are the documentation requirements? What are the patent laws and trade-mark arrangements? Are there any other non-tariff barriers to entry?

Furthermore, Charles and the consultant need to know the characteristics of each market. What is the state of competition in respect of the same type of product or substitute products?

They need information on the possible methods of distribution. What internal channels are available? Should they go direct to consumers?

Finally, they need from information to be able to assess the possible profitability of such a venture in terms of potential sales volume related to profit potential. They need to investigate the short-, medium- and long-term prospects for profit. They need to establish market price levels, related to both their current and their anticipated costs.

All this information can be supplied by government agencies free of charge, and this will enable them to establish whether such an operation is worth while in the first place, and hopefully to establish an order of preference of particular South American countries.

Advice will then be required in respect of the best possible channel to use in the chosen country. Again, the British Overseas Trade Board will willingly carry out enquiries on behalf of British companies, and will investigate, check and recommend a short-list of reliable agents and/or distributors.

Ideally, at this stage, either the consultant or Charles Dupont should visit the short-listed agents in that country to see for himself how efficient and how effective those agents are in respect of the agency products that they already have and are selling in their own country. They should have prepared, bearing in mind the legal constraints of that particular country, a suggested agency agreement, so that when the negotiations take place, they are perfectly clear on what aspects of the agency agreement must be contained in that legal document. It must be clearly established who is responsible for advertising and promotion; who is responsible for the stocks; how payments will be made; what statistics the agent will regularly supply to Dupont. All of these factors must be discussed and agreed.

If this procedure is followed, and provided that the results of the market research are positive, the chances of this operation succeeding are now considerably better than they were in the first instance.

(Students may be interested to know the outcome of this activity. Dupont did, in fact, employ a marketing consultant; they did carry out the research; they did find a very good agent in Brazil; and within 12 months they were selling to Brazil alone in excess of 250,000 units per year.)

4 KARL KRONER GmbH

If I were appointed the new international marketing director of the Karl Kroner group, the first factor that I would establish very clearly is what authority and responsibility I have in respect of all the companies within the group. By visiting at least the major subsidiaries, I would hope to establish good working relationships with the executives of those subsidiary companies.

Concurrent with the visits, I would instigate a full and in-depth analysis of the Kroner group, its strengths, weaknesses, and in particular, its product ranges. I would need to be able to establish exactly what products had been produced, were being produced and what new products were in the pipeline for launching in the foreseeable future. I would need to analyse the state of technology being used, and whether this might become obsolete. I would need to analyse the stages which the various products within the group had reached in their product life cycles, and would need to make a comparative analysis of the type of marketing mix that was being applied.

Only when this initial research had been completed could I attempt a comparative analysis for all Kroner group products in respect of possible entry into the United Kingdom market.

As the company is so large and diversified, it would be absolutely vital to establish clear criteria in order to establish a short-list of possibly suitable products. Products that pass this initial screening could then be put against yet further criteria in order to create an effective short-list of feasible products.

Once this short-list was established, I would then choose the best product emerging from that short-list and carry out an in-depth market research study of the UK market for that particular product. The main criteria here would be: growth prospects; profitability; level of investment; and the state of competition. It may well be that this product does not meet those criteria, and consequently a similar activity would then be carried out in respect of the other short-listed products.

It is, of course, possible at any stage that no products are found to be suitable.

Hopefully this would not be the case, and I would find the opportunity to establish a product opportunity gap. I would then need to analyse fully the significance of that gap, and relate this to other products being offered in similar categories.

The importance of in-depth research into the exact state of the market and competition, related to product opportunity gaps, cannot be overstressed.

I would have to consider, in relation to any gap that emerged, the feasibility of improving upon an existing product that we had, or adapting that particular product, to make it more suitable for the United Kingdom market if it were not, in fact, sufficiently suitable.

Having established an opportunity gap for one, or possibly more than one, product I would then need to research the possible entry strategies.

Just because in the past the Kroner group had found that the problem of competition was a major factor, this may not pose a problem in the future.

The situation in respect of competition must be related to the strength and power of the West German Kroner group. It may well be opportune for the Kroner group to establish a joint venture with a large United Kingdom operation as Kroner may well be in a very good position to offer a reciprocal agreement to the United Kingdom company.

However, this may not be possible. If that should prove to be the case, I would then carry out the following activity.

I would further analyse the product opportunity gap, clearly establishing that the unique characteristics of the product that we have to offer were sufficiently strong either to delay competitive action, or to create a new sub-segment which major UK competition was not particularly interested in or were not adequately capable of dealing with.

I would also research the alternative methods of entry, ranging from the Kroner group making a large financial commitment on a major UK national launch, to a small, regional entry.

One factor must be mentioned. If I, as the new international marketing director, were not an Englishman, it would be essential, in view of the very wide spread of markets and products of the Kroner group, that an experienced English marketing executive be appointed to work in conjunction with me, as there is no substitute for in-depth knowledge and experience of such sophisticated markets as those which exist in Western Europe.

(Students may like to know that the West German group concerned did, in fact, find such a product, and this product will probably be launched in the United Kingdom in 1987. Obviously, security forbids any further information being given in respect of either the company or the product.)

5 FLITCH & KEY LTD

(a) Flitch & Key are not marketing, they are treating sweaters purely as a commodity, and just selling them. There is absolutely no continuity of supply, as is shown by the fact that orders have to be placed six months in advance, and no extra stock can be delivered. There is absolutely no proper marketing planning, consequently nobody needs to establish clearly sales forecasts, and there is no use whatsoever of the various elements of the marketing mix.

Therefore, Flitch & Key do not at the moment have a marketing operation — it is purely production-oriented, and all the time that sales are buoyant no doubt this policy will continue. Nevertheless, it appears from the case that sales are now beginning to drop, and consequently Flitch & Key must take positive action if they are going to overcome this problem.

This will require Flitch & Key having a clear understanding of what international marketing involves, and it may well be the case that they are fully aware of this type of operation in their own country, but lack the incentive, knowledge or expertise to carry this out abroad. One must ask whether, indeed, they are really interested in international business.

Times change, markets change, and customers change. Flitch & Key cannot just rely on their tradition of excellence when such markets are changing, and no doubt competition is increasing.

If they are to successful in the marketing of sweaters in France, the following action should be taken.

(b) Firstly, Flitch & Key must acquire a full and comprehensive understanding of what the marketing philosophy is, and how this differs from the sales philosophy which they are at present adopting. Unless this is done, the revival of the French market will be purely a temporary revival.

Secondly, Flitch & Key must understand the significance and role of planning, and be prepared to plan fully their overseas operations.

Thirdly, they must, by research, establish the significance of export markets to their whole operation.

Fourthly, should that research prove positive, they need to establish a priority in respect of the overseas markets in which they intend to operate. If after thorough research, France does not prove a viable proposition, then they could easily withdraw.

The following courses of action concentrate purely upon the French market, and it is emphasised that what follows should be done by Flitch & Key in conjunction with their French agents, Mode pour l'Homme.

Assuming the French market is significant, they need to carry out research to establish clearly: the state of the industry, and its trends; the state of the company within the industry and trends; and the company market situation in respect of market share.

They then need to carry out research into the needs of the market. What products are being demanded by the French, and what products are likely to be demanded by them in the future? The range of sizes that should be offered; the colours that are the most popular; the pricing policy that is the most acceptable; what promotional activity is required; and how effective are the existing channels of distribution. In other words, how can they best produce the right product, in the right place, at the right time, at the right price?

They must ask themselves, following the results of the foregoing research, whether they are, indeed, capable and willing to carry out any activity that is needed to make the market more successful.

They should then identify any possible constraints that might exist within that market. Only after this activity has been carried out can Flitch & Key, in conjunction with their agents, establish a forecast, and begin to build in the various marketing mix allocations that will enable them to reach this forecast.

Decisions will then be required in respect of the product range, pricing policy and strategy, promotional activities, and the type of physical distribution and type of outlet where these products will in future be sold.

All this takes time, and the plan must essentially consist of a time scale for introduction, which must be linked with the production facilities available to Flitch & Key and the agents' ability to carry out the marketing plan.

Finally, it is vital that regular control techniques are established to monitor on a regular basis the performance of both Flitch & Key and their agents, Mode pour l'Homme.

Index

Page numbers in **bold** type refer to the introductory section of each chapter, those in roman are to questions, and those in *italics* are to answers.

Geo[illegible]

Dropped

in.

Cover designed by London Artist
Kenson Low.

E-mail:- kenson_low@hotmail.com

This Book is dedicated to my good mates,

Mick Findlay
Joe Bowers
&
Algy Caldwell.

And also to all British servicemen past and present.

Geordie Dropped in

(This book contains strong language.)

Wyn jackson

Jackwyn.

e-mail:- jackwyn@btopenworld.com

Published by jackwyn.

This edition printed 2004

By Athenaeum Press Ltd.

Copyright @ August 2004 Wyn Jackson

The right of Wyn Jackson to be identified as the Author of the Work has been asserted by her in accordance with the Copyright Designs and Patents Act 1988.

All rights reserved. No part of this publication may be Reproduced, stored in a retrieval system, or transmitted, in any form or by any means without prior written permission of the publisher, nor be otherwise circulated in any form of binding or cover other than that in which it is published and without a similar condition being imposed on the subsequent purchaser.

Whilst this is a true story most of the names in this publication are fictitious and any resemblance to real persons living or dead is purely coincidental.

Chapter 1

It was two days after my birthday on the l2th August 1952 when having reached the age of eighteen, the dreaded envelope dropped through our letterbox from Her Majesty's Service instructing me to enrol for the obligatory two years National Service in the army to serve my Queen and Country. Upon arriving at the recruitment office, I was full of trepidation as I sat down to fill in the mandatory forms. Subsequently, after passing the medical I was persuaded to sign on for an extra year, having being swayed by the fact that the income paid in the regular army was about three times more than it was for National Servicemen, and also the reality that I would be able to learn a trade was another major motive in my decision.

It was after all the legalities had been concluded that I was consequently drafted into the Royal Electrical Mechanical Engineers, the R.E.M.E, and a few days later, having been supplied with travelling instructions and a rail pass, I boarded a train at Newcastle Central Station to travel by train to my destination, Dorset. I was quite excited not knowing what was in store for me, and sensed this was the beginning of a new chapter in my life. A few hours later, having arrived safely, I together with numerous other apprehensive recruits was assembled, by a brutish Staff Sergeant, to be collectively bussed to Blandford Camp, to commence my six weeks basic training.

On that first day, feeling shell-shocked I found myself being marched, with my compatriots, to the medical room to have three jabs administered, two in one arm and one in the other, maybe it was just me, but the needle felt thick and blunt and I wondered if perhaps they used the same needle for all forty of us. After the platoon Sergeant lined us up, we were ordered to drop our underpants down to our ankles, thus being exposed and feeling acutely embarrassed, most of us modestly tried to hide our tackle behind cupped hands whilst a doctor walked slowly down the line gazing intently at each one of us individually before grabbing our balls and directing us to cough. This, we were led to believe was to determine if we were suffering from a hernia.

It was shortly afterwards that one recruit presumably had a severe reaction to the injections as he became delirious and started fitting and was subsequently whisked off to hospital, I cannot say what happened to him as we never saw him again.

Reality struck when next day, I, together with the thirty-nine other recruits which made up a platoon, was brusquely awakened at six a.m. by one hell of a racket when a Corporal, using a stick, banged on the door with all his might. Still in a state of uncertainty, our platoon was instantly marched to the stores and issued with uniforms and kit. In hindsight, I believe that the soldiers issuing the uniforms must have been mocking us, since most of us were equipped with extremely ill fitting gear. Once dressed, I observed that my compatriots were all laughing at each other, as most of the berets were miles too big, and of course being new, were very stiff and therefore sticking out at a ridiculous angle. In addition, trousers were either half-mast or else hanging almost to the ground; however, one or two of us found we had been lucky enough to obtain a well-fitting uniform. Once attired, and looking almost like circus clowns, we were marched outside to wait for the army tailor who, after a moment or two approached, white chalk in hand and expertly marked the uniforms where adjustments or nips and tucks would be required to make them into decently fitting garments, they were consequently whisked away for modifications.

Next was the dreaded trip to the barber, who seemed to take great gratification in shaving each and everyone's' thick locks off, and was especially enthusiastic when eradicating the Teddy boy's 'Ducks Arses'. Once perched in the chair, it seemed to take only about two minutes to carry out the dirty deed, which left us all identically bald; I glanced down with regret at the rings of my dark hair, jumbled amongst the blonde and red cuttings, now lying wilting on the floor. I glanced in the mirror, and said to myself.

"For fuck's sake, is that me or my grandad?"

Now, the already oversized berets, without our hair to pad them out, were almost touching our noses, however a Corporal who must have remembered his own induction into the army took pity on us and gave advice on how to make the berets more suitable. He recommended that we steep them alternatively in boiling then cold water to shrink, then to press the wet berets onto our heads and push into shape, thankfully this worked.

After a few days, I found army life exceptionally stressful, seeing as I had to endure intense verbal abuse and extreme humiliation, and although incredibly fit I was worked to physical exhaustion.
It was whilst practising drill that I had difficulty with the 'about turn' manoeuvre and no matter how hard I tried, I just could not seem to get the exercise correct. Therefore, after my third clanger the Sgt. Major ordered me to report to the guardroom and inform the Provo Sgt. of my 'crime'. I was soon to feel the full brunt of the notorious Provo Sgt's wrath, the bastard's sadistic method of chastisement was for me to scrub the guardroom veranda, using a toothbrush, a bar of hard carbolic soap and a bucket of cold water. The

backbreaking punishment took me seven hours to complete this meant being constantly stooped down on hands and knees from six p.m. until one a.m. the next morning.

Immediately after I had thankfully completed this humiliating onerous task, the Sgt. Major strode up to me, slid his arm around my shoulders and said,

"Don't worry Geordie; we'll make a soldier of you yet".

My stomach turned cartwheels, and with a raging passion, I cursed him under my breath and called him all the fuckin bastards under the sun and every other filthy oath that I could bring to mind; I was at my lowest ebb and sensed that I was being systematically demoralised.

Having been born in the poverty-stricken area of the infamous Scotswood Road, Newcastle upon Tyne, and having suffered relentlessly at the hands of bullies at school, I had, when eleven years of age, enlisted into the noted Grainger Park Boys Club to learn the art of pugilism. I became very successful, and achieved the honour of becoming Northumberland Champion and Northern Area Champion at the tender age of twelve and subsequently retained the title each year thereafter until the age of sixteen, when after being chosen to represent England I found it almost impossible to obtain opponents so decided to turn professional.

Being a successful boxer meant that in Civvy Street I was respected, and treated almost with celebrity status. I found that complete strangers would approach me to ask questions, such as,

"You're the professional boxer aren't you?"

"Are you Ronnie Jackson?"

"I saw your last fight."

"Good luck for tonight Ron."

Now, I found myself brought down to earth with a wallop and treated like scum, I had to suffer the indignity of being yelled and screamed at, and to meekly accept being ordered around. I was perpetually characterized as 'a stupid little man,' and labelled useless. I rapidly concluded that I detested every single minute of army life and found it very hard to stomach and ruefully regretted that I had signed on for an extra year.

Feeling utterly disconsolate and miserable, I kept myself to myself, I avoided all conversation, and did not speak to any of the other recruits in my billet, although I could not help noticing that most of them felt the same way as myself and several were very emotional and cried themselves to sleep at night. There were forty of us altogether, the majority of whom were reluctantly completing their mandatory two years National Service. In retrospect, I can only assume they must have thought me a particularly weird, strange person, seeing that it was three weeks before I uttered a word to any of them.

There were five recruits in our billet, who stuck together like glue, they considered themselves 'hard cases,' and were always arrogantly strutting about and throwing their weight around.

Every morning, a Corporal brought the mail into the billet and chucked it down onto the first bed inside the doorway; instantaneously the bullies commandeered it and refused to let any of the other recruits near until they themselves had sorted through the envelopes to retrieve their own. After confiscating their personal mail, they gathered the remainder of the letters up and flung them with contempt, onto the floor. Needless to say, most of the envelopes ended up under the bunks and the rest of the lads had to scrabble around on hands and knees to retrieve them.

This performance made my blood boil, because having

suffered first hand intimidation myself as a schoolboy; I cannot tolerate bullies, therefore my stomach tied up in knots with anger, but I was determined to keep my cool and turned the other cheek.

Those first six weeks of training were very gruelling, I had to learn how to wear my uniform correctly, how wear my beret, how to polish my boots, how to march, how to stand to attention, how to salute the Officers, who to call Sir and how to practise square bashing to the satisfaction of the Sergeant Major. The instructors also taught me how to strip and assemble my rifle, which was a bolt action 303 Le Enfield, until I could do it blindfolded. I went on to practice the same procedure with a Bren gun, which is a magazine fed light machine gun; and was methodically trained how to use these weapons until eventually, I was a competent marksman.

Each day as part of our training, we recruits, had to Blanco our webbing packs which was part of our equipment, this chore was carried out in a designated room at the end of our billet which incorporated wooden benches, into which twenty sinks and taps were fitted, however because there were forty soldiers in the billet, there was always a mad dash to be

Me, 4th left, 2nd bottom row.

amongst the first group, as everyone was aware that the last soldier to finish would get the obnoxious job of cleaning all the toilets.

One morning, as usual, I grabbed my kit, hurried to the Blanco room and placed it on the bench next to a sink, only to discover that I had unfortunately left my block of Blanco in my bedside locker. Knowing it would only take a few seconds to single it out, I hurried back through the billet and quickly grabbed it, however upon returning to the Blanco room I discovered that one of the bullyboys was standing at my sink, and my equipment was nowhere in sight.

"What's happened to my kit?" I asked him

He smirked and said, "Look oot the fuckin winda".

I glanced out and was disturbed to see my kit lying in a pool of filthy water, and because the rain was streaming down in torrents it was becoming more saturated by the second.

I was incensed, a red mist seemed to appear before my eyes and I have got to admit, I completely lost it, I lurched forward, grabbed the sneering bully by the throat and dragged him outside, where, ashen with fury, I shouted,

“Pick up my kit you fuckin bastard.”

I was almost throttling him with rage; his eyes were virtually bulging out of his head as he bent down to retrieve my soaking wet kit. I dragged him back into the billet, the dripping water from my kit leaving a wet trail on the floor behind us. I yanked him over to the sink, grabbed HIS kit and furiously tossed it out of the window, and then pinned him up against the wall and said.
“Don’t you **ever**, **ever** cross me again you fuckin bastard”.

I glanced across at his mates half expecting them to come to his aid but they were rooted to the spot, mouths hanging open with disbelief, watching their mate, the tough bullyboy, reduced to a snivelling wreck.
I realised this was the first time that the other thirty-nine recruits in my billet had heard me utter a word, except for me replying to the N.C.O’s so I can only assume that their evaluation of me must have been.
“He’s a fuckin madman”.

When the mail arrived the next morning, as usual, one

of the bullies picked the envelopes up, glimpsed through them, however this time, he strode over to me, handed over two letters and said,
"These are for you Geordie".
He placed the rest of the mail onto a bed for the other recruits to sort through and from that day on, they ceased to commandeer the mail, and to the delight of the rest of the billet, they stopped their bullying.
At least one good thing came out of my outburst.

Immediately after breakfast, the day began with a physical training session, which was held in a large gym that sported excellent contemporary facilities, at last I began to feel more settled, since prior to enlisting, I had trained religiously in Grainger Park gym every single day for seven years. We had four incredibly fit Physical Training instructors who gave lessons; and guided the platoon through exhaustive rigorous training sessions. We were soon made aware that if any recruit made a mistake, he had the choice between two punishments, one, to either carry out fatigues, or two, to spar three rounds with one of the instructors, who, we were informed, was currently amateur Commonwealth

Welterweight Champion.

Since none of the other thirty-nine recruits had ever had boxing gloves on, let alone been in the ring, when they made an error they understandably chose to do fatigues. One day however, it was my turn to regrettably make an error, so was accordingly given the same choice and because I hated fatigues with a vengeance, I said,

"I will box the three rounds."

Surprised, as I was the first recruit to take him up on his offer, the P.T.I. laughingly said,

"You must have done some boxing yourself."

I admitted that I had,

"How much have you done?" he enquired.

I informed him that I'd had at least one hundred amateur fights winning ninety-five per cent of them, and that I had represented Great Britain and had also had five professional fights, winning four of them. His eyes widened with surprise and he seemed generally impressed as he smiled and graciously declined to climb into the ring with me to execute the three rounds.

I found that having boxing in common, led to us becoming

very good mates, and from that day on, all the recruits in my billet wanted to be my best mate and I actually found to my surprise that I was beginning to enjoy army life and began to look forward to the next three years.

Chapter 2

In charge of each platoon was, a Sergeant, two Corporals, and two Lance Corporals, and every morning we rookie soldiers came out of our billets to form into platoons, whereupon the Duty Sergeant would commence the Roll Call.
He ordered us to-
"STAND TO ATTENTION"

He instructed, or should I say screamed at us,

"LEFT TURN"

We were immediately marched to the perimeter of the drill square and ordered to stand smartly to attention before the Regimental Sergeant Major.

It seemed as if this drill square was the R.S.M.'s hallowed ground; he made an impressive picture as he stood upright, his back erect and straight, emitting an aura of self-importance when positioned in the centre of his square ready to inspect the platoons.

One morning the immaculate R.S.M. marched as usual to his spot in the centre of the square and was, to his utter disgust, confronted with a gigantic heap of shit. He stopped short in his tracks, was this a derogatory indication of someone's opinion of him?

The dumped turd seemed to be making a statement as it lay releasing a foul stink on his sacred ground, I could swear that there was steam rising from the heap of shit, or maybe it was coming from the R.S.M. The enraged Sergeant Major's face turned a deep shade of purple, how could someone have the audacity to defecate on his square. The pile of shit was so colossal, that either someone had saved it up for days, or two or three lads had connived together as a group, to do the dirty deed.

The R.S.M considered it a personal insult; he fumed and seethed as he bellowed at the top of his voice,

"Who ever did a heap of shit as big as that must need medical attention; his arse must be in a hell of a state."

He ordered each platoon to march past the pile of shit and bellowed,

"**Eyes right.** Take a good look at the shit, can anyone identify the culprit?"

We recruits were almost doubled up with laughter, as we obeyed his order.

I would not have liked to be the next soldier on fatigues; you do not have to be a rocket scientist to guess what his first job would be.

During the last week before our passing out parade, we were given permission to go into Blandford for a night out, therefore most of us recruits assembled together to visit a local pub. We were drinking and having a good time, grateful to unwind and be able to relax for a change, when after a while, the publican asked if anyone could play the piano. One recruit in our company jumped up and offered to play, but since he was pissed, everyone was concerned that he might show himself up, so said to him.

"Sit down; you don't want to make a fool of yourself, do you?"

"But I *can* play, *honestly,"* he replied.

So, the lads, not knowing what to expect said,

"Go on then, make a fool of yourself, play chopsticks"

Everyone was waiting to hurl abuse and were ready with rehearsed wise cracks, however, when he began to play the whole room appeared to become mesmerised, we could not believe our ears, he was brilliant, his nimble fingers tinkled expertly over the keys, enthralling the captivated audience. Only then, were we informed that he had been a finalist in the Hughie Green Talent Show on Television. His contribution certainly helped in making it a fantastic party, the atmosphere was superb and it was without doubt a night to remember.

After completing my basic training, I found myself posted

to a trade training camp at Borden, Hampshire, to learn the trade of Gun Fitting.

All we new recruits were *welcomed* into the camp by a Sgt Major Proud, who was a veteran soldier with a warped sense of humour. We soon realised just how droll he could be when on the first Muster Parade the Sgt Major told us to answer immediately when our name was called out and to promptly come to attention.

With a sharp,

"STAND AT EASE", the Sgt Major began to call the Roll.

After reading several names from the list of new recruits, he began to pull comical faces, then when about half way through, he paused, squinted at the Roll, took a second hard look and called out,

"Lucy Garnie",

"SIR", a voice answered.

"Lucy? *Lucy?"*

With a whimsical look on his face, the Sgt Major shouted.

"I didn't know we had a lady in our midst."

Everyone chuckled, and it soon became apparent that the

soldier was of Italian extraction, his last name being Lucigarnie. The Sgt. Major continued to call out names and after a moment or two he once again paused, distorted his face, narrowed his eyes, brought the Roll up to about two inches from his nose, then held it out at arms length, and shouted,

"Prince Mohamed Amuridin."

Another peal of laughter from the platoon,

"SHUT UP" screamed Sgt Major Proud

"And as for you, PRINCE, YOUR HIGHNESS, from now on you will answer to "HAMMER IT IN'! 'UNDERSTAND?"

"YES SIR" came the reply

After calling out a few more names, he once more repeated the process of scrutinising the Roll, and with a bizarre look, shouted,

"Squib."

There was a slight delay then the reply came and was the most highly pitched squeaky voice that I have ever heard.

"Sir,"

The platoon was by now reduced to hysterics, Sgt Major was in his element, and he repeated his call,
“Squib, Vincent Squib”
The squeaky voice once more replied,
“Sir,”
Sgt. Major Proud marched up to Vincent Squib and put his mouth right up against his ear, and bellowed,
“SQUIB, IF YOU DON'T WAKEN YOURSELF UP I'LL PUT A SQUIB UP YOUR FUCKIN ARSE, ALTHOUGH IT SOUNDS AS IF YOU’VE GOT ONE UP THERE ALREADY”

Hoots of laughter once more.

Many of the recruits’ received money through the post as a kind gesture from their families, however it was soon discovered that cash was going missing, having apparently been pilfered. The prime suspect was Steve, the Post Corporal; as a result, he was instantaneously arrested and thrown into jail, there to stay until the investigations were finally concluded. No such procedure of ‘innocent until proven guilty’ in the army in those days. Steve had a twin

brother Mark who was serving in the same camp, understandably this situation made things very awkward for Mark who took the brunt of all the accusations, which were flying around. He had to endure the anguish of being verbally goaded and had to stomach the finger of suspicion being pointed at Steve. Mark was especially protective of his twin and vehemently denied the allegations against him. However, there was one soldier who would not let the accusations rest; he publicly declared that Steve was a thief and that he should be accountable for the soldiers' loss, saying he ought to be ashamed of cheating the recruits out of their money. Mark was understandably livid and challenged him to fight.
"Not outside" he declared, "but supervised in the boxing ring."

That night they both entered the gym with a sense of determination, and glared at each other with hatred in their eyes and after quickly donning the gloves, Mark stated.
"No rounds, no minute rests, just let us get on with it, and don't interrupt until one of us has had enough"

Sure enough, after climbing through the ropes, they

proceeded to knock seven different colours of shit out of each other, until finally they ended up battered, cut, bruised and swollen, neither willing to concede and only compromising when a Corporal stepped in to declare.

"Enough's enough lads"

He ordered them call it a day, and although they obeyed and removed the gloves, they vehemently refused to shake hands. Subsequently, after a thorough investigation, it was uncovered that the thief was an employee at the Main Post Office sorting office, therefore Steve was completely exonerated, to the humiliation of the main accuser who reluctantly apologised, although it stuck in his throat to do so.

Derek Powell, a recruit from Tottenham, was posted to Borden at the same time as myself; and was constantly inviting me to his home for weekends, but being quite a reserved person I always declined. However, he was most persistent and continuously badgered me until eventually I agreed to go. Nevertheless, once there I had a brilliant weekend, and was pleased that I had, after all my doubts, consented to accompany him.

Derek's family greeted me warmly, and made me most

welcome, and I was soon to discover that his grandmother, who resided with them, was a true dyed in the wool Geordie, who declared that she had been dying to meet me.

"Eeh hello pet, how ar yi, which part of Newcaastle ar yi from?" "What di yi think of the army? Haav yi settled in yet?"

We began to converse about home and she was most interested as we reminisced about Newcastle and Tyneside, she recalled all the fond memories that she had left behind, and said that her heart would always be in Newcastle and that she longed to return one day. When the time came to return to camp, I sincerely thanked them for their hospitality, and the grandmother insisted that I accept a five-pound note. I felt acutely embarrassed and declined her generous offer; however, she stuffed the note into my pocket and said she would be most offended if I did not accept.

There is one in every Company, in ours it was Raegan, a stereotypical obnoxious bully, who found an easy target in the inoffensive Alan Thomson. He latched on relentlessly to persecute his victim, not only to mentally deride but also to physically abuse him. There was not a day went by without

Raegan taking great pleasure in persecuting Alan until finally at the end of his tether Alan approached me pleading for help. He asked if I would teach him to box so that he would be able to defend himself, I said that I would be only too pleased to help and told him to come to the gym to join in the training. When Alan appeared, the other boxers were taken aback and could not believe he was serious about wanting to learn to box, he being such a harmless non-violent type of lad.

However, after just a few weeks of demonstrating to him the basics of pugilism, which he picked up promptly, and teaching him how to punch correctly with the knuckle part of his fist, he asked me.

"Am I ready Geordie?"

"Ready! Ready for what?" I asked.

"Am I ready to punch the fuckin living daylights out of that bastard Raegan?" he replied.

I perceived by the hatred in his eyes that he was serious, and answered,

"Alan, let me tell you something, boxing in the ring and fighting outside are two completely different kettle of fish, if you are thinking of taking him on, accept the advice that my father passed on to me. 'Always be first.' Whenever challenged, always be first to go outside, especially if it is dark. This will give you an advantage, since your eyes will quickly become accustomed to the gloom. Always stand out of sight and position yourself at one side of the doorway then as soon as your opponent emerges, hit him full force in the middle of the face, when he drops don't let him get up"

Two days later as we were queuing in the N.A.F.F.I. for supper, Raegan performed his usual trick and pushed in at the front of the queue, I leant forward, grabbed him by the collar and said.

"Get to the back of the queue Raegan"

He shrugged and went a little further down the queue and pushed in front of Alan and growled,

"Get out of my fuckin way Thomson,"

Alan was ready; he decided the intimidation would stop there and then, so furiously replied.

"Don't you fuckin push me around, I'll see you outside you bastard".

“I hope you’ve got your first aid box,” replied Raegan.
A murmur, which gained momentum, went around the room,
“Thomson’s challenged Raegan to go outside”
“Bollocks, Thomson can’t fight,”
“But it’s true, c’mon we can’t miss this”

Everyone in the room surged forward as Alan confidently left the N.A.A.F.I. followed a moment or two later by Raegan, with me hot on his heels. Alan followed my instructions to a ‘T,’ and immediately Raegan appeared in the doorway; he bore the full brunt of Alan’s right hand, and dropped like a stone to the ground whereupon Alan went in with both feet.
I quickly stepped in, grabbed Alan, pulled him off and said,
“C’mon Alan, that’s enough, he’s learnt his lesson”.

Arriving back in the billet after supper, we found Raegan lying on his bed, disconsolate and feeling very sorry for himself, he was sporting a real shiner of a black eye which was so swollen it was almost closed. Suddenly two of Raegan’s previous victims entered the billet, walked over to his bed and each threw a punch at the prone Raegan and shouted,

"You got you what you deserved, you Bastard, now you'll think twice before bullying anyone else."
Next morning we were surprised to find Raegan's bed empty, apparently he had gone A.W.O.L.

Posted on the notice board one morning, were Orders that every soldier was required to attend a parade at 11a.m, since this was out of the ordinary, the lads were curious as to the reason for the parade.
We were disturbed to find it was an identity parade, as apparently a local girl had complained to the powers above, that one of the soldiers in our regiment had indulged in sex with her and had consequently made her pregnant. The Colonel was outraged and had subsequently arranged for the young woman to attend the parade to identify the culprit.

We recruits felt very uneasy, and as you can imagine the remarks and jokes were flying around thick and fast as each and every one was accusing the other.
The joking abruptly ceased when the young lady appeared on the square, we were aghast, our mouths dropped open with horror; none of us had ever seen such a repulsive looking girl.

She was ugly beyond belief, with dark greasy hair hanging in scraggy strands, her uneven teeth were yellow, and she was so obese she could only waddle across to the parade of soldiers.

We were desperately shrinking down, trying to make ourselves obscure, believing that she would probably choose a soldier that she fancied, no such procedure as D.N.A in those days. We cringed as she slowly walked along the lines of soldiers; she paused at each individual, gazing intently as she looked him up and down, then each one thankful and relieved when she passed him over to confront the next in line.

However, to everyone's delight she did not identify any one of us and in reality, when the truth became known, she was not pregnant after all; and had not even been out with a soldier. The lads, on reflection, were of the opinion that she must have been so desperate for a boyfriend that she had, to everyone's relief, concocted the whole story.

Chapter 3

After my trade training at Bordon had concluded, I was posted to a transit camp at Arborfield then following the settling in period I was, to my delight, asked if I would assist the Physical Training Instructors. I was ecstatic and grabbed the chance with both hands, as physical training was, at that time, my sole purpose in life, it being my forte.

I soon discovered that when serving in the forces, being a professional boxer or any other athlete for that matter, brought, privileges and respect from both Officers and men alike.

It was at Arborfield that I encountered a young soldier called Ernie Evans, who originated from Sunderland, in the North East of England. Ernie and I bonded immediately and became great mates; I could never comprehend why, but Ernie was the one who was unfortunate enough to be given the most objectionable and dirtiest of jobs. On one occasion, he was ordered to clean the whole platoon's rifles in readiness for the Queen's Coronation Parade.
There were forty guns altogether, and each one had to be meticulously cleaned, oiled and polished, this chore took Ernie a full two weeks to complete. However, he was a tough, strong-minded lad and even though he arrived back at the billet fatigued with his hands and nails ingrained with filth and thick black oil, he accepted the victimisation and it seemed to make him even more determined to accept army life.

One day a travelling fair arrived at Reading, and proceeded to assemble its rides and stalls in a large field in the nearby village of California. This was a novelty for us servicemen and broke the monotonous strict routine we were accustomed to, so we gathered into groups to go to the opening night and experience the 'Thrill of the fair.'

Smartly dressed in army uniforms I, along with Ernie and another three mates, set off to the fairground, where upon arrival, we discovered it was heaving with throngs of people bustling and milling around. The five of us revelled in the electrifying setting, which surrounded us as we slowly sauntered through the crowds. We found ourselves enveloped in the alluring aroma of hot dogs and onions and were delighted with the sound of music blasting out from the rides, so loud in fact, that we could feel the vibration reverberating through our bodies.

We tried our luck, alas, to no avail, on the rifle stalls, and were convinced that the sights on the guns were warped or the pellets misshapen, because, even though most of us had attained high qualifications as marksmen, we could not even win a cheap teddy bear between us.

We stumbled upon a boxing booth with the proprietor

standing on the platform shouting through a loud hailer. He was challenging spectators and urging them to volunteer to box his Irish middleweight who was giving an exhibition on the platform, shadow boxing and punching a heavy bag. The boxer undoubtedly looked impressive as he displayed his skills and looked superbly fit and strong; I guessed that he must have been in his thirties. The proprietor was yelling,

"There will be five pounds prize money for any challenger who can last three rounds with my boxer"

This brought back memories and my mind began to wander as I reminisced about my boxing career, I was however, abruptly interrupted from my daydreams when I became aware of my mates yelling,

"He'll box, he'll box".

I became conscious they were pointing at me, and I suddenly found myself being pushed and manhandled forward, and was pressurised into accepting the challenge.

I reluctantly climbed onto the platform, egged on by my mates,

"Have you done any boxing," the proprietor asked,

“A little bit.” I replied

The booth fighter looked at me and said,

“Don’t worry son, I won't hurt you, remember you can retire any time you want”

“OK” I said

I followed him inside the marquee, which housed the boxing ring, and removed my jacket and shirt then climbed through the ropes. As I stood in my corner, I glanced across the ring to weigh my opponent up and noticed that he was taller and heavier than I was, and had all the usual markings of a pugilist.

However, being supremely fit I was full of confidence, almost cocky in fact. I thought to myself, ‘I can take this bloke any time I like.’ The bell rang, and as the first round began, I walked into the middle of the ring and planted my feet firmly on the canvas; I stood in one spot and called on all my previous experience to bob, weave and block all the punches he threw at me. In fact, when the bell rang to end the round, he had not landed a single blow.

“Ding”, the bell rang and the second round commenced, this

time I moved swiftly over to the booth fighter and threw a short right hook, which connected exactly on target, his chin, knocking him clean out.

The Proprietor was incensed; and point blankly refused to hand over the five-pound prize money, which to my mind I had won fairly and squarely.

“You're not a novice”, he yelled at me.

The people in the audience were furious and began to chant in harmony,

“Give him the money.” “Give him the money”

The proprietor was unmoved and doggedly refused, it was at that point that I grabbed the loud hailer from his hand and challenged his other booth fighter, who again was taller, heavier and older than I, but what the hell, I was feeling elated.

To keep face with the crowds of onlookers, the proprietor felt obliged to accept the challenge, I put into action the equivalent scenario in this next contest. Once again, the fighter never laid a glove on me, and I knocked him out in the second round, which meant of course that the proprietor owed me ten pounds.

Needless to say, I did not receive a penny of the prize money; and as my mates and I made our way out of the booth, we were dismayed to discover that the proprietor had summoned a gang of fairground workers who, in a threatening manner, were advancing in our direction. Upon reaching us, they formed a circle to surround us, each one brandishing a weapon of either a baseball bat or a hammer. We found ourselves outnumbered by about six to one; I was feeling totally responsible for my mates' safety so turned and glanced at the proprietor, I smiled and said,

"Stick the money up your arse".

The circle opened up and we walked through.

The next morning, I was summoned to Sgt. Major Dixon's office, who, we had been informed was the youngest Sgt. Major in the British Army, this was possibly correct as he was only about twenty-six years old. He was a man of colossal stature being at least six feet five inches tall and about eighteen stones in weight. As ordered, I marched into his office, over to his desk and came quickly to attention. I was extremely apprehensive and tried to surmise the reason why I had been summoned. The Sgt. Major looked up from

his paperwork, and said,
"I saw you perform on the boxing booth last night Jackson, well done, well done."
He went on to add,
"There are two thousand soldiers in this camp Jackson and we are regrettably, short of N.C.O's, would you be willing to assist by acting as Physical Training Instructor? I would be extremely appreciative if you would consent."
I was beyond doubt, thrilled and couldn't hide my excitement as I replied,
"I would be delighted to, Sir".
He immediately, placed me in charge of a platoon and said,
"If anyone questions why you are in charge Jackson, inform them it's on my orders,"
"Yes Sir" I replied.

From that day on, every morning, until I was posted overseas, I helped to train the platoon, by putting them through rigorous daily exercises, although we often simply played twenty a side football in the nearest field.

One day as I was emerging from the gym after completing the morning exercise session, a craftsman approached me and said.

"Sgt. Major Dixon wants to see you in his office."

Perplexed, I made my way there and immediately came to attention at his desk, he continued reading a document for a moment or two then slowly looked up and said,

"Jackson I want you to go to the gardens outside the guardroom and pick a huge bunch of flowers, then deliver them to my wife, and tell her they are a present from me".

"Yes Sir, but what if I'm caught Sir?" I asked hesitantly.

"Then be it on your own back, I'll positively deny any knowledge of it. Now go, that's an order Jackson."

"Sgt. Major, can Craftsman Evans come with me to act as lookout?" I tentatively asked.

He readily agreed, therefore I searched for Ernie, and found him just finishing his lunch in the N.A.A.F.I. I explained to him what was expected of us, and then full of apprehension we made our way to the gardens, which were in full bloom with the most beautiful flowers.

Taking turns as lookout, Ernie and I furtively picked huge armfuls of vibrant flowers as swiftly as possible, fortunately for us, without being detected. Then carefully cradling the colourful blooms in our arms we cautiously made our way to the Sgt. Major's home, which was in the married quarters, about half a mile away.

His wife promptly answered the door to our knock and was overwhelmed when we handed over the flowers explaining they were from her husband, but as she clutched them in her arms, the delighted smile on her face slowly faded, when at that precise moment she heard her husband's voice bellow out in the distance. He was screaming oaths and profanities, the air turned blue with his foul language, and even though we were about half a mile away, his voice rang out as clear as a bell. Mrs Dixon was visibly shocked.
"Is that my husband?" she whispered.
"Yes Maam" we replied,
"That's outrageous, him using that kind of language, just wait until he gets home I'll sort HIM out", she said
We were justifiably amused since the Sgt. Major was such an enormous figure of a man and his wife was such a tiny slight little thing, we found her threats hard to comprehend.

It was soon after this little escapade that Ernie applied for, and was duly accepted to take a Parachute Course, which he passed with flying colours, thus obtaining his wings, which he justifiably wore with a sense of pride

Ernie and I lost contact with each other in June 1953 when he was posted to Egypt and I myself was posted out to North Africa, to a camp named Lancia, situated in the Sahara Desert, approximately eight miles from the main town of Tripoli.

I along with several other soldiers boarded a civilian aircraft to fly to Tripoli, and as this was my first experience of flying it was quite unnerving when in mid air, an announcement came over the loudspeakers saying that unfortunately the aircraft had developed engine trouble and we had to make an unscheduled landing in France. Nevertheless, we landed safely, although we were obliged to wait for six hours whilst mechanics worked to repair the fault, to guarantee that the aircraft was once again airworthy. As this was my introduction to foreign soil, I found it truly awesome, the differences in the style of buildings, the scenery, and the atmosphere all captivated me, and as I listened to the foreign chatter, which sounded like gobbledegook, it amused me and made me wish that I could understand the language.

Following the successful repair to the engine, we once again boarded the aircraft and flew to a transit camp in Malta, there to stay for two weeks. This was, we were informed, to acclimatise us to the heat, before being subjected to the relentless intense temperature of the desert. These two weeks in Malta was a new experience for me, it seemed almost as if I were on holiday and I loved every moment, and found to my disappointment that the days passed all too quickly.

Chapter 4

Next stop was Tripoli, and as I alighted from the aircraft, the oppressive heat hit me like a hammer, I reeled back and gasped for air, I could not believe the extreme blistering temperature, it felt as if I had stepped into a sauna. Myself together with the other soldiers from the aircraft clambered aboard a wagon, which was waiting to take us to camp and as we drove along a road, which was no more than a dirt track, we felt conscious of, not only the intense heat, but also the

differences in culture.
We noticed that the 'houses', were constructed from cardboard and corrugated tin and had frayed sheets of either cloth or plastic draped over for shelter.
We passed several bundles of crumpled rags lying at the roadside; it was explained to us that the ‘rags’ were old Arabs who had lain down to die, we were understandably horrified.

We overtook an Arab who was riding on a tiny grey donkey, so small in fact that the Arab’s feet were almost trailing along the ground; he was grasping a rope, the other end of which was attached to an Arab woman who was trotting behind. This must have been difficult enough, without the enormous bundle, balanced on top of her head.
It seemed as if we had been transported hundreds of years back in time to a previous century.

Not much further along the road, we drove through a small village, there I witnessed an Arab clutching a small white goat, suddenly I observed the glint of steel as the rays of the sun reflected off the blade of a large knife. I was appalled when the Arab proceeded to slit the little goat’s throat from one side to the other. Being an avid animal lover, I retched and was almost sick with revulsion, as the blood spurted out, staining the goat's coat and transforming it from brilliant white to scarlet red. The small creature, legs twitching in its last throes of life, slumped lifeless to the ground, a nauseating sight etched in my mind forever. It was explained to us that this was their Country and we had to accept their culture.

We arrived at the camp at mid-day, and as we clambered out of the wagon tired and hungry, one of the cockney lads amongst us shouted over to a group of soldiers who were lounging on a veranda adjoining their billet and asked,

"Cor mate, is it always as hot as this?"

"This is nothing mate, it gets much, much hotter", the soldiers shouted back.

We gasped with dismay, thinking it would be unbearable, however next morning, we realised they had been joking, when headlines in the local newspaper reported it as,

"The hottest day for twenty years, and stated that numerous Arabs had died of heatstroke"

The temperature had risen to an unbelievable one hundred and thirty six degrees.

That first night at camp, we were exposed to a loud continuous wailing, which emitted from the surrounding Arab villages, we were soon to discover that the local Arabs wailed and chanted every single night for hours on end. However, each night at the exact time, almost to the minute, the chanting abruptly stopped, it was almost as if someone turned a radio off, nevertheless, even though this wailing occurred night after night, I never ever got used to it.

The Regimental Colonel in charge of our base workshop was a Colonel Bradley, a veteran ex. S.A.S. Officer who had experienced action during the war and, as I was soon to discover to my delight, he was fanatical about boxing.

I had been stationed in the camp for only two days when Colonel Bradley sent for me, as having evidently read my service history from the records, he had noted my boxing ability and experience, so immediately requested that I train the boxing team.

Colonel Bradley promised that I would have a free hand in all decision making concerning the boxers and training. He stated that if there was anything I needed, I just had to request it and it would be provided without question. Additionally, he put me in charge of the physical training for the whole regiment.

I was assigned to a billet, which housed forty men, and I quickly formed a great friendship with a soldier named Mike Fraser, who had also signed on for three years, Mike was short, being only five foot three, however he was strong and very sturdily built. Mike was always cheerful with a perpetual grin on his face, he was born and bred in Liverpool and had a wonderful sense of humour, he had that dry Scouse wit for which Liverpudlians are renowned. It did not matter how serious a situation was, Mike would always see the humorous side.

Another soldier in my billet was Robbie Bell, another regular soldier who had signed on for three years and although I had never met him previously he was from my neck of the woods, the Scotswood road area of Newcastle upon Tyne. Robbie was precisely the opposite of Mike, he being six feet two inches tall; lanky and as skinny as a beanpole; however, equivalent to Mike, he had a great sense of humour, and a quick sharp repartee, and was always laughing and joking.

The beds in our billet were constructed from tubular metal, and draped with mosquito nets. These were essential since the area was swarming with the little bloodsuckers. The instructions were to lift the bottom end of our beds each morning and night to a height of about twelve inches, and to let them drop onto the concrete floor, we followed these instructions rigidly and were amazed at the amount of beetles and bugs that fell onto the floor each time.

We were warned to check our clothing each morning, since it was possible that scorpions may be hiding in amongst the folds of the garments, and told another favourite place in which they might conceal themselves could be our boots. The Medical Officer cautioned us that a single sting from this particular species of scorpion could prove fatal, which did not instil us with confidence.

One morning, after a long drinking binge the previous evening, our cook was suffering from a massive hangover so

feeling a tad under the weather he forgot to check his uniform. Consequently, as he pulled his trousers up, he felt a sharp sting on his arse; he dropped his pants and to his horror, he noticed a scorpion crawl out from the garment and quickly scuttle away. Realising he had been stung, he screamed and jumped around the billet, tripping over his trousers, which were by then draped around his ankles.
"I'm going to die, I'm going to fuckin die." he was shouting and screaming.

We hurriedly summoned a wagon to take him to our Military Hospital, and tried to calm him down whilst waiting for it to arrive. Five minutes later he was whisked off to hospital where they administered an antidote and after receiving the medication, he was relieved when assured that he would be all right and wouldn't suffer any after effects, except, that when he returned to our billet, he was made the butt of our jokes for days.
After his scary experience, he was understandably especially cautious before dressing, and took ages each morning to scrutinize and thoroughly check his clothing.

My job was to supervise the R.E.M.E. workshops until

lunchtime, then each afternoon, I trained the boxers, and arranged football training, in addition, I organised the training for the athletics team. We had a Staff Sergeant Ball in our regiment, who was, at the time, the current three 'A's British Champion, at shot put, discus and javelin, I approached him to request that he coach the lads who had shown interest in participating in those three events, and he was very willing and pleased to do so.

After working extremely hard, I was thrilled when after only six weeks, I read on Orders of my promotion to Lance Corporal; I felt this was a great achievement, having been accomplished in such a short period.

This meant I had to take my uniform to the army tailor to have the stripes sewn on; however upon returning to the billet Mike, being store-man in charge of equipment, had nicked numerous stripes from the stores. Then he, together with his partner in crime Robbie, had orchestrated a plan to sew stripes all over the sheets and pillowslips on my bed. Furthermore, they had sewn stripes onto my pyjamas, my beret and onto all my underclothes, they had glued stripes onto both ends of my bed and even onto the inside and outside of my locker. I couldn’t help but laugh.

Subsequently for the next few days, each time I uttered a word, being the jokers they were, they instantly jumped to attention, saluted me, and shouted

“Yes Corporal. No Corporal”.

Chapter 5

After having served as 'acting' Physical Training Instructor for several months, Colonel Bradley called me into his office one day, to suggest that I enrol onto a Physical Training Instructor’s Course, saying that I should try to obtain legitimate qualifications. I excitedly agreed to his suggestion. The P.T.I. tuition was to be completed at the British Army School of Physical Training, which was located in Egypt, and involved six weeks of intensive preparation; I was exceptionally enthusiastic and eagerly waited for the arrangements to be finalised.

A few weeks earlier, a soldier named John Bowes, who originated from County Durham had arrived at our camp, he was an exceptionally fit, good-looking blonde lad who was fanatical about sport. He particularly excelled in football, having played for the team of Bishop Auckland, who at the time were amateur champions of England. John was designated to my billet, and immediately became good friends with myself, Mike and Robbie. Upon discovering that I had enrolled onto a P.T.I. Course, John was especially enthusiastic and said that he had aspirations of becoming a physical training instructor himself. On his request, I approached Colonel Bradley to request that he be allowed to attend the same P.T.I. course. As a result, because qualified Physical Instructors were few and far between, the Colonel readily granted permission.

Several days later, it appeared on Orders that, Corporal Jackson and Craftsman Bowes were to be posted to Moascar Garrison in Egypt to attend the next P.T.I. Course which was due to commence the following month. The following weeks passed rapidly as we both waited eagerly for the day to arrive when we would depart for Egypt.

When that day finally arrived, John and I were full of enthusiasm as we travelled to Tripoli Airport to board an R.A.F. aircraft. After settling ourselves down for the journey, we chatted, letting our minds run wild with expectations of what was ahead. We had been airborne for about three quarters of an hour, when I casually glanced out of the window; I was confused and said to John,

“I’m sure that's Tripoli down there.”

I leant forward to quiz a Sergeant who had appeared from the cockpit and had taken the seat in front of us. I asked him if it was indeed Tripoli beneath us, he confirmed it was, saying that the crew had forgotten to fill up with fuel, leaving us no other option than to return. To our amusement, we found ourselves back on the tarmac of Tripoli Airport, and after the aircraft was duly filled up, we once again took off, this time to reach our destination without any further hitches.

Arriving in Egypt, we excitedly disembarked from the

aircraft and walked through the airport to the pavement outside to discover a wagon waiting to transport us to camp. As we clambered aboard, we noticed the two guards, who were escorting us, were carrying armed machine guns, and were positioned either side of the wagon. We observed them furtively glancing around and noticed they were very alert and nervous; they informed us that having arms and live ammunition was essential for protection, since terrorists were very active in Egypt, their main target being our British troops.

John and I were quite apprehensive during the journey, which conveyed us to a transit camp, however we arrived intact and made our way to the N.A.A.F.I., and being ravenously hungry we appreciated the food, which was on offer. Afterwards, we were informed that we had been assigned to guard duty and duly instructed to report to the guardhouse. There the duty Sergeant Major issued us both with a Sten gun and with two magazines of live ammunition.

That night stays especially vivid in my memory, I recall it being particularly dark and eerie, and as we patrolled around the perimeter fence, we could hear the rat-at-tat-tat of machine gun fire, which was uncomfortably close and deafeningly loud so we both felt very vulnerable in this volatile situation.

"I've had enough of this," John grumbled.

He began to look cautiously around until eventually, to his relief, he found a large cavity in the sand; he furtively crept inside and huddled down to shelter for rest of his guard duty. I myself felt very exposed and vulnerable, but being, I believed, a dedicated soldier I felt it was my duty to carry on patrolling and therefore continued.

The loud gunfire caused me to reminisce back to my childhood days, back to when, being only five years old, I was bewildered by the sudden weird piercing incessant sound of a siren, the usual warning of imminent attack in wartime. Our neighbours came rushing out of their houses in sheer panic, shouting

"We're at war."

They gathered in small groups, arms gesticulating as they anxiously discussed the repercussions they believed war would bring to their lives. Apparently, the Rt. Hon. Neville Chamberlain had just made an announcement on the radio informing the nation that, **THE COUNTRY WAS AT WAR WITH GERMANY.** The time was 11.15.a.m. on Sunday morning the 3rd of September 1939. The atmosphere amongst the clusters of women was of disbelief and horror; then a sense of hopelessness seemed to fill the air, and even though I was so young, I realised that something was very amiss.

I lived with my family in Maughan Street, which ran vertically up from the famous Scotswood Road, on which a massive factory, namely Vickers , was located, and was in fact situated directly at the bottom of our street.

Vickers 's was a munitions factory which manufactured tanks and guns designated for the British Army, consequently everyone believed, rightly as it turned out, that the factory would surely be a prime target for the enemy. This meant that we, being in such close proximity, would be at great risk, and likely to be caught up in any bombing raids directed at the factory.

The panic and apprehension was quite scary for me, however it turned out to be quite exhilarating and exciting for us kids in the neighbourhood. Directly the sirens sounded, we observed the urgency of neighbours extinguishing their lights or making sure their windows were obscured with black material to conceal any lights left on during the blackouts.

Everyone seemed caught up in the fear of anticipated air raids, also the realisation that enemy bombs would be dropping and exploding in our immediate vicinity became a reality as we huddled together in air raid shelters. Our street, was in fact, strafed several times by Nazi aircraft, however as soon as the 'all clear' siren sounded, we kids eagerly went out onto the streets searching for shrapnel to collect as souvenirs.

Father ushered me outside our front door on several occasions, to observe dogfights in the sky between our Spitfires and German Fighters. This was a thrilling sight, we watched as the aircraft dodged and evaded each other. We scrutinised the amazing spectacle of gunfire spitting out from the aircraft, creating bright yellow flashes, which streaked through the darkness of the night sky, virtually simulating huge firework displays.

The aircraft also had to contend with enormous barrage balloons floating in the sky, as a deterrent to enemy aircraft; these were large, sinister grey shapes quite daunting for a small boy. In the background, we could hear the deafening noise of a huge anti-aircraft gun, nicknamed Big Bertha, manned at nearby Lobley Hill, and each time the enemy aircraft approached, it came into action.

Families by their hundreds were evacuated to farms and houses in the depth of the countryside; the logic being, that being in isolated, rural areas they would be safer and less likely to be harmed by the enemy, as primarily, the bombing targets were factories and commercial premises. Children of all ages were name-tagged, supplied with gas masks, which hung around their necks and then herded off to Newcastle Central Station for transportation by train to safer destinations, usually Cumberland. Older children, as a rule, would be without parents, whilst babies and younger children had the pleasure of their mothers to chaperone them. Our father however, refused to allow our family to be evacuated, instead he elected that we stay home, his reasoning being,

"It doesn't matter where you are, when your time is up, its up."

Suddenly, back to reality, and thankfully, morning was breaking and my stint on guard duty was due to end. John crept out of his sanctuary and we made our way back to the guardroom, to be informed that the shooting, we had heard during the night, was retaliation, aimed at terrorists who had stealthily crept up to and tragically killed a British Soldier who had been patrolling the perimeter immediately next to John and me. My heart sank with the realisation that it could quite easily have been me and I remembered my father's words, I could only surmise that this time was not my time.

Chapter 6

Early next morning, John and I boarded the wagon, arranged to take us to the Physical Training School at Moascar Garrison. On arrival, we jumped off and enquired where the toilets were, seeing that after the journey, we were desperate for a 'jimmy riddle.'

A Corporal showed us to a location named the Roundhouse, which was a large round wooden structure, built around a deep pit, which measured roughly about twenty feet across.

This 'toilet' consisted of a narrow wooden shelf curved around the entire pit, and since there were no doors to give privacy, the user had to sit on the shelf, facing outwards, and was therefore exposed, and in full view of all and sundry. Not only was it extremely embarrassing, but the stench was, understandably, disgustingly stomach churning.

As John and I approached the Roundhouse, we observed a thick black column rising up into the sky from the stinking pit, at first, we assumed it was a pillar of black smoke, however as we neared, we realised that it was indeed, a dense concentrated column of flies. It was so nauseating and repulsive that we turned away in disgust and went discretely into the bushes to attend to the call of nature.

John and I were to be stationed in Egypt for eight weeks; and we soon discovered, to our disappointment, that the weather was oppressively humid and sticky, far removed from the beautiful climate we enjoyed in Tripoli.

The first week was designated to normal duties and recreation, and then to our delight, the six-week P.T.I. course commenced, we were introduced to the Physical Training Instructors and were instantaneously impressed with their outstanding physiques. They were all identical in build, being broad shouldered with extremely well defined muscular arms and shoulders, each sported the tiniest of waists and all had prominent six-packs, and were conditioned to the utmost standard of fitness and strength, John and I could only gaze on in envy.

Finally the training was set in motion, with the Instructors demonstrating the obstacle course; they being so fit and flexible made it look effortless, a piece of cake, we wondered just how long it would take for us to reach such a pinnacle of excellence.

The days were structured into forty-minute periods, which included road runs, swimming, obstacle courses, and gymnastics which I had never done before, although after a few practice sessions I quickly learned the basics of balancing, floor exercises, rope climbing etc.

It was after learning the fundamentals, that we trainees were selected into teams of eight, when every morning each team competed against the other and against the clock to test our ability and determination. Regrettably our team of eight was lumbered with an overweight, lazy Greek lad who weighed at least fifteen stone.

Situated right in the middle of the obstacle course was a ten-foot wall, where two soldiers from the team, stood with their backs against it and cupped their hands. The other six team members ran forward individually, placed one foot into the cupped hands, then jumped up to grab the top of the wall. He then pulled himself up and stayed to help the next soldier before dropping over to the other side. This manoeuvre was repeated until all eight team members were safely up and over.

However, to our dismay, every single day, our team finished a dismal last, the cause being, that the Greek soldier would just plonk his foot into the cupped hands, and not even attempt to reach for the top of the wall. He just stayed there like a lump of lard therefore the soldiers holding him had to strain with all their might and try to push him up. However, it took another two soldiers leaning over from the top of the wall, calling on all their reserves to yank him up and over; this

P.T.I. Course, myself top row, 2ndleft.

meant of course that we lost valuable time.

Each morning the same commotion transpired, therefore the soldiers in our team were becoming more and more frustrated and angry with him, so one morning, as I was running behind the Greek lad, I leant forward, grabbed a handful of fat from around his waist and said to him,

"Make an effort this time, you lazy bastard."

He spun around, furious, his eyes wide and glaring with rage, he whispered,

"Tonight, when you sleeep, I creeep to your tent, I coot your throat, I keel you."

I replied angrily,

"Fuck off you lazy bastard."

The P.T.I. Sergeant who was in charge, overheard his threats, and said.

"If I were you Geordie, I'd be very, very careful."

There were seven other trainee P.T.I.'s sharing my tent, and they agreed amongst themselves to take turns to stay awake and keep vigil, just in case the Greek lad tried to carry out his threat. I myself put on a brave face and retorted,

“I'm not loosing any sleep over that stupid bastard,”
Nevertheless, I must admit that I was very apprehensive, and that night lay awake for several hours. To their credit, my good mates, fearing for my safety, kept lookout on four consecutive nights, then, eventually realising that he must have been making idle threats, they began to relax.

There was one free period set aside each day, in which to run through our weakest exercise, and while everyone else was intent on practising, the Greek lad stood in the middle of the gym and shouted at full volume,
“LOOK AT ME, LOOK AT ME”.

Eventually, believing he had each and everyone’s attention, he performed handstands; and on completion, he strutted around, looking incredibly conceited and arrogant.
The trainees tried their best to ignore him, but found this was impossible, so ultimately, feeling utterly sick to the back teeth with him, they yelled insults.
“Shut your fuckin mouth you conceited wanker”.
“Fuck off you ignorant prick”.
“Go fuck yourself”.

and other similar expletives, but he was either so thick skinned, or maybe it was that he didn't understand English oaths and foul language, since the verbal abuse ran like water, off a duck's back.

Incorporated into the P.T.I. course, were two boxing sessions, and it was at the beginning of the first lesson, that the Greek lad jumped up in front of the audience and bellowed at the top of his voice,
"ME HAVE ONE HUNDRED AND FEEFTY FIGHTS, ME HAVE ONE HUNDRED AND FEEFTY KNOCKOUTS".

Everyone burst out laughing and the Sergeant stood shaking his head in disbelief, then as you can imagine, the trainees once again bombarded him with obscenities until I believe, the message eventually got through.

Finally after eight weeks in Egypt, and even though six of them had been exceptionally, physically, demanding, I had enjoyed every minute, and was exhilarated when, at the conclusion of the course, I was notified that I had achieved my longed for qualifications as a Physical Training Instructor.

John and I on the P.T.I. course in Egypt.

I was duly presented with the badge of Crossed Sabres, which I wore, with a sense of achievement and pride. I am pleased to say that to his delight John also passed.

A week later John and I were instructed to travel to Port Said, to begin the return journey to Tripoli, this time by sea, which was a new experience to look forward to. We were driven to the wharf by an army wagon, where upon arrival we leapt out of the vehicle onto the dock, however it being late at night we found ourselves in complete darkness, then unexpectedly I heard a broad Geordie voice shout from out of the shadows,

"Howway lads, wear yi gannin man"

Turning round, all I could see in the gloom, was a set of brilliant white teeth, and the whites of two eyes, however after finally managing to focus, I realised the eyes were staring out of a face as black as the ace of spades. I was flabbergasted when realising that it was he who was speaking with the broad Geordie brogue; I began to converse with him and asked,

"Where did you get that perfect Geordie accent?"

He explained that he had been attached to the

Northumberland Fusiliers for numerous years so had picked the brogue up from them, which made sense.
He escorted us to the quayside to embark onto the boat, which we discovered was a flat-bottomed Landing craft; heavily laden with, amongst other equipment, four wagons and two, twenty-five pounder artillery guns, all of which were securely fastened onto the deck with exceptionally colossal chains.

There were twelve soldiers, including John and I travelling to Tripoli on the boat; we found the cabins were sparse, although adequate, each fitted with four bunk beds meaning that John and I shared a cabin with two other lads.

In due course, we cast off and put out to sea, John and I stood on the deck, leaning nonchalantly against the rails, watching as the land disappeared from the horizon. We delighted in the pleasure of the sea breeze fanning against our bodies, it was a complete contrast to the oppressive heat, that we had endured in Egypt, and which we were both relived to be leaving.

We were in our element as we savoured the pleasure of the gentle wind wafting on our faces; we revelled in the relaxing surroundings and listened to the waves gently lapping against the boat. We watched the wake, foaming and frothing to form a white trail behind us as the boat gently glided through the sea.

The next day, we were all in agreement and decided,

"This is the life for us." "What a brilliant vocation, we MUST join the Navy."

For the duration of the firsts two days of sailing, we either sun bathed on the deck or leaned against the rails, watching as dolphins swam alongside, flanking the boat, leaping and twisting in unison above the water as they followed us for miles, this was heaven, we thought.

Then suddenly, without warning the unpredicted occurred, the weather abruptly changed for the worse, the sky blackened to an eerie purplish hue, and the waves began to swell higher and higher, until they became gigantic frothing monsters. We were alerted to the fact that we were caught up in a typhoon, and were immediately ordered below to our cabins and warned, for our own safety, to stay below until further notice. Once there we waited with apprehension as the boat, being a flat-bottomed craft, was being thrown and tossed around in the sea like a cork, it was indeed, a terrifying experience.

The cargo of wagons and guns, were literally being thrown from side to side, when the boat rose out of the water, they slid across the deck, first to one side with a deafening clunk, then across to the other side with an almighty crash, each time straining against the chains, which creaked and clanked as if they would snap. The waves were relentless as they crashed over the boat and we were all of the opinion that it must surely capsize. The boat was undulating so violently, that at first, we could only observe the sea, then a moment later, the sky, then the sea, the sky, we all turned a pale shade of green and most of us were severely seasick.

Because the weather was so perverse, it was too perilous to attempt to come in to dock, so we had to endure two more days of this extreme weather, anchored outside the port, we could vaguely distinguish the lights of Tripoli in the distance and could only fantasise about dry land.

Eventually the weather subsided, going from one extreme to the other, as when finally, the sea calmed, it resembled a

millpond, and only then were we able to navigate safely into harbour. Upon disembarking, John and I could hardly stand, let alone walk, the sensation of swaying from side to side was a convincing factor, the pavement seemed to be undulating beneath our feet and the feeling was dreadful.
Who suggested joining the Navy? -

"NO FUCKIN WAY."

Back on dry land, after John and I had finally found our 'land legs' we both admitted that after the six strenuous weeks of concentrated training, we felt incredibly fit, much fitter than we had ever felt before, so fit, I felt as though I could have jumped over the roofs of houses.

Subsequently, after returning to Tripoli, I noticed, on Orders, that I, with about ten other soldiers was instructed to take a written educational exam, together with a trade test. I entered each test full of confidence and was jubilant when being informed that I had passed both with flying colours. I was immediately promoted to full Substantive Corporal, meaning the only way I could be demoted was by a Court

Martial. I felt fulfilled and very satisfied with my life, having grown to thoroughly enjoy being a soldier, the disillusionment of basic training just a far distant memory.

Chapter 7

Being promoted to a fully qualified Physical Training Instructor, meant that I was put in charge of the Athletics team, who at the time were training hard for the Open Championships in Libya. We had a Craftsman Williams in our unit, who, in Civvy Street, had been a professional runner; his preferred distance was the half mile, so was firm favourite to win that race. However, because the second best runner in the team had unfortunately sustained a leg injury, I was invited to substitute for him, consequently I began training extremely hard and as a result, when the day of the Championships finally arrived I was superlatively fit.

I gave the race some deliberation, and decided, that during the race, my tactics would be to shadow Williams and stay as close to his shoulder as possible, then on the final bend, I would, hopefully, increase my speed to gain a couple of yards, to subsequently creep up alongside him. The instant the race commenced, I stuck to my strategy, which worked out exactly to plan, and on the last bend I began to feel that I could beat him, so on that assumption, I sprinted as fast as I could, and to my bewilderment I overtook him, leaving him, the professional, trailing behind. Unpredictably, to my delight I won the race by several yards, then subsequently went on to win both the one-mile and the three-mile races.

It was three weeks before the next Open Athletic Championships were due to take place that a Craftsman McGraw was posted to our unit; he was a small inoffensive, harmless type of lad, who, at most, was only seven and a half stones in weight. One evening as usual I was drinking in the N.A.F.F.I. with my three regular mates, Mike, John and

Winning the three-mile race

Robbie, when out of the blue McGraw approached me and asked.

"Corporal, how do I get into the Athletics team? I would love to take part in the one mile race".

Being half pissed, we took advantage of his naivety and told him to,

"Run around the camp, it's about a mile in distance; we'll time you to see if you're good enough to join the team."

Off he went, looking very pleased with himself, the group of us continued to drink and dismissed him from our minds until suddenly he reappeared in the N.A.F.F.I. out of breath.

Puffing and panting he eagerly asked,

"How did I do Corporal? Am I good enough?"

Since we had forgotten all about him, I said spontaneously,

"Sorry, but it was not quite good enough, do it again and try harder this time"

Off he disappeared into the night.

This in fact happened three times in all, until eventually, he arrived back almost dropping with exhaustion, I suddenly felt truly guilty and ashamed, as we hadn't even had the decency to time him. I felt a surge of sympathy towards him and said. "You did absolutely great McGraw, I will definitely grant you a place in the team, report for training first thing tomorrow morning".

He was jubilant and seemed to almost skip on air as he left the N.A.F.F.I.

McGraw was in fact, first on the scene for the training sessions every day for two weeks, until finally the morning of the Athletics Championships dawned. I being the defending Champion of the one-mile race was feeling quite positively confident, as we, the competitors lined up at the starting line. McGraw who had trained exceptionally hard was also an entrant in the race and standing right next to me, we both stretched and flexed our muscles and were hyped up and raring to go.

The starting pistol went off, and we immediately moved forward, McGraw took me completely by surprise when he shot off like an arrow, I struggled to keep up with him and tried to assure myself that he could not possibly keep up the rapid pace.

However, he did, and no matter how resolutely I ran, how

hard I tried, I just could not catch him, he seemed to leave me standing. He won the race, beating me into second place by at least five yards, I felt humbled and quite humiliated. Craftsman McGraw undoubtedly had the last laugh.

A favourite place for us soldiers in Tripoli was without doubt, a long private sandy beach; kept exclusively for British personnel. Located on the beach was a well-patronised N.A.F.F.I. where hot thirsty soldiers could purchase ice-cold beer to help cool down. It was a haven, offering shade from the scorching sun, as temperatures normally rose to at least 130 degrees Fahrenheit during the summer months. Additionally situated on the beach were changing rooms fitted with cool refreshing showers, used to wash the fine sand off our perspiring bodies.

A wooden raft measuring about ten feet square was conveniently anchored out at sea, and was located about half a mile from the shore. Therefore, my mates and I regularly swam out to it, to simply use it as a platform to laze about on, resting and sunbathing before swimming back to the beach, or alternately to use it to practice diving.

We were absolutely devastated one morning to read an

Order on the notice board, which prohibited swimming at our beach, the order stated,

"Swimming will be out of bounds until further notice, due to dangerous sharks basking in the area."

Since swimming was, our favourite pastime and we religiously went to the beach every afternoon to swim and to cool off, we felt especially frustrated. However, several days later, we were jubilant to read on Orders, that the hazard from sharks had passed, therefore the sea was now safe, and as a result, the beach was now within bounds.

That same afternoon immediately after work, we could hardly contain ourselves with anticipation and the thought of the cool refreshing sea, as we grabbed our swimming trunks, jumped into a truck and drove directly to the beach.
In his rush to get into the water to cool down, Robbie quickly discarded his clothes and shoes and sprinted onto the sand, regrettably he failed to remember that the sand would be sizzling hot, subsequently he began to hop up and down, screaming in agony as the soles of his feet were literally

cooking.
Some of us, who were still wearing sandshoes, raced forward, lifted him up and carried him onto the promenade, then, realising he needed hospital treatment for his severely burned and blistered feet, we immediately sent for an ambulance.

Whilst everyone was hanging about waiting for help to arrive, I turned to gaze at the sea; the water appeared cool and invigorating, it was so inviting and seemed to be beckoning me like a magnet. I could not resist the temptation so waded into the water to swim the half mile to the raft. Upon reaching it, I pulled myself aboard and lay resting for a short while until I had regained my breath. Then finding my second wind, I decided to swim back to shore, so lowered myself slowly down into the water and began to leisurely swim towards the beach. A moment or two later, to my absolute horror, I became aware that a shark was pursuing me, it is commonly said that when your life is in danger your whole life flashes before you, I can assure you it is true. My imagination went into overdrive as I contemplated the gruesome way in which I would die, I visualised being literally torn to pieces, limb by limb by those razor sharp teeth.

Driven by sheer panic, I swam faster than I'd ever swum in my life, I moved at such a high-speed, that I think I must have broken the world record, Johnny Weismuller didn't have a look in, regrettably to my terror, the shark was relentless in its pursuit, as it silently, stalked me. I felt my heart pounding and beating so hard and fast, that it must surely burst out from my chest.

My mates stood on the beach watching in bewilderment, my arms flailing like a windmill, my legs kicking like pistons, moving me rapidly through the water, then mercifully I reached shallow water only to become conscious that the 'shark' was my own shadow.

I was engulfed with a feeling of enormous relief, and then a moment later I felt particularly ridiculous, especially when my mates began questioning,

"What on earth was all that for Geordie"? "Are you training for the Olympics?"

Still feeling exceptionally ludicrous and knowing that I would be ridiculed if they ever discovered the truth, I answered nonchalantly,

“Oh I just felt like having a hard work out.”

Another day I swam out to the raft, only to discover four strangers lounging there, it soon became apparent to me that they were soldiers from another regiment, and whom should I notice sitting amongst them, but my two best mates, Mike and John. As I began to clamber aboard, the visitors were of the opinion that I was an Arab, as having served in Tripoli for over two years the sun had turned my skin to a dark nut-brown colour and since having almost black hair, in retrospect I can understand their blunder.

They point blankly refused to allow me to climb onto the raft and each time I tried to pull myself up; they pushed me away shouting,

“This raft is reserved for British personnel only, there are no foreigners allowed, fuck off”

“But I **am** a British soldier; I'm serving with the R. E. M. E.” I was yelling,

My pals Mike and John, as usual decided to clown around, so made the decision to join in with the banter,

“He’s **not** a British soldier, we know him, he’s an Arab cleaner, who works in our camp”, “Get off you bastard”, they bellowed.

However, after a while, they conceded and helped to pull me on board the raft, where we all saw the funny side.

Chapter 8

One afternoon a young soldier parked a huge wagon immediately outside the window of Colonel Bradley's office; as a result, it blocked out the sunshine and cast a large shadow across the room, thus darkening his office. This infuriated the Colonel who instantly stormed to the office door; he threw it open with passion and ordered a passing soldier,

"MOVE THAT FUCKIN WAGON,"

To which the soldier sheepishly replied,
"Sorry Sir, I can't drive."
"WHAT? WHAT? CANT DRIVE" the colonel roared,
"RIGHT, EVERY ONE IN THE REGIMENT WILL TAKE DRIVING LESSONS AND BE ABLE TO DRIVE WITHIN SIX WEEKS, THAT'S AN ORDER."

Sure enough, a notice appeared on Orders the very next morning, stating that everyone who held a full driving licence were appointed with immediate effect, to be driving instructors, also pinned on the board was a roster, whereby every hour, every day, there were compulsory driving lessons for the non-drivers.

The lessons were executed in our large wagons and to begin with, were confined to within the camp boundaries, however after a few days practice; they progressed on to the deserted sandy roads outside the camp.

Subsequently after two weeks of concentrated lessons, the driving instructors sorted out the learner drivers into two categories, the first group consisted of learners who in their opinion were ready to take the test, and the second group still novices who they considered would need extra tuition.

I was astonished to be selected, as the first soldier they thought good enough to take the driving test, I supposed that it may well have been that I was a full Corporal and so given preferential treatment.
However, on the day of my test, I was feeling very apprehensive as I sat behind the wheel of the wagon with the examiner, who was one of our Sgt. Majors in the passenger seat. He instructed me to drive out through the camp gates, and to continue along the track, which led into Tripoli, it being a distance of some eight miles.

I arrived safely in Tripoli, with no mishaps, and drove past the magnificent King's Palace, which faced the sea front; regrettably, as I approached an enormous roundabout, I found myself suddenly confronted with obstacles that I had never experienced during my limited driving lessons.
To my dismay, there were actually other obstacles on the road, such as,
'Vehicles, donkeys, horses, carts, and pedestrians.' "Fuckin hell, what do I do now?" "**Help**".

The Sgt. Major instructor ordered me to take a right turn, and to drive through an archway, which happened to be the gateway into the Old City; I dutifully carried out his instructions only to find myself in a narrow street, which, to my disbelief, was not much wider than the wagon, which I was driving. Suddenly to my alarm, I noticed dozens of Arabs who were sound asleep and lying on either side of the narrow road; apparently, this was the time of day for their Siesta.

Since I lacked the experience of driving amongst even the lightest of traffic, never mind a crowd of sleeping people, I obviously panicked and stamped onto what I believed was the brake, but shit, it was the accelerator, consequently the wagon lurched rapidly forward. To this day I can still see the chaos this caused, I can plainly visualise the fear on the faces of the Arabs, when after being so rudely awakened, they leapt to their feet screaming in terror as they scattered in all directions, frantically throwing themselves out of the path of this three-ton monster which was bearing down upon them. Many jumped into doorways, others darted into narrow alleyways whilst the remainder flattened themselves against walls.

Eventually, after a period of time, which felt at least five minutes, but in reality was probably only a few seconds, I managed to compose myself and my foot automatically found and hit on the brake. I quickly calmed down and after collecting myself, turned to look at the Sgt. Major who was visibly shocked.

“I think we better return to camp don’t you?” he said.

Dejected, I thought to myself,

“Well, I’ve made a right balls of that.”

Upon arriving back at camp, I was marched into Colonel Bradley’s office, accompanied by the Sgt. Major, the Colonel who was perched behind his desk enquired,

“Well Sgt. Major, how did Corporal Jackson do?”

I sheepishly stood and listened as the Sgt. Major quickly enlightened the Colonel, giving him explicit details of my escapade. Colonel Bradley who well known for his sense of humour grinned and replied,

“Do you think that with a bit of practice Corporal Jackson could do better next time?”

“Yes Sir I'm sure he could.” Sgt. Major replied.

“PASS” bellowed the colonel.

Although flabbergasted, since it was the last thing I had expected, I was obviously delighted, but then was utterly stunned when, an HOUR later my name, Corporal Jackson went up on Orders, I was now officially a,

"DRIVING INSTRUCTOR."

Sure enough after six weeks of intensive driving lessons, all the soldiers in our regiment had indeed passed their tests to become qualified drivers, whether we would have passed in civilian life is questionable. However all passed, with one exception, and that was a very quiet soldier, a Craftsman named Hill who took his driving test four times and failed miserably on each occasion. Our Colonel was extremely frustrated, and accused him of wasting everyone's time, then as an after thought, he ordered that Craftsman Hill be taught to ride a motorbike.

One day, about three weeks later, a group of engineers had the task of repairing a tank gun, positioned outside our workshop next to a large metal reservoir, this reservoir contained acid and was used to dip and clean metal parts of vehicles in preparation for re-painting. Unpredictably Hill, who was having another of his countless motorbike lessons, came roaring from around the corner with the instructor as pillion passenger perched nervously behind. Hill was driving so fast that he could not stop and lost control of the bike and the inevitable happened. We all stood helplessly watching as the bike rammed into the acid container, as a result, the traumatized instructor catapulted through the air, over Hill's head and to everyone's shock, dropped like a stone into the tank of acid.

Fortunately, the numerous soldiers who had witnessed the whole travesty, raced to his aid, pulled him out, and fortunately had the insight to immediately hose him down with copious amounts of water before whisking him off to hospital. Mercifully, there were no adverse effects, and the fact that he was wearing close fitting goggles, meant that luckily his eyes had been protected.

Chapter 9

Serving in our regiment was an older Sgt. Major, who originated from Scotland, he, being a career soldier, had proudly served his country and had been involved in numerous battles and skirmishes throughout the Second World War. Consequently, the breast of his uniform was covered with medals awarded for actions of bravery, however being in his late fifties he was nearing retirement age.

This Sgt. Major was greatly respected and held in high

esteem, he was regarded as a grandfather figure by all the young soldiers in our regiment who, in times of stress, would turn to him for advice. If any of the lads were experiencing problems, no matter how trivial, they would approach him for guidance. Being very understanding, he always lent a sympathetic ear and gave first class counselling.

In his soft Scottish brogue, he constantly talked lovingly about his wife, he praised her to the extreme and made it clear to us that he could not exist without her, he said she was his right arm, and he loved and respected her, he undoubtedly had her up on a pedestal. There were six Scottish lads in our regiment who went everywhere together and it came like a bolt out of the blue when one day, to our amazement, they began to brag to us, that each and every one of them was having full intercourse and oral sex with the Sgt. Major's wife. They said she was a nymphomaniac and was game for anything, including group sex. We did not believe a word of it and thought they were having a sick joke; we accused them of fantasizing and talking bollocks, we warned them to shut up, saying that they would ruin her reputation.

One night, one of the Scotsman, who was in our billet, a

Craftsman Campbell, asked Mike, John and myself if we wanted to accompany them to the Caledonian Club for a social night of music, dancing and drinking. The Caledonian Club was situated on the sea front in Tripoli, and was patronised by Scottish servicemen, their families and invited guests. After a short discussion, the three of us decided that it would make a pleasant change from our usual routine of drinking in the N.A.F.F.I. so accepted. We changed into our best civilian clothes to meet up with the group of Scottish lads and together we made our way to the club in Tripoli and had a thoroughly enjoyable night.

As we were leaving, the six Scotsmen were just behind and followed us out into the street; we were mystified to witness that the Sgt. Major's wife was accompanying them. She was strolling in-between two of the soldiers, who both had an arm around her and were pawing her, we could not help but notice that one soldier had his hand inside her blouse and the other had a hand up her skirt, and she seemed to be in ecstasy. Even though they were trailing about five yards behind us, it was clearly visible that she had a hand inside one of the soldiers' trousers and was giving him a hand job.

Suddenly, Campbell who was holding her around the waist shouted out to me,
“Geordie, come and join us, you can shag her”.
I looked at him in disbelief; he turned to her and asked,
“You'll give Geordie a good shag, won't you?”
“Yes you know I will, the more the merrier.” she replied,

I shuddered with revulsion, she was almost as old as my granny, and was a skinny old hag that I would not touch with a barge pole.
I vehemently declined and said “No thanks”.
As we hurried away, Campbell shouted,
“You don’t know what you’re missing Geordie”.
I muttered under my breath that I did not want to know.

The three of us were absolutely gob-smacked in the realisation that they had been telling the truth all along and it did not take any imagination to realise what antics she was going to get up to with the six soldiers. Mike, John and I felt truly sorry for the Sgt. Major, our hearts truly went out to him and we desperately hoped that he would never find out what his *lovely* wife was getting up to.

Mike, John and Myself.

Two other corporals in my billet were a Cpl. Nichols and a Cpl. Atkinson, both older soldiers, in their late thirties and both having previous experience of active service during the Second World War. Cpl. Nichols was exceedingly well spoken; and if you did not know better you would naturally assume that, he must be an Officer.

Together, even thought they were not Scottish, they organised the Tombola, which was held once a week at the Caledonian Club, and were employed as caller and number checker.

One day Cpl. Nichols, during conversation with Mike, John, Robbie and I, suggested to us,

"I've had a great idea, why don't you come to the club to play Tombola? arrive early before the rush so you will be guaranteed seats in the font row. Then during the game, if any of you need only two or three numbers, mouth the numbers up to me and no matter which number I pick out of the bag, I will call your number out and afterwards we'll all share the prize money".

We believed this to be a great proposition, thinking that it would be enormously funny, especially if we got away with it. We carried out the scheme for five weeks and considered it a good laugh. We, as arranged, mouthed the required numbers to Nichols, subsequently we won every single time, and afterwards met up with Nichols and Atkinson to share out our ill- gotten spoils, which was invariably spent on booze. Naturally, it was only a matter of time before our scam was detected, that night came when it was Mike's turn to shout, "House".

Suddenly a woman who was participating in the game, jumped up, pointed to us and shouted at the top of her voice, "It's a fix, they win every week, I insist the board is checked". Cpl. Nichols had the presence of mind to say nonchalantly, "Yes of course, madam, no problem".

However as he stood up,

"Oh shit," he *'accidentally'* tipped the wooden board over, consequently the numbers on the board and all the uncalled numbers from the bag were *unfortunately* scattered all over the floor, making it virtually impossible to verify the claim.

Needless to say, to the objector's delight, Cpl's Nichols and Atkinson were instantly sacked and advised their services were no longer required.

Chapter 10

There was only one tree in the whole of our camp area; this was a beautiful Palm tree, located outside Colonel Bradley's office. Because he preferred to be out in the fresh air, rather than to be stuck indoors in his hot stuffy office, he commandeered the tree by positioning a table and chair underneath the cool shade of the foliage. Colonel Bradley was an ex S.A.S. Officer, and a very heavy drinker and every day without fail, he gathered his work together, then armed with a bottle of Scotch he sat in the sanctuary of the Palm tree, to complete his paperwork, and to drink from the bottle of scotch until it was empty.

One evening, the usual gang of six, myself, Mike, John, Robbie, Cpl. Nichols and Cpl. Atkinson, were drinking in the N.A.F.F.I. however, being thoroughly bored; we decided to play a game called Pokey Die. This is a game played with two dice; and involves a great deal of the mixing of alcoholic drinks, inevitably, we became so intoxicated that we began to look for mischief. Previously, tomfoolery by us was normally no more harmful than breaking into the cookhouse to cook ourselves breakfast, usually at about 3 o'clock in the morning.

However, this particular night, having drunk more than usual, we were extremely inebriated, and Nichols, being the mastermind, slurred,

"I've got an idea; I know what to do, follow me".

It was two o'clock in the morning as we drunkenly trailed behind him as he made his way to the storeroom, once there he started to grope around until finally he singled out an object, which he slung over his shoulder. He marched, or should I say drunkenly staggered, across the square, the rest of us following like sheep in a single file, singing at the top of our voices,

“Hi Ho‘, Hi Ho’ ’It’s off to work we go.”

Hands on heart, we honestly didn't realise what his intentions were; maybe it was because we were pissed out of our minds, however upon arriving at the Palm tree we could only look on in disbelief as Nichols took a large axe from his shoulder and systematically set to work and chopped the palm tree down. That instantly sobered us up, the only vegetation for miles, the Colonel's favourite shaded drinking place, gone, what on earth would he do? We could only imagine his reaction.

Next morning, whilst the regiment was on Parade, the Colonel's Land Rover came roaring into the square and screeched to a halt; out jumped the Colonel who stopped in his tracks to stare down, in disbelief at his treasured tree, a sorry sight lying limp in the sand.

“WHAT THE FUCK” he screamed.

He went off on a tangent; he ranted and raged I had never

ever seen him so infuriated, he insisted that the perpetrator give himself up, however, understandably being fearful of the consequences, no one was ready to take the blame so we all kept silent.

"Everyone in the camp will be confined to Barracks," the Colonel bellowed,

"This punishment will continue until the culprit owns up." he seethed.

As the days passed by and no-one came forward to admit to the crime, the Colonel, after his initial fury, began to feel proud that the soldiers in HIS regiment had stuck together, and were steadfastly being loyal and faithful to each other by not coming forward to incriminate their guilty comrades. He believed that this was how a regiment should be, honourable and dependable, thereby lifted the confinement order.

Situated a few miles from our camp was an American Base, which had its own radio station that transmitted music twenty-four hours a day and since our camp had access to the music, it was broadcast into our barrack rooms, the N.A.A.F.I. the British bars in Tripoli as well as to the beach.

The most popular type of music played was Country and Western, and as this is my favourite music, I was in my element.
This American radio station ran a request programme to collect donations for charity, the programme was broadcast every single night and anyone who wished to make a charitable monetary gift telephoned the station. These conversations were broadcast live over the air, and the individual contributing, requested their choice of record and stated the amount of money they were donating, subsequently the requested record was played repetitively, over and over again, until someone else pledged a higher donation to take it off the air.

It was two weeks after the tree chopping down incident that my mates and I were drinking in The Corner House, which was a British bar in Tripoli, when suddenly Cpl. Nichols vanished without saying a word. A moment or two later we were flabbergasted upon hearing an upper class voice coming loud and clear over the American radio request programme. There was no mistaking that cut glass accent; we knew immediately that it was Cpl. Nichols, who said,

"The Corporals Mess at Number One Base Workshops is pledging twenty-five pounds to charity, the record is specifically requested for our Colonel Bradley and is, The Woodchoppers Ball".

My mates and I glanced at each other, eyes wide open with disbelief, then we burst out laughing, this was typical of Cpl. Nichols who, a moment later came nonchalantly strolling back into the bar, he looked at us and said innocently,

"WHAT?"

The Woodchoppers Ball was played loud, clear, and was repeated over and over, again and again, until hours later that night, someone else made a higher donation to request another record.

Next day Colonel Bradley made it known to the regiment that he had heard the request and even though it was rubbing salt into the wound, typically he took it in good humour and the subject was never mentioned again.

It was at breakfast time that we British soldiers definitely did not appreciate the American radio station. Queuing up for breakfast, which was usually porridge and it being so thick and sticky would not drop off the spoon so the cooks had to knock the ladle onto the edge of our plates for the portion to fall off. This was bad enough without having to endure the lazy drawl of an American voice coming loud and clear over the air.

"C'mon guys, wakey wakey, it's another nice mornin, if ya don't hurry up ya'll aall miss breakfast. We gat haam, eggs, burgers, mushrooms, pancakes and home made blueberry pie, we've had fresh milk flown over from Germany so cum an git it."

Our lads moaned and shouted obscenities; some even took their boots off to throw at the loudspeakers before sitting down to consume our thick, barely warm, porridge.

Izzy, a civilian worker in our workshops was my interpreter, he was Jewish and spoke perfect English and was also fluent in Arabic and Italian. Izzy was married and lived with his wife and parents in an apartment situated in a three-storied block of flats in the centre of Tripoli. One morning Izzy invited Mike and me to a rooftop party, which was being organised by the residents of the flats, the majority of which were American servicemen and their families.

We arrived at eight p.m. to find the party was already in full swing, with some of the guests sitting astride a three-foot wall, which encircled the flat roof. The American soldiers had brought boxes full to the brim with Country and Western records, and everyone was singing, dancing, and having a great time.

The guests were offered free booze all night so obviously after a while; some of the guests became the worse for wear. I was sitting on the wall next to Mike, beer in hand and on my right was a Yank serviceman. Suddenly out of the corner of my eye, I was horrified to notice the American begin to slowly fall backwards. It seemed almost as if it were happening in slow motion; however, my reflexes were so finely tuned that I was able to grab him before he fell the forty feet onto the concrete to almost certain death.

Although extremely inebriated and visibly shaken he managed to mumble,

"God daamit maan, how caan I thank yah, yah saved mah life".

At that precise moment, a female voice, presumably his wife's, screamed.

"Yah stupid arsehole you're always drunk, I'm sick of yah.

Why don’t yah just jump an git it over with”.

She, herself completely smashed, staggered over to hurl herself at her husband, nails at the ready, however her husband clumsily grabbed her and began to kiss her passionately saying,

“C’mon babe, yah know yah luv me”.

A moment later, they left the party embraced in each others arms, swearing undying love to each other.

It was not until seven thirty the next morning that the party finally broke up, and it was while making our way back to camp that we passed a café and decided to buy a cup of tea to try to sober up. We were sitting at a table happily chatting, when this guy came up to me, and said.

“I’d recognise that Geordie accent anywhere.”

He introduced himself as Sammy Curle, and said he originated from County Durham; he was about thirty years old, good looking in a rugged way and immaculately dressed in civilian clothes. During conversation, he explained he was in the East York’s Regiment and being fluent in Arabic was employed as an instructor attached to the Libyan Army.

Subsequently, on several occasions, when out drinking in Tripoli, we met up with him and his wife. It was during one of those meetings and when in our usual drinking den, The Corner House, that some of the many American servicemen at the bar, began to move the tables to the outer edge of the room to allow a black soldier to take to the floor to tap-dance to the music emitting from the juke-box. He was fantastic, so supple and agile, we watched on in amazement as he frantically tapped to the loud ovation from the audience, however it was half way though his dance that Sammy Curle rose from his chair and said,
"I'll show him how it's done."

Because he had drunk several pints of beer, Mike and I were worried that he would make an ass of himself so restrained him, however his wife leant forward and said,
"Let him get up,"
To our astonishment, the landlord introduced him as, '***Sgt. Major*** Curle,' he had certainly kept that a secret.
He walked into the centre of the floor and began his routine; you could have knocked us down with a feather. We could not believe our eyes, he was spectacular, not only was his tap-

dancing breathtaking, but he also threw in the most athletic moves imaginable, back flips, forward flips, somersaults, he even did the splits, the audience showed their appreciation of his performance with thunderous applause.

Eat your heart out Gene Kelly.

Outside the barrack gates, was an area, which was designated as a taxi rank for several horse drawn carriages, locally known as Garri's, as this was a very cheap convenient way to travel, they were habitually used to transport soldiers into the town of Tripoli. One night, Mike and I decided to go to the Corner House, and after changing into our best civilian clothes were clambering into a Garri when suddenly a Craftsman Thomson, who was in our regiment, approached and asked if he could accompany us saying he would share the travelling expense, we readily agreed.

As we reached the town centre, the Garri stopped at a junction to allow traffic to clear, then unexpectedly a young girl reeking of cheap perfume, hopped into the carriage and sat down on the vacant seat next to Thomson, who was sitting opposite Mike and me. She was an attractive girl and although of Arabian appearance was attired in modern western style clothing and even though slim, had a more than generous bust with plenty of cleavage showing. She immediately began to touch Thomson sexually and as her slim hands quickly found his crotch, she asked quietly,

"You want to fuck me Jonnie?

I had a fleeting pang of jealousy, and thought the lucky bastard; however, these thoughts were quickly dispelled when remembering the film clips shown to us when first enlisting, which showed the horrors of venereal diseases.

Mike and I were amused to notice that Thomson was instantly aroused by the bulge in his trousers, which was increasing by the second.

Thomson was visibly trembling with excitement, his face flushed with expectation and as they scrambled out of the Garri, he said,

"I will see you in the Corner House in half an hour,"

"More like five minutes," we said flippantly.

We were not far wrong, since it was only a matter of minutes after Mike and I had crossed the threshold of the Corner House that a red-faced Thomson came running in like a 'Bat out of Hell' .

"That didn't take long," we laughingly said.

Thomson almost incoherent, stuttered,

"I was ready to shag her, but when I put my hand down to steer my dick in, she wasn't a '*she*' after all, '*she*' was a '*he*,' and to pour salt onto the wound his dick was twice as big as mine".

We were doubled up with laughter and advised him to visit an optician.

Chapter 11

There was great rivalry between the American servicemen and us British troops, and when 'boozed up' there were numerous punch-ups, mostly at weekends and mainly in the Corner House, they were so frequent in fact that they almost seemed to be traditional and expected.

One night an American who was truly inebriated was holding a pint of beer in one hand, the other fist was thumping his chest whilst yelling at the top of his voice,

“Mah daaddy caan beat anyone in Arizona; aan aah caan beat mah daaddy”.
At that precise moment, a British soldier who wanted to place an order for beer began to push his way through the drinkers congregating around the bar when accidentally he bumped into the American, causing him to spill his beer.
“Ya Limey mother fucker,” he screamed, “Aahl pull yer fuckin head off”

He lurched forward, grabbed the offending soldier, and was trying to throttle him, I saw red, *how dare he attack one of my compatriots*. I stepped forward and threw a short right which floored the American, who although dazed, looked up and said,
“Aahl remember you, you Limey bastard.”
I said. “Get stuffed” or words to that effect.

In the centre of Tripoli was a very exclusive gambling club named the Del Mahari, which was frequented by American servicemen, they being the only ones who could afford to patronise it. However, one night myself and three of my usual mates had been playing three-card brag in the N.A.A.F.I and had been on a roll and won several pounds, therefore, believing it was our lucky night, we decided to indulge ourselves and visit the casino to play roulette.

Upon entering, we purchased our beer and began to make our way over to the gambling tables, when suddenly Mike nudged me and nodded his head over to the end of the bar, and who should be standing there but the American I had downed two weeks earlier. He instantly recognised me and I noticed he was gesturing and pointing at me so I realised that he was explaining the previous incident to his compatriots, and the word was noticeably being spread around the hundred or so Yanks who were drinking at the bar, soon menacing looks were being thrown in our direction and Mike solemnly said,

"Try not to look conspicuous, but walk backwards until we reach the door,"

We took his advice, and sipped from our glasses whilst nonchalantly taking a couple of steps backwards, we repeated this procedure until we were about three yards from the door, then quickly glanced at each other and shouted,

"Go."

We began to run as fast as our legs would carry us, laughing so much that we were almost crying.

"We felt like actors in a wild west film!"

Another day Mike and I were making our way back to camp after having had a typically heavy boozing session and as we were walking through an Arab village, we found, due to the excess amount of alcohol we had consumed, that we were very unsteady on our feet. Unfortunately, I stumbled sideways at the precise moment that a local Arab Police Officer was cycling past.

In the ensuing collision, he was regrettably thrown from his bike to land in a crumpled heap on the ground and as he lay motionless, the villagers, who seemed to appear from nowhere, moved forward to encircle us, muttering and mumbling as they closed in.

Mike and I were in a quandary wondering just what to do next, when thankfully, out of the blue, one of our army Land Rovers appeared on the scene, and two Military Policemen jumped out. However not being able to speak Arabic, they were confused and unable to understand what the villagers were saying, however by the angry gesticulating and shouting they thought, for our own safety they had better take us back to camp. Consequently, to our disbelief, they promptly arrested us and threw us into jail.

Upon hearing the details of what happened, all the lads in my billet were warning,

"You've done it now Geordie, you will get at least two years confinement in an Arab jail."

"You'll need to be Houdini to get out of this one Geordie."

The next morning Colonel Bradley immediately sent two Red Caps together with an interpreter to the village to take a statement from the Police Officer cyclist, then a couple of hours later, having received the signed evidence, the Colonel, requested I attend his office at once.

It was whilst anxiously standing to attention at his desk that I noticed the Colonel was frowning deeply, so I felt extremely nervous and wondered just what my fate would be, maybe my mates were right, I visualised myself languishing in an Arab jail.

Suddenly the Colonel began to read aloud the Arab's statement, which accused me of deliberately and maliciously

pushing him off his bike.
“This can’t possibly be true Corporal Jackson?” The Colonel enquired in a disbelieving voice.
“No Sir, of course not, it was a pure accident” I replied
“I thought as much. This is a whole load of bollocks,” he said, and with that, he tore the statement into little pieces.
“Dismissed Corporal Jackson.”
“Sir.”

Phew!

Next morning I was summoned to Colonel Bradley’s office, this time he instructed me to go to the Armoury to contact the duty Sgt. Major and request that I be issued with a Bren gun and to also draw all the unused boxes of ‘out of date’ ammunition from the stores.
The Colonel said I had to use all the ammo up to get rid of it, however it was not until I was issued with numerous boxes filled to capacity with hundreds of rounds of live bullets, that I realised it would take me most of the day to carry out the task.
The layout of our Station Workshops was as such, the site

was surrounded by a high brick wall and there was an open sandy square in the centre. This design meant that the work units, stores and offices were built around three sides of the perimeter, and constructed at the other end of the square, was a firing range which was created from an elevated sand bank, it was to this firing range that the store men carried the boxes of ammo. I settled myself into a comfortable position, loaded the Bren gun and began firing into the sand bank; I continued this laborious task for about two hours when unpredictably the gun jammed. I assumed that it was caused by overheating so decided to remove the magazine, as I casually reached forward, 'fuckin hell' the butt of the gun dropped heavily onto the ground thus freeing the blockage, as a result the gun, being on automatic, began to move slowly from side to side firing rapidly and indiscriminately. Shit, I was shocked to notice the bullets were ricocheting off the top of the walls and onto the work units, and both soldiers and workers alike were screaming and dodging bullets as they ran for their lives.

Quickly composing myself, I somehow managed to grab the butt of the gun to control the line of fire, and just carried on with the repetitive task of firing at the target.

Well I had to break the monotony somehow!

I was set in a regular routine, life for me was, every morning I organised the work in the workshops and made sure that the jobs were running smoothly, then early afternoon I went to the beach with my mates to swim before taking part in sporting activities later in the day, then of course not forgetting boozing every evening. Each day was identical, until Christmas Eve of Nineteen Fifty-Four, it was because four of our usual drinking buddies were on guard duty and therefore unable to accompany us that Mike and I decided to celebrate Christmas Eve, with just the two of us going into Tripoli at about two o'clock in the afternoon.

When we British servicemen were first posted to North Africa, on arrival it was strongly recommended that we never, ever drink the local beer. My mates and I had always adhered to this advice, but on this specific Christmas Eve after having drank several of our usual brew, which happened to be a Maltese beer, Mike and I were quite tipsy and unwisely thought it would be a good idea to visit one of the local café/bars for a change.

After downing a couple of pints of the 'forbidden' local beer, we considered that we'd had enough alcohol and summoned a

Garri to take us back to camp.

Being Christmas Eve, everyone at camp had been celebrating, and all and sundry seemed to be the worse for drink, including the Officers, the Duty Sergeant, the N.C.O's and also the drivers so we found ourselves having to step over several prone figures of drunks slumped on the floor.
Mike and I were both due a stint of guard duty, which was due to commence at six o'clock that afternoon, and somehow, even though we'd had 'one over the eight' we managed to stumble to our billet and change into our best uniforms. This accomplished, we clambered aboard the wagons, to be driven to the guardhouses, to relieve the regimental Police on guard duty. Mike was driven to One Base workshops whilst I was driven to Station workshop, where being full Corporal, my duty was, guard commander, which meant I was in charge of changing and checking guards, and also responsible for writing out reports.

It was about one-thirty in the morning that I began to feel dreadful and very weird, I caught sight of a reflection in the glass door of the guardroom, and I could not quite make out

the bizarre image that was peering back at me. I saw a grotesque, hideously distorted face, swelled up to about twice its normal size, I was shocked by the spectacle staring back at me, it resembled a monster from a horror movie, I soon realised to my despair that it was my own image.
I panicked and frantically shook my second in command, to rouse him from his sleep; he sat up, took one look at me, reeled back in shock then hastily telephoned a guard who arrived a few minutes later with a wagon, they helped me into the passenger seat and drove me to the British Military Hospital in Tripoli.

We arrived at the hospital at 2 o'clock a.m., Christmas Day morning, to find the usually hectic accident and emergency department deserted, and there did not appear to be any staff on duty. I was told the staff were either, still partying, or had crashed out and were sleeping off the effects of the booze. Eventually, the driver, after some frantic searching, managed to find a Staff Nurse to attend to me; she took one look at me, and not being able to determine my condition, immediately summoned a doctor, who incidentally, had to be awoken from a deep drunken sleep. Even though I felt extremely ill, I could not help noticing his breath, which nearly bowled me over as it reeked strongly of whisky.

After being briefly examined and questioned by the doctor, he said in his opinion, the local beer had poisoned me. He instructed the Staff nurse to admit me into the hospital at once, and wrote out a prescription for medication. I was escorted to a bed in one of the wards, whereupon the nurse began to remove my clothes, however feeling extremely embarrassed I insisted that I undress myself. I clumsily fumbled about until I eventually managed; and then struggled to don the army pyjamas, which the nurse had issued to me. Finally when I was ready, the nurse helped me into bed and administered an injection, this was an exceptionally thick needle attached to a massive syringe filled with liquid; I went out like a light falling asleep instantaneously. Finally waking up, I felt much better and aware that I was ravenously hungry; I sat up and requested breakfast from a nurse, who said,

"Oh you're back with the living!"

To my astonishment, she told me that it was not Christmas Day, as I strongly believed, it was in fact Boxing Day, meaning I had been comatose for thirty hours. I was shocked to say the least, fancy missing Santa Claus. Although I was, feeling much improved and my face thankfully back to normal; the doctor's orders were, that I be kept in hospital for five days under observation.

Eventually after being given the all clear, I was finally discharged from hospital and arrived back at camp, where, after assuring everyone that I was fine, my pals began enquiring,

"Have you heard about your mate Mike?"

"No" I answered.

They all laughed and said,

"Go and ask him what happened."

I walked into the billet and found Mike sitting on his bed; peering quizzically at him I asked,

"Well, what have you been up to now, what is everyone laughing about?"

He sheepishly explained,

"On Christmas Eve, the guard, knowing that I was your best mate, thought I should be informed, that you had been rushed to hospital, and that you might be seriously ill, so he rang to tell me."

Mike said that upon being told that I had been whisked off to hospital, he being exceptionally drunk had thought,
"If Ron is ill then I must be ill."

He immediately called a guard saying that he was feeling terrible; as a result, the guard had instantly summoned a wagon, to take him to hospital. Upon arrival, being extremely late, about three o'clock in the morning, the doctor, who had diagnosed my illness, was once again interrupted from his sleep and called upon to examine Mike. However, this time he was justifiably, extremely irate, especially when he realised he was confronted with a time waster.
The doctor ordered the Staff nurse to give Mike a bed for the night, then gave instructions for a specific treatment, to be administered to him the following morning.

After a deep drunken sleep Mike awoke on Christmas morning to the aroma of breakfast, consisting of bacon, eggs and tomatoes, which was being served to the patients, Mike began to pester the nurses by constantly asking,
"When am I going to get my breakfast? I'm famished."
However, they completely ignored him.
After a while the Staff nurse marched up to Mike's bed and

said,
"The Doctor said it is essential you receive your treatment turn over please,"
She thereupon administered an enema, and then ordered him out of bed; she instructed him to get dressed and then threw him out of the hospital, needless to say, without any breakfast.
Mike said he had begged for transport to bring him back to camp, however his plea's fell on deaf ears, they said he was a malingerer and point blankly refused; therefore, he was forced to walk the eight miles back to camp.

Mike said he only made it to the hospital gates before the enema took effect, he said he left a trail of liquid shit behind him as he stumbled from the hospital to the camp gates. I could visualise it as plain as day and was in hysterics, the whole billet was in an uproar with everyone splitting their sides laughing.

I remembered that someone once called him 'a little shit.'

It was soon after this, that our camp was hit by an outbreak of dysentery and out of the three billets, which each housed forty soldiers, there were at least seventy men struck down with the debilitating bug.

Each day upon returning to the billet following completion of work, we would find another bed empty as yet another soldier yielded to the weakening infection. Mike, John and I were lucky enough to escape the virus but our pal Robbie unfortunately succumbed to the bacteria.

A few days later, the three of us decided to visit Robbie in hospital but upon entering the ward, we almost collapsed as the stench overwhelmed us it was so nauseating.

Whilst there, every few minutes we witnessed one soldier after another frantically shout,

"Nurse, bed pan, NURSE."

Then would quickly leap out of bed, run towards the toilets desperately holding his arse, but nine out of ten times, he failed to reach his destination in time. We were retching with revulsion as we rushed outside to thankfully gulp in mouthfuls of fresh air, we couldn't get out of the hospital gates quickly enough, leaving behind the poor nurses to mop up the stinking mess on the floor.

Chapter 12

One morning our Sgt. Major sought me out to inform me that Colonel Bradley wanted to see me in his office at once. I knew the Colonel respected and thought highly of me and I firmly believed this was because he was an avid boxing fan and admired my boxing skills. I was curious to know the reason why he wanted to see me so urgently, although upon entering his office I was soon to discover the reason why, when he ordered me to,

“Stand at ease Jackson”.

He began to read out aloud, details from a document, which he was holding; it soon became apparent that it was the record history of a soldier who had been posted to our camp and due to arrive the following day.

The soldier’s name was Craftsman Ferguson, who was twenty-seven years old and originated from Leeds. He was serving in the army as a regular soldier having initially signed on for twenty-two years. However, it was reputed that he had the most vicious short temper imaginable and had only just been released from Military Prison after serving a four-year sentence for extreme violence, having horrifically wounded two soldiers with a glass bottle.

Colonel Bradley peered at me; I could swear there was a hint of a smile at the corner of his mouth as he said,

“Jackson, take the day off work tomorrow and wait for the wagon, I want you to sort this tough guy out, I won’t tolerate any intimidation from him, I want you to put him into your billet and keep a stringent eye on him, I‘ve got every confidence in your ability to keep him under control. ”

Trying to stay cool, I replied.

"Yes sir."

The next day I stayed off work and lounged about on the steps of the veranda, attached to our billet, to await the wagon, my stomach was churning with apprehension as the wagon appeared and stopped just a few yards away. I watched as Ferguson stood up in the back of the wagon, he was a dark haired, good-looking man, about ten stones in weight, with a very good physique, which was understandable after serving four years in detention, seeing that prisoners are forced to run everywhere and are required to carry out all tasks at double time. In addition, most of their spare time is spent implementing physical exercises, so I could fully comprehend just why he had such a phenomenal body. He lifted up his kit bag, threw it onto the ground and as he jumped off the wagon, I approached him and said,

"Ferguson, you are in my billet, your objectionable reputation has preceded you, and I have heard all about your unsavoury past, but understand this, I won't stand for any trouble, so don't go throwing your fuckin weight around "

"Give a dog a bad name." He mumbled under his breath.

Sullenly he dragged his kit bag into the billet and threw it onto the bed, which I said had been allocated to him; he plonked himself down, stretched out and lay very quiet and sulky.

In reality, over the next few weeks Ferguson made quite a lot of friends, as, when sober, he was very affable and well liked, although when drunk was very aggressive and obnoxious.

A month later, I was once again called into Colonel Bradley's office, to find myself going through the same rigmarole as before with Ferguson. Yet another tough guy, this time, an ex Sergeant, who had been demoted down to Craftsman, he, like Ferguson, had served time in Military Prison for excessive violence, and having just been released had been transferred to our camp and was due to arrive the following day.

This ex prisoner's name was Anderson, once again, I sat on the steps waiting for the wagon to bring him to camp, Anderson had a strong Glaswegian dialect, he was a big guy in his mid thirties and weighed about fourteen stones, he was fair-haired and sported a handlebar moustache. I went through the same instructions with him as I had with Ferguson and told him I would not stand for any nonsense, and then directed him to his bed in my billet.

A moment later, Ferguson strolled into the billet, noticed Anderson and yelled with astonishment then beaming with delight, he went straight over to Anderson and they hugged each other and shook hands vigorously, obviously overjoyed to see each other. It seemed as if they were long lost brothers. It transpired that they were the best of pals having served time together in Military Prison. The rest of my mates in the billet gave me a knowing look; we all had the same thoughts going through our minds:

"Trouble with a capital T."

That very first evening, Ferguson and Anderson decided to have a night out in Tripoli, so in preparation, they showered and changed into their civilian clothes. I acknowledged that they would surely get pissed out of their minds so cautioned them as they left the billet saying,

"I don't care what time you get back, just don't make a nuisance of yourselves, be quiet, and don't waken everyone when you come into the billet".

"Right Geordie," they both mumbled.

I couldn't sleep that night and lay waiting in trepidation, expecting the worst, then low and behold, at one o'clock in the morning, I heard them staggering about outside the billet, both drunkenly slurring at the top of their voices,
“Ahh belang ti Glasgy.”

I heard Ferguson say, “Shh, shh, Geordie’ll hear yi”
“Aal nay shh, I don’t give a fuck aboot Geordie, A’m ganna kick the fuckin door doon.” Anderson shouted.

He proceeded to kick the billet door open with such ferocity that it almost came off it’s hinges, he switched on the lights, then switched the radio on blasting it up to full volume. By then I had reached him, I grabbed him by the neck and bodily threw him down onto his bed and said,
“I’ll deal with you in the morning when you’re sober.”

I turned the radio off and apologised to the other lads, telling them to try to get back to sleep, I switched out the lights, and just as I was climbing back into bed, I heard an almighty commotion. All hell broke loose; I ran over to the switch and turned the lights on, only to see Ferguson and Anderson knocking the living daylights out of each other, I shrugged my shoulders and decided to let them get on with it. Next morning, bloodied and bruised they both came and apologised to me and promised that it would not happen again, and to give them credit, it did not.

About three months later, Ferguson (Fergie) actually, being a very good soldier was promoted to full Corporal so, as expected, began to use the Corporals Mess, which was a separate room at one end of the N.A.F.F.I. Regrettably he was habitually getting stoned out of his mind and wanted to fight all and sundry. As a result, he was resented and loathed by quite a number of the soldiers, especially by a certain heavyweight boxer from Liverpool, a Cpl. Hood.

Subsequently, due to him persistently fighting, Fergie was once again stripped of his rank and demoted back down to craftsman, this meant of course that he wasn't allowed into the Corporals Mess. Nevertheless that same night, ignoring all protocol, he strolled, larger than life, into the Mess, whereupon Cpl. Hood immediately ordered him out. As usual, Fergie became very antagonistic, and consequently demanded a punch-up,

“Cummon you bastards, I’ll fight anybody.” he shouted. He confronted Cpl. Hood and challenged him to go outside and fight, Cpl. Hood willingly obliged, however, being much bigger and heavier than Fergie, he downed him with a couple of short rights. Fergie picked himself up, and bloody nosed came staggering back in to the Corporals Mess, determined to start more trouble. His intentions were obvious when he advanced towards me and proceeded to verbally abuse and provoke me; he challenged me to go outside to fight, shouting,

“I can take you any time I like, you Geordie bastard. You think you’re fuckin tough don’t you? Come outside, I’ll knock your fuckin head off”.

I thought to myself, for fuck’s sake not again. As a professional boxer these confrontations had happened numerous times previously, I began to feel like a gunfighter who, because of his reputation was forever being challenged. I was annoyed at being confronted in front of all my mates, so not wanting to loose face I followed him outside, he turned around, wild eyed, fists clenched, he pointed to his chin and shouted,

"Go on Geordie, stick one on there."
I immediately obliged by throwing a short right hook from about twelve inches, he dropped instantly to the ground, I waited to see if he was going to get up and fight but he lay motionless. I stayed until he began to stir to make sure he was all right, and then rejoined my mates.

The next day the regiment was celebrating the Queens official birthday, which started with a full dress parade in the morning, then after lunch everyone played crazy football, which is a game involving the Officers on one side against the rest of the men on the other. The N.A.F.F.I arranged the evening's entertainment, this included tombola, and free booze which was laid on for the entire night,
"As much as you can drink," we were told.

Fergie was feeling embarrassed about the previous evening and was in a sulky mood, as a result he refused to join in any of the activities and decided to go alone, into the centre of Tripoli, to The Corner House, which was usually frequented by both British and American soldiers.

That night however, Tripoli was deserted of British soldiers, seeing that they were all celebrating at camp; therefore, the bar was overrun with American servicemen who were curious to find one lone British soldier. They quizzed Fergie asking,

"Where are all your Limey mates?"

Fergie explained that it was the Queens birthday and everyone was celebrating back at camp with free beer. Some of the Americans, who were intoxicated, began to make derogatory remarks about the Queen and disparaging comments about the British Army. Fergie, being fiercely patriotic was livid, so he picked up a metal tubular chair and started to thrash about violently, hitting several soldiers in the process.

However, being seriously outnumbered, they quickly restrained him, then threw him down onto the floor and held him down, whilst to his horror one of the American soldiers pulled out a knife and screamed.

"Guys, Aam gonna have this Limey mother fucker."

He thrust the knife at Fergie and sadistically stabbed him five times.

Fergie sustained serious injuries and was bleeding profusely from deep wounds to his chest and stomach. The horrified proprietor of the Corner House immediately summoned an ambulance, which rushed him to hospital.

Back at camp, we were unaware of the crisis, and carried on with the evening's festivities, with everyone joking, drinking and having a great time. However, the room suddenly went quiet when two Military Policemen arrived and made a beeline for the Sgt. Major. They immediately engaged him in a serious conversation and a moment later, a very grave looking Sgt. Major climbed onto the stage and took the microphone to make an announcement. He said that it was with great regret that he had to inform us that Fergie was lying critically ill in hospital and had lost so much blood that he required numerous transfusions, he appealed for volunteers to donate blood.

We soldiers immediately forgot our antagonism towards Fergie and I think that each and every one of us in the regiment volunteered blood. Fergie lay dangerously ill for three weeks, but thankfully went on to make a full recovery and was back to his normal cheeky self within a couple of months, he would proudly lift his shirt to display his scars,

"War wounds" he called them.

Not many months later, a notice appeared on Orders asking volunteers to join the S.A.S. Fergie applied and was duly accepted, and that was the last we heard of him.

Chapter 13

The Royal Engineers had a tremendous football team who had won their way through to become the supreme champions of the Middle East, their reward was a sightseeing tour of the area which would incorporate playing matches against all the other regiments stationed in the locality. They, the Champions, finally arrived in Tripoli and a football match was duly arranged between themselves and our team from Number One Base Workshops.

One of the players in our team was a ginger haired Geordie lad called Wilkinson who played the position of Centre Forward, he in fact, whilst in civilian life, had played football for Bishop Auckland, a team who at the time were amateur champions of Great Britain. Wilkinson, being such an outstanding player, was nicknamed, The Cannon Ball Kid, a name he thoroughly deserved. The match was appropriately organised for a Saturday morning and was so well publicised that all the other regiments in the area arrived at the ground to watch the game.

At the time, our team had numerous talented players; and had previously played eleven matches that season without defeat. In hindsight we realised that the Royal Engineer's must have done their homework on our team players' ability, because their centre half, who was a Cockney lad, had only one purpose in mind, and that was the sole intention of crippling Wilkinson, our star player. During the match, the Cockney centre half made no attempt at all to play the ball, he shadowed Wilkinson relentlessly and tackled him at every opportunity, coming in hard with both feet until Wilkinson, was eventually callously injured and, writhing in agony, was

carried off on a stretcher.
Since substitutes were not allowed, we were forced to finish the game with one man short, so we were more than pleased with the result of a one-one draw.

Our Colonel Bradley was enraged with the opposing teams' centre half's tactics, he accused him of being unethical and unscrupulous, however since the result was a draw, a rematch was appropriately arranged and was to be played four days later, on the following Wednesday.
Arriving back at camp after the match, I was summoned to the Colonel's office, whereupon he duly gave instructions,
"Corporal Jackson, you will be selected to play in Wednesday's rematch, and your one and only job will be to nobble that Centre Half bastard. Show him no mercy, I want him off, that's an order, UNDERSTAND?"

My heart sank as I replied,
"Yes Sir".
Being proud of my reputation as a clean sportsman, and previously having played in dozens of games, firstly as a youngster for South Benwell School, then as a youth for

One base workshops football team.

Me, centre, bottom row.

Grainger Park Boys Club and then as an employee for Fenwick's department store. I had never ever fouled an opposing player, nor even been cautioned by a referee, so this order to play dirty went against the grain and I felt very uneasy.

Wednesday arrived, and our team was in high spirits, morale was soaring as we anticipated that a win was within our reach. As I was preparing to run onto the football pitch, the Colonel confronted me to remind me of my task,

"Jackson, remember you have a job to do.," he said solemnly.

Normally I felt elated and excited before a match, but this time I had mixed feelings, my emotions were varied and I felt very uncomfortable about the whole situation.

During the first half of the match, the cockney Centre Half fouled me three times. Each occasion transpired when one of our wingers crossed a high ball to me, and as I was jumping up to head the ball, the Centre Half leapt up next to me and elbowed me in the solar plexus so hard that I dropped to the ground. As I picked myself up, he gave me such a mouthful of verbal abuse that I slowly began to seethe, and changed my

mind about being a gentleman; I was becoming more and more infuriated as each second ticked by.
During the halftime break, our Colonel came into the dressing rooms and reiterated his orders,
“I’m relying on you Corporal Jackson”, he stated.

After the fifteen minutes breather, our team ran back onto the pitch to commence the second half, but no sooner had we began, when the Centre Half fouled me yet again.
“Oop's sorry”, he said sarcastically, with a sly smirk on his face.
This was like waving a red rag to a bull.

A moment later I ran at him and tackled him as hard as I could with both feet, I took his legs away with such ferocity that he was brought down with an almighty thud, then crying like a baby he was immediately carried off.

Our team was jubilant as, when the final whistle blew, the score was ‘two - one’ to us. However as we triumphantly ran off the field to the loud ovation of all our supporters, a woman, who, I was informed later, was the Centre Half's wife, ran out from the crowd like a demented mad woman,

screaming like a banshee, she yelled.
"You dirty fuckin bastard".

She threw a right hook, that Henry Cooper would have been proud of, which landed smack on my chin. This was so unexpected that I was quite dazed for a moment, she screamed more profanities and lurched forward once again. However my mates anticipating her intentions, managed to restrict her, it was at that precise moment that the Colonel strode forward to proudly pat me on the back.
"Well done Jackson, well done," he said.

The next morning I discovered that my left testicle had swelled up to about twice its normal size and I had another swelling in my groin.
I immediately set off to see the doctor, who, upon examination, thought that I might have ruptured myself and ordered me to hospital. Once there, I sat in the waiting room until my name was eventually called. I was limping very badly as I walked into the examination room, then became acutely embarrassed to discover that the doctor was a very young lady, not much older than myself, and seeing that mine

was a very personal injury, I felt extremely self conscious. This feeling was made doubly worse, when, after being ordered to drop my trousers, the doctor seemed to step back, her nose crinkled up and with a look of distain she reached forward to obtain a pencil from her desk. Then, as if my dick was something relatively disgusting, she gingerly raised it up with the tip of the pencil to inspect the swellings.

I peered down at my dick; it didn't appear to be any different from any of the other lads', what was her problem? Maybe she was a dyke! Yes, I assured myself, that was it, she must be a dyke.

"Groin strain", "Take two weeks complete rest", she said.

Chapter 14

The British Army employed twenty young Arab men, who were engaged at our camp as cleaners, they worked conscientiously and meticulously being very grateful for the work since receiving regular wages meant their standard of living was a great improvement on their counterparts. Each day an army wagon collected the workers from a picking up point near their homes in Tripoli and brought them to our camp, where their work included cleaning and polishing the billets and barrack rooms. The Arabs worked diligently every morning until lunchtime, and then were transported back to Tripoli.

The dropping off and collection point at our camp, happened to be just outside my billet, consequently while waiting to be picked up after work the young Arabs frequently joked and fooled around with us soldiers who usually congregated on the balcony. It was during one of these humorous teasing sessions that one of the Arabs pulled a colleague from out of the bunch and against his will, pushed him towards the balcony and ordered him to lift up his Jellaba (tunic). The young man was obviously exceptionally embarrassed and very reluctant, he therefore shook his head and refused, however the others insisted. They grabbed the bottom hem of his Jellaba, and pulled it up to his waist and since he was not wearing underpants, it was promptly revealed that he was very well endowed. The Arabs pushed their chests out and proudly shouted,

"Shufti zubric."

Pointing down to the embarrassed lad's private parts, they stated,

"All Arab men beeg like theez".

"Eengleesh men no good, too small," they teased, making small inch signs between index fingers and thumbs.
This banter continued for days; however, our lads took it all in good humour.

Since there were forty soldiers in our billet, shower time was not a time to be self-conscious or embarrassed, so I could not help noticing that soldiers with average sized dicks would either throw their towels over their shoulders or sling them around their necks. Other's who were more than averagely endowed would arrogantly strut around naked, smugly showing off their tackle to all and sundry. Then there were the unfortunate lads with less than average proportions so would, out of humiliation, wrap themselves in towels, tucking them around their waists to conceal themselves for fear of being ridiculed.

One day a wagonload of new recruits arrived at our camp, having just been posted from England, amongst them was a Craftsman Newman, who was allocated to our billet. Newman was a real nice lad, quite shy and quiet and for several days, we could not help but notice that he waited until all the soldiers had used and vacated the shower room, which was situated at the end of the billet. It was immediately after the lights went out that he would silently make his way to the shower room and proceeded to wash in private.

Another soldier in our billet a Corporal Lindsay was especially perplexed about this; and was certainly preoccupied with the reason why Newman would not shower jointly with the other lads. He puzzled to himself,

"Was he shy?"

"Was he embarrassed?"

"Was his dick tiny?"

He was so preoccupied with it, that he decided he had to solve the mystery, therefore one night, Cpl. Lindsay waited until Newman had finished using the showers, then as he walked through the billet with his towel wrapped tightly around his waist, Lindsay jumped off his bed, switched on the lights and swiftly grabbed and flicked Newman's towel off. All the soldiers gasped, there was a deathly silence, and everyone's eyes were out on stalks as they stared in disbelief. Newman had the biggest dick that I, and probably any of the other lads had ever seen, it was awesome, it was unbelievable, it could be described as being comparable to a toddlers arm. Newman was mortified and blushed scarlet red, he was extremely self-conscious and felt so humiliated that he was almost reduced to tears as he grabbed his towel back from Lindsay and hurried to his bed.

This cleared up the mystery, which had been baffling me since the day Newman had arrived at the camp wearing long trousers. I, as his Corporal, informed him that it was obligatory to wear shorts; however, he explained to me that he had been excused, on medical grounds, from wearing shorts, and then proceeded to show me an official letter confirming the fact. I was confused to say the least, and was extremely baffled and curious to know the reason why.
It was now crystal clear, Newman's dick, was so long it almost reached down to his knees, so would invariably hang down from the leg opening of his shorts and be exposed.

Corporal Lindsay was in his element, he was ecstatic and could not wait until the next day for the Arab cleaners to congregate outside our billet, it was immediately after they had assembled, that Lindsay grabbed Newman, yanked him to the front of the veranda and told him to drop his trousers.

Newman was disgusted, and vehemently refused.

"Drop your trousers Private, that's an order,"

Cpl. Lindsay shouted,

Newman, near to tears, grudgingly obeyed his command, and when the Arabs saw the size of his enormous dick they reeled back, their eyes widened with disbelief, their mouths dropped open.

"That's a typical British soldier's dick." Corporal Lindsay casually said.

Needless to say, that was the end of the Arabs daily repartee.

A few days later, we were on an important Brigadier's Parade; and our Colonel was proudly presenting our battalion to the Brigadier accompanied by his small army of Officers who were fussing about and full of their own importance. It was when one of the underling Officers who was inspecting us, upon reaching Newman, stopped and shouted,

"Why isn't this man wearing shorts?"

Our Sergeant Major discretely leant over and whispered into his ear.

The Officer stepped back, looking flabbergasted, then after a conversation with the other big brass, the Brigadier himself marched over to Newman and quietly murmured something into his ear. Newman blushed scarlet red, and looked acutely embarrassed, and then the Brigadier to Newman's hand and vigorously shook it, winked at him, cleared his throat and walked on.

You do not have to be Einstein to know what the talk in the Officer's Mess would be about that night.

Most of the lads were envious of Newman, and the vulgar remarks came thick and fast, but in all honesty they really shouldn't have been jealous at all, as I was soon to find out when a few nights later, when on guard duty with Newman, I realised that he was utterly depressed and feeling exceptionally sorry for himself. I felt a surge of compassion towards him and tried to cheer him up as he, almost reduced to tears, explained his predicament.

He said he would willingly change places with any of the other lads in the billet, and would jump at the chance and give anything in the world to have a normal sized willie. He mournfully explained that even though he was twenty years old he had never ever had sex; he told me that as soon as a girl comprehended how enormous his willy was, she would run a mile. It made me realise that the colossal size of his willy, would in all probability, inflict terrible internal injury during intercourse.

Chapter 15

There were two workshops situated in our camp, Station workshop, and One Base workshop, these were units, which carried out repairs to guns and vehicles. The British Army employed several civilian Italian tradesmen who worked together as a team with us Military craftsmen and one day I was approached by one of the Italian engineers, who spoke perfect English; he proceeded to engaged me in conversation, and told me that he was heavily involved in running a boxing gym in Tripoli. He said he had been informed about my boxing career and invited me to train in his gym, saying that I would be more than welcome. He said it was a new ultra modern gym, which had all the usual amenities; I willingly jumped at the chance and after being given directions to the locality, I arranged to meet him there the following night.

The next night upon arriving at the gym, which was situated in the middle of the town centre, the Italian engineer greeted me and made me feel most welcome I changed into my training gear and made use of their excellent facilities by training particularly hard, and I had a tremendous workout. The manager of the gym seemed suitably impressed and asked if I would be willing to spar with his best middleweight boxer, and although he was a weight heavier than myself, I agreed and sparred four rounds with him, happily, due to my previous experience I came through unscathed.

I must have made an impression with the managers of the gym, as they immediately asked if I would consider boxing on their next promotion, which was to be held two weeks later. Missing the exhilaration and the adrenaline of fighting professionally I promptly agreed and for the next two weeks, I trained exceptionally hard, therefore, on the night of the fight I was supremely fit and won the contest easily, the referee stopping the fight in the third round to save my opponent from further punishment.

After the contest, I changed back into my civilian clothes and stood at the back of the hall to observe the remainder of the bill, when unexpectedly a Sergeant, who I noticed was from the American Air Force, approached me, he had apparently been a spectator in the audience, and had seen my contest. He said he had thoroughly enjoyed my performance and asked if I would consider boxing as 'Top Of The Bill' at a show which was being organised at the American air base, a few miles away.

He went on to explain they had an ex World Champion middleweight boxer who originated from Philadelphia, his name was Angel Face Barker, and although stationed in Germany, he said they would fly him over to Tripoli if I agreed to the contest. The Sergeant said that even though Angel Face Barker had been World Champion, he was now in his thirties so was probably past his best.

I considered his proposition for a moment, appreciating that not only was he ex. World Champion with experience in abundance but that he was also a weight heavier than I was. However being twenty years old and in my prime, with confidence in abundance, after weighing up the pros and cons, I decided to accept the challenge.

I had ample time in which to get fit and began to train in earnest so naturally I abstained from alcohol during this period. I had unconditional help without any strings attached firstly, from the regimental boxing team, who offered me heaps of first-class sparring, secondly from the cooks who provided extra food and said that anything I needed, or wanted I only had to ask and it would be provided. Consequently, after completing my training, I was aware that I was superbly fit.

I made a request to the promoter that he match my chief sparring partner from my regiment, with an opponent to allow him to also fight on the bill. This lad, Craftsman Thomas, was an amateur middleweight boxer, who had previously won an A.B.A title in Civvy Street, and was ecstatic when the promoter enthusiastically agreed.

Whilst I was training in the gym one night, a Sgt. Major, who originated from Liverpool, asked if he could act as my corner man and since he was very knowledgeable with the basics of pugilism I was happy to accept his offer.

The Boxing Programme was to be held at the American Camp, in a magnificent open-air stadium, this out-door arena could seat two thousand spectators and on the night of the promotion, it was bursting to capacity with American servicemen.

Craftsman Thomas and I made our way to the dressing rooms where we changed into our boxing shorts and boots, and then the Sgt. Major bandaged our hands expertly in readiness for our bouts. When my cue came, I walked slowly down the aisle and climbed through the ropes into the ring, the adrenalin pumping furiously round my body.

I felt exhilarated and apprehensive, however a moment or two later, 'Angel Face' Barker clambered through the ropes on the opposite side of the ring. As he turned around to face me, my mouth must have fallen open, Angel Face! What a joke, I can only describe him as the most repulsive looking pugilist I had ever seen. His brow was deeply furrowed with anger, he had a broad flattened nose that was, I assumed, through boxing, spread across most of his face, his eyebrows were thickened with scar tissue and protruding out over the glaring bulging wide eyes that were staring out from a black face that seemed to be mocking me.

His lips were curled and snarling and I could feel his hatred focussed on me, and to make matters worse, he had the fabulous physique of a weight lifter, having exceptionally broad shoulders, a tiny waist and a well-defined six-pack. A light smearing of oil accentuated his toned muscles; he was truly an awesome figure with the qualities and the persona of Adonis.

"What the fuck have you let yourself in for?" a little voice in the back of my head whispered.

The bell rang to commence the first round, and as I was beginning to rise off my stool, Angel Face ran across the ring and hit me with a solid right, since I was only half way up onto my feet this was so unanticipated, stunned, I dropped onto the canvas. I must have lost a few seconds because the next thing I became aware of, was the referee counting, four, five, I weakly pushed myself up onto my feet only to experience a glove hammering into my face once more, dumping me yet again onto the seat of my trunks for a second time.

I scrambled unsteadily to my feet simply to be on the receiving end of a torrent of punches, down onto the canvas once more, this time for a count of six.

To this day, I cannot explain how, but I managed to survive that bruising first round and could only feel a great sense of relief and gratitude when I heard the bell ring to end it. Instinctively I staggered to the safety of my corner where I slumped down onto the stool to appreciate the reprieve from the bombardment, I was truly thankful to have the minute rest and to listen to the words of encouragement from my corner man, the Sgt. Major. Feeling somewhat refreshed I came out of my corner for the second round, prepared for anything that my opponent could throw at me, I realised that he had hit me with his hardest punches and I had survived. I felt my conditioning begin to click in and began to feel more confident as I felt my strength returning, I survived this second round and gave back as good as I got.

However, in the third round, Angel Face Barker gave me a

lesson in fouls that I will never forget. I had never experienced such dirty boxing throughout my entire career, since British boxing is famously noted for being extremely clean, the referees always make sure of that and any sign of dirty fighting, the boxer is harshly warned or even disqualified.
Nevertheless, in this round, Angel Face shamefacedly butted me, scuffed me with the heel of the glove, elbowed me, hit me below the belt, and thumbed me in the eyes. Each time my opponent fouled me, I expected the referee to step in to verbally warn or caution him, but he did neither, I was amazed as he completely ignored the fouls and dirty fighting.

As I came out for the fourth round, I realised that Mr Barker had shot his bolt, he had visibly tired and was gasping for breath and his punches had lost some of their power and sting. Recognising this lifted my spirits and gave me great encouragement. I had found my second wind, so stepped up a gear and took great pleasure in administering the same dirty tactics that Mr Barker had taught me in the previous rounds. I was an excellent pupil and soon learned that I could also fight dirty, so proceeded to give back some of his own medicine.

It was during the fifth round that I connected with some of my best punches and dumped Angel Face down onto his arse twice, he was hanging on for dear life gulping in mouthfuls of air, gone were the conceited leering looks, these were substituted by remorseful dejected glances.

Sixth round was a very painful round for Angel Face, with yet two more trips to the canvas, I knew I could have finished it there and then, but I wanted to teach him a lesson. I was not finished with him yet, I wanted revenge, so knowing that the referee was not likely to step in, I held him up against the corner post with my left hand and punished him by continuously throwing punches with my right fist until the bell rang to end the fight.

The judges' verdict was a draw; I was delighted with the decision, as Angel Face Barker being ex. World Champion, meant this was, I believed, quite an achievement for me.

Chapter 16

Ours was a small unit consisting of only one hundred and twenty men, therefore, because we had three camps on which to mount guard, this meant that all the None Commissioned Officers had to move up a rank, therefore I, being full Corporal was promoted to "Acting Sergeant." The guard duties were coming thick and fast, and every one was certainly tired and feeling the strain, then one day a new Sgt. Major was posted to our regiment and on his first night at camp, he accompanied our 'Orderly Officer of the day,' on his guard duty. When their truck approached the gates of Station Workshops, the soldier who was on Guard duty, as usual, challenged the Orderly Officer who immediately revealed the password and instantly produced his identification. However because the Guard recognised the new Sgt. Major, he foolishly allowed him to enter without requesting proof of his identification.

The Sgt. Major was incensed and at once jumped out of the truck to confront the Guard, then proceeded to tear a strip off him, calling him an incompetent bastard, screaming that absolutely *no one* gets past a guard without first showing identification, EVER. He was so irate that he instantly put the Guard on a charge and ordered that he be escorted straight to the cells.

Two days later, the Sgt. Major himself was the acting Orderly Officer of the day; this meant everyone was on their toes. That night, the Guard Commander, who was a canny Scot, wanted to prove our proficiency so instructed the duty Guard to,

"Summon me as soon as the Sgt. Major arrives at the gates. I want the pleasure of personally challenging him to show him just how efficient our Guard duty is normally carried out."

Accordingly, the Sgt. Major arrived at the gate promptly at twenty-three hours; therefore, the duty sentry instantly informed the Guard Commander who arrived without delay and immediately ordered the Sgt. Major and his driver out of their vehicle, and demanded to see identification.
The driver promptly produced his credentials and handed them over to the Guard Commander, who scrutinised them, nodded and handed them back. The Commander immediately turned to the Sgt. Major who was frantically fumbling about in his pockets, he was extremely embarrassed when he realised that he was unable to show his identification as he had inadvertently left it in the pocket of his civilian jacket.

The Guard Commander took immense pleasure in instantly arresting the Sgt. Major, saying,
"*No one* gets past the guard without first showing identification."
He ordered that the Sgt. Major be thrown into the cells, where he spent a most uncomfortable night, seeing that the cell was

utterly bare, being devoid of bed, mattress or even a blanket, he certainly got a taste of his own medicine.
Fortunately, he had a very good sense of humour, and joined in the laughter with the rest of the unit when they found out.

It was a daily occurrence for new soldiers to arrive at our camp and one of these, was a Lance Corporal who was posted to us from England; consequently he was allocated a bed in our billet. He was a very quiet, unassuming guy, who after introducing himself, unpacked, then proudly proceeded to stick a large photograph of his wife on his locker door.
As soon as the other lads in the billet spied the photo and because she was such a strikingly attractive girl, they all crowded round to admire her, they raved over the picture and told him just how lucky he was, saying they were envious and wished they could have such a pretty wife/girlfriend.

After settling in, the Lance Corporal began to look in earnest for a civilian place to rent, so that he could bring his wife over to Tripoli and after a few weeks, he eventually found an apartment that was suitable, and accordingly arranged for her to be flown over from England the following week.

His wife was even more attractive in the flesh, and she seemed to settle quickly and she being a qualified nurse, found employment almost immediately in the American Air Force Hospital at the nearby camp.

A few weeks later, Mike, John and I were having a usual boozy evening in one of the drinking dens, which we often frequented in Tripoli, when we met up with two Military Policemen who were good pals of ours. In conversation, they told us they had been under orders to keep surveillance on a soldier's wife, who was in fact, the spouse of one of the lads in our camp, saying he actually worked in our workshops. They said they had just carried out a forced entry at her flat, to discover her, stark naked in bed, being shagged by two American Airmen and to cap it all, there were another two American Servicemen sitting in the living room, nonchalantly passing the time away playing pontoon, awaiting their turn.

The Military Policemen told us there had been an anonymous tip off about this scenario, which had apparently been going on for some weeks, and was fact, every time that her husband was on guard duty. However, they were ordered

by their superiors to stay cautious and wait until they had unequivocal proof before raiding the premises.
They had therefore, kept observation, watching and waiting, cataloguing a stream of American soldiers frequenting the apartment, until finally; they decided they had enough evidence to support a raid on the premises.
Forcing an entry, they said she was mortified when confronted; and began to sob uncontrollably, she begged them to keep their discovery secret from her husband. The Policemen ordered her to get dressed, and bundled her into their Jeep to covertly whisk her off to the airport, there to be escorted onto the next aircraft flying back to England.

We were stunned upon being informed that it was the Lance Corporal's wife, and upon meeting him face to face next morning, we observed that he was exceptionally quiet and very subdued. Realising that he must be feeling utterly devastated, Mike, John and I felt exceptionally sympathetic towards him, so decided unequivocally, to keep the appalling facts about his wife a secret from the other lads in the billet. The Lance Corporal did not have an inkling that we were aware of the truth, and we made sure it stayed that way;

however, within two days he was transferred to another camp.

He wasn't such a lucky bastard after all.

Another posting to our camp, which caused quite a lot of amusement, was a Sergeant, who took great pleasure in relating some astonishing stories about his war service and his past experiences.

He had the medals to prove that, without doubt, he had at least served in the army during the war, but the problem was, that his stories were so far-fetched and unbelievable that you could only smile.

His favourite story, which he was always relating to anyone who would listen, was that during the Second World War, he was fighting the enemy in mountainous terrain, dodging bullets, and crawling through thick mud. He said he was always cheerful and a great inspiration to all his comrades, he stated that on one mission he single handily took out three machine gun positions. Then after marching for miles, carrying a wounded comrade, his boots were worn to tatters, so he had no other option than to kill six German soldiers before he found a pair of boots that fitted him comfortably.

We had of course all heard that story before, usually in films.

He outdid himself one morning when he picked up an English newspaper, which sported a full-page photograph of a stunning, famous film actress posing in all her wedding finery next to her new husband in the grounds of a church. He angrily slammed the paper down onto the table and shouted.
“I don't believe it, the fuckin bitch, how could she do this to me, she's my fiancée, we're engaged to be married. When I left England she promised faithfully, that she would wait for me.”
Everyone looked up into the air with disbelief and thought of Coo-coo land.

Whilst Colonel Bradley was in charge of One Base Workshops, it was a Colonel Gibson who ran Station Workshops; however, the day came when it was time for Colonel Gibson to move on.
His replacement was a middle aged Colonel who’s wife wanted a ‘hands on’ approach to the unit, and was intent on becoming involved with the running of the workshops. She was a staid upstanding no nonsense woman, and decided that Saturday night in the N.A.A.F.I. would be an ideal time to

have a singsong with 'her boys' as she called us. She came prepared, music in hand to sit and play at the piano to the music of mostly, Vera Lynn songs. This situation occurred for about three weeks, then the lads rebelled, they were completely sick to their back teeth of having to be on their best behaviour, having to mind their P's and Q's and not being able to let their hair down as customary .

The next Saturday the Colonel's wife was in her element as she stood conducting the lads who were merrily singing along; however, one voice suddenly began to bellow out a filthy song, which involved a Queen Farina, fornication and dirty dogs. No sooner had he uttered the first two words than the rest of the N.A.F.F.I. joined in to sing the raunchy song at full volume The Colonel's wife was aghast, her chin hit the floor, could these be 'her boys'?. Her husband moved forward, put his arm around her and said, "Come along dear, I think it is time we left." They departed to the uproarious cheers of the lads who were stamping their feet and thumping loudly on the tables.

We quickly got back to normal, and looked forward to a typical Saturday night of drinking swearing and fighting.

Chapter 17

One lunchtime to my utter dismay, I read a notice on Orders, from the War Office, of my transfer from One Base Workshops to the Kings Hussars Regiment who were stationed about thirty miles away.

My heart sank with a heavy feeling as the thought of leaving my job, my best mates and the teams of athletes I trained became a reality, our Sergeant Major Wilson instructed me to pack my kit in readiness for transportation at eight o'clock the next morning. I was feeling disconsolate and down in the dumps when about an hour later, the Sergeant Major approached me and ordered me to his office. Once there he stated that he had had a meeting with Colonel Bradley who was furious about the transfer saying that he was not going to let me go, because I was an important member of his unit.

"If Jackson goes, who will train the boxing team, the football team and the athletics team?" he said.

He devised a plan, and that was for me to disappear into the town of Tripoli each day until further notice.

I was instructed to make myself scarce and to make certain I was not at camp when the wagon came for me the next morning. Accordingly, at six a.m. I dressed in civvics and quietly slipped away from my billet, hiring a Garri to take me into the centre of Tripoli. I was utterly bored having to waste hours in Tripoli by aimlessly wandering around and couldn't help glancing over my shoulder every so often believing that I would surely be arrested by the Red Caps and charged with being **A**bsent **W**ith **O**ut **L**eave. I had countless cups of tea in café's or went window-shopping until finally tea time arrived and I could return to camp. Arriving there I was immediately surrounded by my pals who enquired,

"Where the fuck have you been Geordie?, everyone's been frantically searching for you."
However I was sworn to secrecy.
This continued for ten days, until one evening the Sergeant Major approached me to say,
"I don't fucking believe this Jackson, I don't understand how many strings he had to pull, but the Colonel has managed to stop your War Office transfer to the Hussars, and change it to a transfer to our own Station Workshops, so you can report for work as usual tomorrow. I've been in the army nearly all my life and I've never ever known this to happen, you're a very lucky bastard."
However the Colonel being an ex. S.A.S. Officer was used to getting his own way and to my delight it meant that I was to stay in my own camp my own billet and continue to train my teams as normal.

At the beginning of July 1955 I was summoned to Colonel Bradley's office to discuss the fact that I was almost due to be demobbed, the Colonel showed me a document which specified details of a promotion, which was for myself to be promoted from Substantive Corporal up a rank to full

Sergeant. He said it was a great opportunity for me, which would lead to prospects of a great army career, saying, in his opinion; I was Officer Material and would move quickly through the ranks. However, this meant I would have to sign on for a further three years.

The proposition was extremely tempting, especially as I had grown to thoroughly enjoy serving in the army, but after a moment of deliberation, I decided that my true objective was to resume my professional boxing career and I could only achieve this in Civvy Street. Nevertheless, I could not help but to feel very honoured, as this promotion was an achievement to be proud of, having being accomplished in just three years.

I informed the Colonel, that regretfully I had decided to decline the offer, and explained the reasons why and even though he was disappointed, he fully understood and accepted my decision. He shook my hand firmly and wished me the very best of luck for the future in Civvy Street and with my boxing career.

On one hand, departing was such a wrench, since I would be leaving behind all the good mates, which I had accumulated in Tripoli over the past two years, with the exception of Mike, whose army service had also concluded so was therefore being demobbed simultaneously.

It was together that Mike and I made the sentimental journey back to England, stopping off en-route to stay for another week in Malta, where on the first morning, whilst being inspected on parade, the Sergeant Major's face lit up when he observed I was wearing the Crossed Sabres badge of a Physical Training Instructor on my sleeve. He promptly ordered me to take the platoon on physical exercise.

Collecting a football from the stores, I assembled the platoon, took them for a short run; actually to the nearest field, then to their delight, we proceeded to pass the time away by kicking a football about for two hours.

A week later, Mike and I boarded an aircraft to bring us back to England, and after an uneventful flight we landed safely at Gatwick Airport and having been issued with rail passes; we made our way, by train, to Aldershot. During the journey, Mike explained, that he had decided he was going to have a couple of weeks relaxing at home, and then was going to join the Merchant Navy. He tried to persuade me to accompany him and was persistent in begging and cajoling

me, I must be honest when I say that I was sorely tempted, but since boxing was first and foremost on my mind, I declined.
I often wonder why, when after over two years, of being the closest of mates, we did not even exchange addresses; we simply shook hands and said,
"See you."

Then walked away in different directions without even a backward glance.
I believe this is generally recognised as the traditional,

'Soldiers Farewell.'

I was to stay in Aldershot for a week, before being granted the obligatory two weeks demob leave, I drew my pay, collected my ticket and boarded a train, to take me back to my hometown of Newcastle.
By this time, I found that I was looking forward to seeing my family again, after three years of separation.

As I alighted from the train in Newcastle, I experienced a weird feeling as having being away from home for such a long period, the locality felt unfamiliar and alien. I felt like a stranger as I strolled out of Newcastle Central Station to join the back of a queue to wait for a bus, which would take me home.

Thirty minutes later, I arrived at my parent's house, to be confronted with a tremendous welcome from my family, who had organised a surprise coming home party and even though I am not the partying type, it was great to be home. I could barely recognise my younger sisters, Jeanne and Lillian since they had grown so much.

That first night home, I accompanied my father to the Hydraulic pub on Scotswood Road for a celebratory drink, there happened to be a stranger standing at the bar with a pint of Newcastle Brown Ale, in hand. He was bragging about his army experiences and reeling off all the Countries that he had supposedly served in, and was describing the actions, which he had been involved in during the war.

At first, most of the regular drinkers were predominantly intrigued and listened to his stories intently, however because he ranted on and on, bragging and boasting, soon everyone lost interest and became thoroughly bored. They assumed that he must be romancing and believed the stories must be fictitious considering the tales that were unfolding were so outrageous. Undeterred, he puffed out his chest and proudly alleged.

"I have a medal with a bar."

Father having a very dry wit, casually piped up,

"I have **three** bars."

The strangers jaw dropped,

"THREE?" he said in disbelief,

My father nonchalantly quipped,

"Yes, three, The Hydraulic, The Hammer and The Gun."

These being three of the most popular bars on Scotswood Road.

Everyone in the pub burst out laughing, and with that the stranger drank up his beer and left.

In reality, my father, being a coal miner, had been exempt from enlistment into the forces, meaning that the sole extent of his 'Army Service' was that he was conscripted into the Home Guard.

However, because father was rather addicted to the booze,

when he was supposed to be 'on duty', he would, more often than not, be either drinking in the local pubs on Scotswood Road, or gambling in the hoying schools which used to be held in the local back lanes. These hoying schools were well patronised by the local men, some of whom habitually, to the despair of their wives, gambled away all their hard earned weekly wages in just a few hours.

Inevitably the ‘powers that be’ discovered that father was shirking his duties so I believe he must be the only person in history ever to be 'dishonourably discharged' from the Home Guard.

When I was a child, father explained to me that he was forced to ‘stand to attention’ while the buttons and flashes were ripped from his jacket, but because he was an impressive joker, I never did determine whether this story was true or whether it was another of his fabrications.

During the final months of the war, father was recruited into fire watching duties, so was accordingly assigned to a large local grocery store, namely the, Co-operative. Father was, in theory, supposed to be on ‘lookout’ at the store from six p.m., which was the time the staff departed after completing their working day, and was supposed to continue his guard duty until Seven-thirty a.m. the next morning. Needless to say, as soon as the local pubs opened their doors at seven p.m. father disappeared from the store to go boozing with all his cronies. After supping Newcastle Brown until 'hoying oot' time, he would return to the store, however by this time he was generally half cut, so would find a quiet corner, make himself comfortable and sleep through the rest of the night.

Being desperately poor, our family was fed with thc cheapest food, which meant mother having to purchase scraps of the most inexpensive meat, stale bread, broken biscuits, bruised fruit etc, now the floodgates were unexpectedly thrown wide open, what a golden opportunity, the mind boggled with the prospect of father being let loose in a food shop.

I remember mother scribbling shopping lists for provisions, which she gave to father, long lists that usually incorporated corned beef, spam, cheese, butter, and bacon, eggs, sugar, jam, tinned fruit, milk, bread, vegetables, fruit, tea and OVALTINE. It was the first time I had ever tasted such a delicious drink and to this day, I can still savour the aroma from the steam rising from the cup.

Father would clandestinely pack the food into a cardboard box and mother would furtively creep up to the back door of the store at about six a.m., to collect the groceries before the shop assistants arrived on the scene. Because mother's upbringing had been very religious, it went against the grain and she felt incredibly guilty, but being a devoted mother to myself, my brother Stan, my three sisters Eleanor, Jeanne and Lillian she felt grateful that she could at last give us something decent to eat for a change. We took great pleasure in secretly eating this delicious, scrumptious food, and relished it with gratification, I believe we must have been the only family in the area to gain weight during those lean hard war torn times.

This help-yourself food continued until the war ended, and then, regrettably it was back to cheap poverty food, no more sumptuous feasts for us, and unfortunately no more of my favourite Ovaltine.

After the initial pleasure of coming home, I soon began to feel despondent and at a loose end since all my pre-army mates were now either in the army themselves, or courting, so having been accustomed to the constant companionship of close mates over the past three years, I was feeling incredibly lonely, A few nights later and being thoroughly bored I decided to make my way to the Oxford Galleries, which is a local dance hall situated in the centre of Newcastle.

The Oxford was a famous, popular, meeting place for young couples, and it was widely accepted that more than fifty per cent of the local population met their future spouses there. I was generally milling amongst the crowds of young people, whilst listening to the live music playing at full blast from the raised stage. I watched as couples danced together on the highly polished floor while the compulsory revolving bulbous glass hanging lights created diamonds of lights, which flickered across the room. Suddenly my eyes were drawn like a magnet to a girl, it was her eyes that first captivated me, big, dark brown Latin type eyes, she looked at me, and our eyes met. I felt my heart begin to race, it may sound corny, but it was love at first sight, I could not believe my emotions, me

the tough, supremely fit athlete reduced to this weak-kneed trembling wreck,
"So this is love?"

I instinctively decided to make my way over to ask her to dance, so began to push my way through the crowds towards her, however upon reaching the spot, I could only feel disappointment when I discovered that some other guy had beaten me to it. I was determined to introduce myself so lingered at the edge of the dance floor waiting for her to walk by. When the music finally stopped, I seized her hand and asked her for the next dance, and held her closely as we made our way onto the floor, we happily chatted as we danced to the music.
She was slim with a trim petite figure; and had an aura of elegance about her, she was small, being only five feet two inches tall, although wearing stiletto heels gave her another four inches in height. I discovered that she was seventeen years old, her name was Wyn, and she worked in a Solicitors office, and coincidently, lived very near to my home, in fact, on the private housing estate, which was just at the top of my street. Wyn and I courted for seven months, meeting every

single day, before taking the ultimate commitment of marriage. I jokingly said that I had been half way around the world, and then met, fell in love with and married a girl from the top of my street.

Chapter 18

Finding myself back in Civvy Street, after completing my army service, I was undecided upon which occupation to pursue, and since I had been quite frugal in the army had consequently saved several hundred pounds so I reached the decision that I should become self-employed.

In that era, most of the properties in the neighbourhood had open fires on which they burned coal and logs, so I decided that it could be quite a good little money earner if I bought and sold logs to housewives around the local streets.

I scrutinized through the advertisements in the 'Commercial vehicles for sale' column in the local newspaper and noticed a Hillman van which I thought would be suitable, it was described as being reliable and clean, and was only forty-five pounds; as it sounded ideal for my requirements I arranged to inspect and check it over.

On initial examination, the van seemed to be in good nick, so I purchased it there and then, however at that time there were no such restrictions as M.O.T's. now, in hindsight, I'm convinced that if there had been such checks, the van would never have passed, not in a million years. In retrospect I realise it would have failed miserably, and I believe it would surely have been consigned to the scrap heap.

I normally parked the van overnight in the back lane, outside my parents' house, which was on an incredibly precipitous hill, and each day I requested that father accompany me, primarily for companionship, and the other reason being, to keep him out of the boozer for a few hours.

Every morning I drove to a nearby local colliery to purchase logs, which were old pit props that had already been sawn up, by the miners, into the correct size. We arrived at the pit to load the logs into the van, cramming them in as tightly as possible, and on the way home, stopped in each of the streets that we drove through, to sell the logs to the residents. The van was invariably empty by the time we reached home, since this being an economical way to produce heat, meant the logs were extremely popular and in great demand.

It was during this winter that we were experiencing an unusually sub-zero spell, so on an especially bitterly cold morning, the temperature being several degrees below freezing, when I tried to start the van it was unresponsive. After numerous attempts and still getting no reaction, (being a clapped out wreck this was nothing unusual). I began to feel anxious, thinking that the battery was becoming flat, so I said to father

"Get in; I'll try to bump start it down the hill."

I disengaged the handbrake and began to freewheel the vehicle down the steep bank, I tried letting the clutch out several times but the van was dead as a doornail. I was becoming rather desperate as I was nearing the road junction at Scotswood road, I therefore made one last frantic attempt and finally to my relief, the engine burst into life.

I assumed that if I took my foot off the accelerator to brake at the junction, the engine would, in all probability cut out, and almost certainly would not start again. I kept my fingers crossed that the road would be clear of any morning commuter traffic that could be approaching at that exact moment and wrenched the steering wheel round to the right then recklessly careered onto Scotswood Road.

It was at that precise moment, as the van hurtled around the corner leaning over, almost on two wheels, that, without warning, the passenger door flew open and unpredictably the passenger seat with father still perched on it, shot out of the van and landed slap bang in the middle of the road, father still sitting as if entrenched into it.

I quickly glanced into the mirror and saw father, still perched bolt upright and motionless on the van seat. He appeared to be frozen with fear, not moving an inch, and seemed as if in a trance, the knuckles of his hands white as he clutched onto the sides of the seat, hanging on it seemed for dear life, as the passing traffic swerved left and right to avoid him. Appreciating that father hadn't come to any real grief, apart from his dignity and maybe his arse being bruised, I made the split decision to stay in the van to keep the engine running, firmly believing that if I took my foot off the accelerator to go to his aid, the engine would more than likely cut out.

I could not help laughing at the hilarious spectacle he made, I leant out of my door and shouted,
"COME ON FATHER, YOU CAN'T SIT ON YOUR LAZY ARSE ALL DAY, WE'VE GOT WORK TO DO, GET BACK IN."

He stood up and shouted
"AAD JUST AS SOON HOY MEESELL OFF THE TYNE BRIDGE AS GET BACK INTO THAT FUCKIN WRECK, IT'S A HEAP OF CRAP."

With that, he picked up the seat, brought it over to the van, opened the back doors, threw it in, slammed the door and stormed off. The next week the engine seized up and the van took its long awaited place of honour on the scrap heap.

During the few weeks prior to being demobbed, I had suffered bouts of severe stomach pain, and since this was persistent, the Military doctor advised me, upon arriving home, to seek medical advice from my own civilian doctor. I carried out his instructions, and after consultation and examination, I received medication in the form of daily medicine and tablets. I continued the treatment for several months, but in spite of this, the problem persisted and I suffered from unrelenting pain.

After Wyn and I married, I was still having frequent spasms of pain, together with bouts of sickness and spells of vomiting blood, as a result, my local doctor referred me to a specialist at the Newcastle General Hospital for tests, these involved having a barium meal and stomach X-rays. Unfortunately, the analysis disclosed that I had a duodenal ulcer, which was probably caused by the excessive drinking over the previous three years. This to my distress meant that I would not be able to resume my professional boxing career until it had healed.

The hospital doctor instructed me to go on a strict dietary routine, and he gave me a diet sheet of do's and don'ts, I also purchased a book, "How I Cured My Duodenal Ulcer," which I had seen advertised in a local newspaper. The author recommended eating steamed fish, creamed mashed potatoes and peas, this to be followed by milky rice pudding, the meal had to be consumed every day for six months. Even though it was particularly bland and monotonous, Wyn made sure that I adhered to it, and dutifully cooked the meal every single day for me. I ate the boring food religiously day in day out, devoutly sticking to the diet, until finally, after many months, the ulcer seemed to have disappeared, and I was relieved when hospital X-Ray's confirmed it.

Finally, I was pain free.

Since my ulcer had disappeared, I decided to apply to have my professional licence reinstated, and took the mandatory medical examination, which I passed with flying colours and obtained the longed for boxing licence.
I decided that my next initiative was to start another business as being self-employed would mean I could arrange my boxing training around my work and would be able to take time off whenever necessary to follow my boxing career.

After careful consideration I came to the decision that a travelling greengrocery shop would be ideal, so I purchased a van by bidding for it in a local commercial vehicle auction. It was a three-ton, three-way loader for which I paid sixty pounds, I drove the van home full of aspirations and hope, and began what was to become a very lucrative business. I created a worthwhile round with regular customers who relied on me to supply them with fruit and vegetables and I was soon earning a good living. Every afternoon after my greengrocery round had finished, I trained exceptionally hard and soon became quite successful in the ring I fought several top class boxers and had twenty-five professional fights.

The wholesalers, known as the 'green market' usually opened for business at six o'clock every morning and was always bustling and incredibly hectic as buyers from shops and supermarkets, together with street traders, vied for trade and haggled prices with the vendors. It was so chaotic it was virtually impossible to find a barrow on which to stack the purchased sacks of vegetables and boxes of fruit.

One morning, a few days after my fight with a boxer called Brian Husband I was, as usual, buying produce at the green market for my travelling round. After wrangling and negotiating the best prices for my purchases, I was pleased to notice an empty barrow tucked away in a corner. Since barrows were in short supply as there were never enough to go round, I felt fortunate to find this one. I walked over, bent down, took hold of the handles and started to push it to where my stock was stacked.

Suddenly the salesman from whom I had bought my supplies said, with a look of horror written all over his face,

“Oh my God, take a word of warning from me, don’t touch that barrow. It will be more than your life’s worth, it belongs to the toughest, hardest barrow boy in the market. Nobody but nobody is allowed to use it but him.”

At that exact moment a thunderous voice behind me hollered “Put that fuckin barrow back, I'll pull your fuckin head off, no bastard touches my barrow; I'll knock your fuckin teeth right down your fuckin throat.”

The voice was getting nearer and nearer, louder and louder until he was immediately behind me.

At that precise moment I slowly lowered the barrow to the ground and turned round to face him, he stopped dead in his tracks, apparently recognising me, his face drained of all colour and he went a deathly shade of grey, he stuttered,

"Eee Ron Jackson? Eee I'm sorry, I didn't realise it was you, I saw you fight Brian Husband the other night, it was a fantastic fight. I didn't know you came to the market, you can use my barrow any time you like; just take it, any time, any time."

I couldn't help muttering under my breath, "Arse licking creep."

Another morning, having left the greenmarket after buying supplies from the wholesalers, I was driving my travelling shop down Bath Lane, which is in the centre of Newcastle when in my mirror, I caught a glimpse of a Police Officer riding a motorbike and following closely behind. He began to overtake me and as he drew alongside my van, he leant over, thumped twice on the side of the van with his fist, and waved me down to stop.

I pulled over to the side of the road and turned the engine off, wondering what on earth was happening, as I was sure I had not committed any driving offences, I wound the window down and asked,

"What's wrong Officer?"

He let loose with a tirade of foul language screaming at the top of his voice,

"What's fuckin wrong? **You** know what's wrong. You're a stupid fuckin arsehole, you're a brainless twat, where the fuck did you learn to drive you fuckin idiot, you're a menace, you shouldn't be allowed on the roads."

My stomach began to churn I was seething and felt incensed at being spoken to like that, and even though he was a Policeman I was on the verge of jumping out of the van to confront him, he must have noticed my fury as he swiftly lifted his visor up to expose his face whereupon he burst out laughing. He was doubled up and said,

"I wish I had a camera, your face was a picture, how are you Geordie?"

Then and only then did I recognise him as a soldier who had served with me in basic training in the R.E.M.E. this was typically characteristic of him, he was always the joker, always clowning around, we shook hands and chatted for a while before both going our separate ways.

My boxing career culminated on the 5th September 1959, with a bout against Tommy Molloy, who at the time, was reigning British Welterweight Champion. During the contest, which was held at New St. James' Hall, I felt I was doing particularly well and firmly believed I was ahead on points when unfortunately I sustained a very badly cut eye, which forced the referee to step in and stop the fight.

Although disappointed, this was not altogether unanticipated because regrettably, my five previous successive fights had also been stopped when suffering extremely deep cuts to the same eye. My doctor warned me that the protruding scar tissue was a serious weakness and would always cause problems, therefore having my best interests at heart he advised that I should seriously consider retiring, I was reluctant to do so but on reflection, I felt that his medical advice should be adhered to, so agreed.

Chapter 19

After about six years of civilian life, even though happily married with two beautiful daughters I realised that I was missing army life, not only did I miss the charisma of being a physical training instructor, but most of all I missed the companionship of my mates. Once again, I began to yearn for the aspiration that I had craved to achieve whilst in the regular army but was always too busy to accomplish and that was the ambition to become a member of the Parachute

Regiment. Finally, I decided that I would make my dream come true and enrolled at the Gateshead headquarters of the 17th Battalion of the T. A. Parachute Regiment.

It was there that I did the R.I.S.C. (Recruits Initial Select Course) this course is deliberately made exceptionally difficult with the sole object of selecting suitable men as candidates to enter the Parachute Regiment.
The course was incredibly arduous and the men would be exhausted after executing the laborious tasks, which included a particularly difficult obstacle course, a log race and a milling competition (boxing).

I myself being strong and fit passed the selection course and was delighted to be selected to go forward on to the next phase, which was a parachute course at Number One School Training Centre at Abingdon. There were forty soldiers in my platoon, all enthusiastically waiting to begin the course, where one of the first pieces of equipment on which to train, was 'The Fan', which is located at a height of fifteen feet, from there; we were taught how to fall accurately so as to make a safe landing. Afterwards we progressed to the Death

Tower, which is located seventy-five feet above ground level; we had to jump from this contraption and slide down a wire to ground level.

We trainees were shown film clips of correct landings and incorrect landings, in addition we were shown horrific film clips of 'Roman Candles,' these are parachutes, which fail to open, it was disclosed later that they had used dummies in the demonstrations, nevertheless, the effect was daunting.

It was immediately before our first 'bona fide' jump that we were advised that the most important thing to remember before jumping was to,

"Cross your left leg over your right leg."

"Why Sir?" A voice piped up.

"So we know which thread to screw you out of the ground if your chute fails to open." The instructor answered.

We looked at each other and gave a faint-hearted laugh.

This training course consisted of eight jumps; two of which were made from air balloons situated eight hundred feet above ground level, the other six jumps were executed

On Parachute Course, me on left.

from either Beverley or Hastings aircraft. Upon making my first jump, I seemed to automatically go through the motions; however my second jump seemed much more nerve-racking and frightening, this was I believe, because I realised the dangers, and had been given an insightful of just what could go wrong, however I'm pleased to say I completed all the jumps.

Out of the forty of us who started the course, five failed and therefore dropped out, nevertheless the remainder of us passed with flying colours and were proudly presented with our wings by Bomber Harris V.C.

On my return to the T.A. Headquarters in Gateshead, the Officers, having obtained information relating to my previous regular army experience, immediately promoted me to Lance Corporal, then within two months I was once again promoted, thus obtaining a second stripe making me up to full Corporal.

Being a qualified physical training instructor, I was immediately put in charge of the P.T. and given the assignment of supervising the boxing team and promptly promoted to full Sergeant.

I attended the T.A. centre every Wednesday evening, and was

Sergeant Parachute Regiment

readily available to attend camp almost every weekend; I also attended the mandatory annual camps, which lasted for two-weeks. These annual camps were sometimes held in Great Britain but more often than not, they took place overseas, usually Germany or Cyprus, I also travelled throughout the country attending tournaments with the boxing team.

One specific Wednesday night, as usual I changed into my uniform to attend the T.A. centre, however, realising that I would be drinking, I declined to take the car, and instead, caught a bus to meet up with my mates in the centre of Newcastle. From there, we walked across the Redheugh Bridge, which spans the River Tyne to reach our destination, the T.A Drill hall in Gateshead. Once there, we practiced the compulsory drill for a couple of hours before having the mandatory few drinks. At the end of the evening session, my mates and I left the drill hall and were merrily walking back across the bridge to Newcastle intending to catch a bus home. As customary we were joking, and carrying on and I was falling about, laughing heartily, when all of a sudden as I gasped for breath, I sucked the air in so violently, that I swallowed my tooth palette.

It was a few years previously, whilst competing in a boxing contest in Tripoli, that a blow to my mouth caused one of my front teeth to become slightly loose, I attended the Military dentist who advised me not to worry as the tooth would more than likely tighten up again. Unfortunately, the next day, I was playing football when a player on the opposing side, collided with me as we both jumped up to head a high ball. On impact, he accidentally butted me in the mouth, and to my disappointment, my tooth fell out. I made an appointment to attend the Military Dental Hospital, where they took impressions of my teeth and fitted me with a palette. From then on, I wore the denture, which had one front tooth attached, but understandably, after a few years through wear and tear it had become relatively slack.

That night when I swallowed the palette, I thought I would surely die as I was choking and unable to breathe, my mates at first thought I was larking about, then realised just how serious it was, I was literally dying in front of their eyes. In sheer panic, I stuck my fingers down my throat to try to retrieve the palette, but only succeeded in pushing it further down. In desperation, writhing about, I finally managed to hook a finger round the palette to pull it back into my mouth and spit it out.

I was gasping for breath with blood pouring from my mouth, since the palette, having jagged edges, had torn my throat to shreds. Feeling enormously lucky to be alive, I summoned a taxi to drive me home.

The next morning I made an appointment to see my doctor, who upon examining my throat, said I must have been the luckiest man on earth to survive, he said it was apparent by the injuries to my throat, just how far down the palette had been.

He said,

"Take a trip to the Hancock Museum, there is an oesophagus in a jar which has a palette wedged across, and it's not as far down as yours was.".

One weekend our Company together with the whole Battalion of eight hundred men attended a huge exercise on Otterburn moors. As usual, before boarding the aircraft, we were marched to a hanger to be briefed by Major Swinburne who was our Company Commander. As customary, he instructed us to treat the exercise as a genuine assault, therefore he ordered us be as silent as possible when being dispatched and to descended and to land as quietly as possible.

As this was a night time exercise, we found ourselves stepping out of the aircraft into complete darkness, however once we had released our containers and were floating down to earth, a voice piped up,

"Who dat down der?"

The answers came instantaneously,

"Who dat up der?"

"Who dat down der saying who dat up there?"

This was met by the thunderous voice of Major Swinburne

"SHUT UP, Corporal Kennedy, I recognise your voice ."

"It's not me Sir, I'm over here."

"No, I'm over here Sir" from the other direction.

"I'm over here Sir" from yet another spot.

"SHUT UP" Screamed Major Swinburne.

Several voices in unison shouted,

"Fuck off Sir."

The whole Battalion was in an uproar, it must have been the noisiest decent in history.
As soon as the exercise was concluded, the Major gave us a good dressing down, although he could not hide his amusement and was secretly laughing to himself.

I was to experience a few scary moments during my parachute regimental service, I refer to one day when our platoon was carrying out an exercise and parachuting onto Otterburn moor in Northumberland. It was after I had been dispatched from the aircraft that I unfortunately found myself swinging through the rigging lines of another soldier‘s parachute, this being called a 'bird in a cage'.
The two of us were swiftly thrown into a predicament, which is commonly known as a 'daisy chain', which resulted in my chute causing the other chute to collapse, and then the other chute resulted in mine collapsing. However with my heart thumping as if it would burst, I somehow managed to disentangle myself to float free and luckily we both landed unharmed.

Another dilemma I experienced, was an incident that is

generally recognised as a blown periphery; this is when my rigging line whipped across my canopy splitting it wide open, from one side, right across to the other, this resulted in my parachute being sliced into two halves. As I was hurtling towards the ground like a ton of bricks, an Officer on the ground was screaming instructions through his loudhailer,
"PULL YOUR RESERVE NUMBER TEN, PULL YOUR RESERVE."

I instinctively reached for the handle on my reserve chute but realised that I was only about three hundred feet above ground, so my mind went into overdrive and a little voice seemed to whisper,
"If you pull your reserve, your main Chute will close and there won't be enough time for your reserve to fully open."

Therefore, I refrained, and resisted the temptation to pull, and just hoped and prayed, as I dropped like a stone. A second or two later I hit the ground with a resounding wallop and felt myself very lucky to walk away with only severe bruising.
On yet another occasion, while attending an annual camp, this time in Wales, and although the weather conditions were

Myself stick 5 behind brother Stan

exceptionally bad for parachuting the Officers decided to allow the exercise to go ahead. Understandably, the Battalion taking part in the jump suffered numerous casualties including countless broken bones. The ambulances were kept busy shuttling the wounded men backwards and forwards to hospital, I myself experienced a very hard landing, and since my ankle immediately swelled up to twice it's normal size the medic suspected that it was broken. Yet I was told I had to walk the five miles to the ambulance dispatch point for transportation to hospital to have it X-Rayed.

I was in intense pain as I hobbled to the pickup point, then when I eventually arrived at the hospital I discovered the waiting room was full to bursting point with wounded soldiers lying in every nook and cranny. Whilst waiting for medical attention, I was chatting to a Para who had sustained two broken ankles, I was commiserating with him and discussing the extreme weather conditions in which we had executed the jump. I mentioned that he must have had an extremely hard landing, then to my amusement he informed me that he had made a perfect landing before collecting his chute to walk in darkness towards voices he could hear nearby. Then unpredictably, to his horror, he felt himself falling into space, as unbeknown to himself he had been blown off course and as a result had landed on the flat roof of a building in the near vicinity.The most seriously injured men were on trolleys and the less severely wounded were laid on the floor of the corridor, where a carpet of bodies stretched from one end to the other. After a lengthy wait, I was at last attended to, and had my ankle X-rayed, this proved that luckily, there were no broken bones, however I had suffered tendon damage and sustained very bad bruising; the doctor prescribed painkillers then I was taken back to camp in a Land Rover.

My next chilling experience was when, just before one of my annual camps, a Major Taylor who was our adjutant, requested that I attend a training course, at Abingdon, which would be to obtain qualifications to become a jump dispatcher. However, because this training course was to take place the week preceding my two-week annual camp, I hesitated, believing that the extended time away from my family wasn't realistic, primarily because my wife Wyn was suffering from a severe case of bronchitis, and both my daughters were ill with chickenpox, so after long deliberation, I reluctantly declined.

My assistant who was a P.T. Instructor from Middlesbrough, pleaded with the Adjutant to allow him to take my place, and after careful consideration; the Adjutant consented to him substituting for me, consequently he was ecstatic as he travelled to Abingdon to undertake the course.

The following day, I heard a report on national television, which gave details of a Military aircraft exploding in mid air, killing all personnel aboard; I was totally fazed out when I discovered that the P.T.I who had substituted for me, was aboard the aircraft. Apparently, friction from a loose bolt had caused a spark, which ignited the fuel tank. I was devastated about losing my assistant in such a tragic accident, and could not help feeling that someone up there must like me.

Chapter 20

Soon afterwards, I was placed in charge of the R.I.S.C. for new recruits, it was on one of these courses, that I became aware that an Officer recruit was having problems completing the obstacle course, and even with encouragement, he was beyond doubt having great difficulty scaling the wall. Since I was sitting astride it, I leant down, yanked him up and helped him over, he was particularly grateful, since completing the obstacle course, meant that he was selected to go forward to undertake the Parachute course at Abingdon, where he eventually obtained his wings. Later he approached me saying,

"Thank you very much Sgt. I would never have achieved my wings without your help."

This Officer, who, after acquiring his wings, was immediately promoted to the rank of Lieutenant and placed in charge of the one hundred and twenty soldiers in 'A' company, and was to supervise us at the next annual camp, in Germany.

In preparation for what was to be a N.A.T.O exercise, our Company travelled to Salisbury Plains to draw weapons, ammunition and rations which were required for the two-week camp.

The following day, after gazing at a map, and given that we had a few hours to spare, the Lieutenant shouted,

'A' company, fall in. Since we are located only a few miles from Stonehenge we must grab this opportunity to visit the site."

As a result, off we went on foot, all one hundred and twenty of us, marching and jogging the eight or so miles. However, upon arriving at the site we were confronted by a wire fence, surrounding the gigantic stone artefacts. Upon observing us, a uniformed attendant sporting a moneybag, moved forward to collect entrance money, as this was completely unforeseen, the surprised Lieutenant turned to me,

"Do you have you any money Jackson?" he said,

"No Sir" I replied.

"Has anyone in the Company got any money?" he shouted,

"No Sir" the reply came in harmony.

The Lieutenant grinned,

"Well lads, there's only one thing for it. OVER THE FENCE!"

In unison, the whole Company scrambled forward and scaled over the fence to the horror of the ticket collector,

"There was no need for that, I would have opened the gates," he said sullenly.

Upon seeing the ancient relics I was most impressed, particularly with their enormous size, I was led to believe that some of the individual stones weighed a colossal fifty tons, and since there is no natural stone within the locality, the stones must have been transported a distance of two hundred and forty miles, the mind boggles.

Although I could not see the significance of them, I was pleased to have had the experience of standing in such a hallowed place.

The next morning we boarded army aircraft and flew to Germany to begin the exercise in earnest. It was a few days later that the Lieutenant was ordered by our Company Commander to check the depth of a river which was approximately two miles away, this was to determine if it would be possible for our wagons to cross. The Lieutenant requested that I, together with another eight soldiers, accompany him on his assignment. This request was duly granted, so we quickly kitted up and set off on our mission. However when the Lieutenant began to purposefully stride towards a thickly wooded area I turned to him and said,
"We should follow the tracks on the map Sir."
"No Jackson, we'll do it by the book, we'll go cross country, using the compass." he replied.
"But Sir, we are in a dense, heavily wooded area, and the compass won't work." I answered.

However, he would not listen to reason, so off we trundled

into the forest, but sure enough, exactly as I had predicted we found ourselves completely and utterly lost, with not even a stream, let alone a river, in sight. Since we had been allocated a period of three hours in which to accomplish our task, and because time was running out, the Lieutenant was becoming rather anxious, and was wondering what on earth he could do next so I suggested,

"There is only one thing for it Sir. Go back to base and when the Officers debrief you, just tell them that the river is about ten feet deep and much too deep for the wagons to even attempt the crossing, they'll be none the wiser."

The Lieutenant's eyes widened and a look of relief swept over his face,

"That's a brilliant idea Jackson, I'd never have thought of that, I owe you one." he said.

Chapter 21

Upon being appointed regimental-boxing trainer, I taught some very good local recruits the art of pugilism, including Pte Norman Marshall, from Wallsend. I had noticed him during the milling contest on his selection course, when he caught my eye after knocking his opponent out. I was very impressed with his style and asked him how many fights he had had, he explained to my astonishment, that it was the first time in his life that he had ever donned boxing gloves. I asked him, if, after obtaining his wings, he would like to join the boxing team, he was very eager and said he would be delighted to.

Wings duly obtained, Marshall was posted to ‘A’ Company and after tuition and hard training, developed into a very talented hard punching boxer and went on to become the Territorial Army bantamweight champion of Great Britain. An identical situation was repeated with a Pte. John Hudson, who hailed from Newcastle and even though he had never boxed before, he quickly developed into a stylish and courageous boxer, who became a credit to our team and also attained the honour of becoming regimental champion at lightweight.

Other successful boxers under my wing included, Kevin Jones, a light middleweight from Middlesbrough, John Lawson, light welterweight and Ron Embleton, welterweight both from South Shields, all of whom I am proud to say, also achieved the honour of becoming regimental champions. My assistant trainer Ronnie Iveson, whom I regularly relied on for support and help, was himself an experienced ex professional light heavyweight having had approximately twenty professional fights during his career.

It was while attending one regimental tournament that I was introduced to Robert Carr, who, at the time was boxing for the 12th/13th battalion of the Para's; and was having his first ever fight. I being his corner man, was appalled by him being exceptionally overweight, he was noticeably flabby, and being unfit was gasping for breath during the rounds, but to give him credit, he stopped his man in the third round.
Upon winning his contest, and having his arm held high by the referee, he became ecstatic and was so elated that he began to jump all over the ring, and immediately the decision was announced, several of his mates hopped over the ropes, into the ring and were leaping up and down, excitedly chanting

"He's going to be world champion" repetitively.

I shouted above the racket "Calm down, there is no way that he'll be world champion as long as he has a hole in his arse."
The next time I encountered Robert, I barely recognised him,

since the visual transformation was incredible, the flab and fat had miraculously disappeared, it was obvious that he had lost about three stones in weight. His now impressive physique sported solid bulging muscles with a well-defined six-pack and he was as fit as a flea, It was hard to appreciate it was the same fighter.

Eventually, having won all his contests throughout the heats, Robert finally reached the Territorial Army Championships, which were held at the White City, London. I, being his trainer, accompanied him to the venue, together with Norman Marshall who had also won his way through the heats to qualify for the finals.

Norman's first contest was held during the morning session and he excelled himself by boxing impressively and winning his bout hands down. However since there wasn't an opponent for Robert in this first round, he was given a bye, this meant that we had several hours to waste before the next session of bouts, scheduled for that evening.

Since the three of us were bored rigid, and tired of just sitting around waiting in the smoky atmosphere of the venue,

Norman suggested that we stretch our legs; therefore, Robert recommended we walk to Hyde Park, suggesting the fresh air would lift our spirits.

All in agreement, we began to make our way to the park, and found ourselves walking down Greek Street, in the notorious area of Soho, as we strolled nonchalantly along, we couldn't help but notice two '*ladies*' hanging around waiting for '*business*'. They were standing on the opposite pavement and both obviously advertising the fact that they were whores, by their outlandish attire. One wore a short, bright shocking pink, phoney fur jacket over a tight red leather skirt, so short it barely covered her derrière; her boobs were hanging out of a skimpy top. She was plastered with makeup so thick you would need a trowel to scrape it off; her obviously bleached hair was the colour of straw with new growth of dark roots showing through. The other 'lady' was wearing an 'off the shoulder' shiny gold top, which left nothing to the imagination and was sporting a black leather skirt, which was as short as her companion's. She was teetering on red stiletto high-heeled shoes and her face resembled an artist's palette sporting colourful splashes of bright blue, scarlet red, black and brown all dabbed onto a background of orange, her hair

was dyed jet blue black, and hung down to her shoulders in scraggy strands.
Robert shouted across to them. “Hello pet.”

They looked over in anticipation and doubtlessly thinking they had picked up some trade, began to cross the road in our direction.
“Will a fiver cover it?” Robert shouted.

Realising he must be taking the Mickey they stopped dead in their tracks, turned and walked back to the opposite pavement.
“A fuckin door mat wouldn't cover it.” Robert yelled.

Chapter 22

On another T.A. training week-end, in the Lake District, this time in the heart of winter, the one hundred and twenty men in our company, were ordered by our Officer, at six o'clock every morning, to dive into the nearby lake. This lake would be frozen over with a layer of ice, consequently upon entering the water we gasped for breath, and it being so excruciatingly cold, we found the pain was almost unbearable, but of course we were 'Para's' and it was expected of us, however to give him credit, our Officer was always the first man in.

During one night, when enduring the sub-zero temperatures out in the wilderness on the moors, and almost numb with cold and fatigue the group I was with, found a stone circular shelter. Relieved to find some protection at last from the extreme elements, we gratefully crawled in and lay down, and with a warm sensation engulfing us, being utterly exhausted we instantaneously fell asleep.

Dawn broke and upon waking, we found that the weight of our bodies had subsequently sunk us down, until we were almost completely submerged into fresh soft cow dung, apparently the 'shelter' turned out to be an area in which manure was stored. We stank to high heaven and for once, we were grateful for the dip in the lake.

Another memorable episode in the Territorial Army was, the time we were executing a weekend exercise, out in the sticks near Hexham, Northumberland, the whole of 'A' company were practicing house-to-house clearance, led by our Company Commander, Major Swinburne.

He together with a Sgt. Major Smith, who himself was a very

experienced soldier, having served in active service during the war, set out to booby-trap a specially designated house, using trip wires etc. The rest of the Company were sitting on the ground waiting until the traps were placed into position. Major Swinburne asked a rookie Lieutenant called Kilpatrick, who was in charge of the platoon, if he had any experience of house clearance.

"Yes Sir, I have." Kilpatrick quipped up confidently.

"Right, you go in first." Major Swinburne ordered.

Kilpatrick grinning from ear to ear, and screaming at the top of his voice immediately charged forward. Upon reaching the door, he kicked it open with such ferocity it almost came off its hinges, he instantly threw a thunder flash into the darkness. This caused an almighty explosion and subsequently all the front windows shattered and blew out, spraying glass everywhere.

A moment later, Kilpatrick charged up the stairs and after a split second, we heard a loud scream, and unpredictably he came surfing backwards, lying face down on a door. The door was a booby trap, which had been strategically placed out of

sight on the darkest, steepest part of the stairs.
As he descended, the door gathered speed, and crashed into the framework of the front door. Kilpatrick catapulted through the opening flying about ten feet into the air before landing with a loud thump onto the ground, to the thunderous cheers and hearty laughter from the rest of the company.

Suddenly, from out of nowhere it seems, a land rover came roaring onto the scene and screeched to a halt, and an irate farmer jumped out screaming.
"WHAT THE FUCK DO YOU THINK YOU'RE DOING?"

Major Swinburne casually turned to face him and looking down his nose he answered in his pretentious voice
"We've got permission to use this house."

"NO YOU HAVEN'T, YOU'VE GOT PERMISSION TO USE THAT HOUSE."
Pointing to another about fifty yards away.
With that, we made a speedy departure.

It was in July of the summer of 1966 that our regiment the

17th Para's were flown to Cyprus to perform the obligatory annual two weeks exercise. The nominated dropping zone was a sandy beach, from where we were force-marched to the Troodos Mountains to commence the exercise.

The most experienced parachutist in our battalion, having executed well over three hundred jumps, was a Colour Sergeant Stevens, therefore I, having myself landed safely from a Beverley aircraft, was shocked to witness the Colour Sergeant hurtling unconscious to the ground and land heavily only a few yards away from myself. Apparently, almost immediately after being dispatched from the aircraft, another soldier's container had, without warning, struck him on the head knocking him clean out. This meant of course that he was not able to release his own container, nor have control over his decent or his landing. Although not life threatening, he suffered severe injuries, including a broken thigh, ankle, arm, shoulder and collar bone, however this did not deter him and when fully recovered he went on to execute numerous other jumps.

Finally we reached our destination, the Troodos mountains and the exercise commenced in earnest, amongst our ranks and in my section, was a Corporal Maguire who was an excellent soldier having previously served in the regular Para's, and being so experienced he did not suffer fools gladly.

Following thirty hours of virtually non-stop pushing forward and having had only an occasional half hour shut eye, and after climbing six, six hundred feet high mountains, we were hot, tired, dirty and all feeling the strain.

A regiment from Liverpool, namely The Green Jackets, were our 'enemy,' and they, having served in Cyprus for two years, knew the territory like the back of their hands. Consequently, we found ourselves being frequently ambushed, fired upon and challenged. Each time this happened we were subjected to disparaging comments from numerous Scouse voices, which seemed to come from all directions, as they echoed loud and clear from the mountains.

"Yoo Hoo girls, come and get us."

"You're all a load of fuckin crap."

"Call yourselves elite, you couldn't wipe our arses."

We Para's were becoming more and more frustrated and

the threats from our ranks were coming thick and fast.
"Wait until we catch up with the wankers, we'll knock seven different colours of shit out of the bastard crap hats."

Suddenly we found ourselves ambushed yet again and one of our Lieutenants, out of sheer frustration, called upon Corporal Maguire to bring his Bren gun into action.
"Where is the enemy located Sir?" the concerned Maguire asked.
"Just fire." ordered the Lieutenant.
"Fire? **Fire where?**" Asked the irate Maguire.
"Just carry out the order Maguire shouted the Lieutenant.
"I can't see the bastard enemy, where the fuck am I supposed to fire?" Screamed Maguire who by now was incensed.
"Just obey my orders." yelled the Lieutenant.

By this time the exhausted and frustrated, Maguire finally lost control and screamed at the top of his voice.
"You tosser, call yourself a fuckin Officer, you're a fuckin useless twat, you couldn't lead Boy Scouts around a camp fire."

With that, he picked up his Bren gun by the barrel and smashed it onto the ground, where it shattered into smithereens; and the remnants left in his hands were hurled over the cliff.
A Sergeant Major from 'A' company quickly strode forward to defuse the situation, he calmed Maguire down and took the Lieutenant aside when after a short discussion, they returned and the incident was never mentioned again.

This was the last annual camp I was to attend as having started a plastering contracting business several years previously meant that time was becoming evermore limited as the pressure of work increased.

I reluctantly felt it was time to hang up my boots and decided to bid farewell to all my good comrades.

THE END.